MASTERWORKS OF
ECONOMICS
VOLUME 1

MASTERWORKS OF
ECONOMICS
VOLUME 1

DIGESTS OF

MUN: ENGLAND'S TREASURE BY
    FOREIGN TRADE

TURGOT: REFLECTIONS ON THE FORMATION
    AND DISTRIBUTION OF WEALTH

ADAM SMITH: THE WEALTH OF NATIONS

MALTHUS: AN ESSAY ON THE PRINCIPLE OF
    POPULATION

EDITED BY LEONARD DALTON ABBOTT

McGraw-Hill Book Company

New York • St. Louis • San Francisco • London • Düsseldorf

Kuala Lumpur • Mexico • Montreal • Panama • Rio de Janeiro

Sydney • Toronto • Johannesburg • New Delhi • Singapore

CONTENTS

ENGLAND'S TREASURE BY FOREIGN TRADE

by *Thomas Mun*   1

REFLECTIONS ON THE FORMATION AND DISTRIBUTION
OF WEALTH

by *Anne Robert Jacques Turgot*   29

THE WEALTH OF NATIONS

by *Adam Smith*   53

AN ESSAY ON THE PRINCIPLE OF POPULATION

by *Thomas Robert Malthus*   181

ENGLAND'S TREASURE
BY FOREIGN TRADE

by

THOMAS MUN

CONTENTS

England's Treasure by Foreign Trade

1. The means to enrich this Kingdom

2. The particular ways and means to increase the exportation of our commodities, and to decrease our Consumption of foreign wares

3. The Exportation of our Moneys in Trade of Merchandize is a means to increase our Treasure

4. Foreign Trade is the only means to improve the price of our Lands

5. The diversity of gain by Foreign Trade

6. The observation of the Statute of Employments

7. It will not increase our treasure to enjoin the Merchant

8. The undervaluing of our Money cannot decrease our treasure

9. The order and means whereby we may draw up the balance of our Foreign Trade

10. The conclusion upon all that hath been said, concerning the Exportation or Importation of Treasure

THOMAS MUN

1571–1641

THOMAS MUN was the son of a London merchant of Queen Elizabeth's time. He enjoyed the advantages of wealth and education and was early engaged in mercantile affairs in the Mediterranean region, especially in Italy and the Levant. In his *England's Treasure by Foreign Trade* (or *England's Treasure by Forraign Trade,* as the title is spelled in Mun's archaic English) he describes the growth of the port of Leghorn as he personally observed it, and tells how Ferdinand I, grand duke of Tuscany, lent him forty thousand crowns, free of interest, for transmission to Turkey, where he was about to obtain merchandise for Italy. In 1615, as a well-known merchant, he was elected a member of the East India Company. From that time on he was active in promoting the interests of the company.

In 1621 Mun published a book entitled *A Discourse of Trade, from England unto the East-Indies; answering to diverse Objections which are usually made against the same.* The purpose of this book was to meet the growing criticism of methods employed by the East India Company and, in particular, to defend the right of the company to export bullion.

The period was one in which the "bullionists" held full sway. The reigning economic doctrine was that money, if not the chief form of wealth, was at least its chief embodiment, and that the wealth of a country was best represented by the amount of coin and bullion within its borders. In support of this doctrine the English government had legally prohibited the exportation of specie and had attempted to control not only international exchange but also the individual transactions of merchants in their commerce with foreign nations. The entire issue had been dramatized when, in 1613, one of the ships of the East India Company, carrying a large amount of bullion, had been shipwrecked.

It was Thomas Mun's contention that the government policy was based on false premises. The East India trade, he argued, was profitable to England because it brought into the country necessary and useful commodities which could be purchased elsewhere only at a higher cost. He maintained that a large proportion of these goods were re-exported at a profit, so that the net result was an inflow rather than an outflow of bullion.

The ensuing debate—the first important economic controversy in England—involved Gerard de Malynes, an assay master at the English mint, and Edward Misselden, a prominent member of the rich and powerful merchandising company known as the Merchants Adventurers. Malynes, a bullionist, attacked Mun's argument, while Misselden defended it along lines which anticipated Mun's subsequent position.

Mun's second and best-known book, *England's Treasure by Foreign Trade, or, the Balance of our Foreign Trade Is the Rule of our Treasure,* was written about 1630 but was not published until after his death. It broke definitely with bullionist doctrines and laid the foundations for what was coming to be known as the mercantilist position.

The mercantilists were nationalists in an era in which the emergence of nations was all-important. They were called mercantilists because they held that England's prosperity was bound up in the possibilities of foreign commerce or merchandising. What they sought to achieve was a system of industrial protection that would develop to the utmost the national resources. For Mun, as for every mercantilist, the index of prosperity was to be found not in a "balance of bargain" (based on the regulation of individual transactions) but in a "balance of trade" which would encourage exports in the mass and restrict imports in the mass.

Mun declares in *England's Treasure* that the object of national policy should be "to sell more to strangers yearly than we consume of theirs in value." He compares the prudence of a kingdom with that of a private person, and argues that just as an individual can get rich only by spending less than his income, so also a nation can get rich only if it spends (imports) less than it sells (exports).

In a series of clear admonitions he advises England to cultivate its wastelands, to reduce consumption of foreign wares and avoid frivolous changes of fashion, to be clever in selling to foreign nations, and to ship only in English bottoms. He recommends that taxes be removed from raw materials used in manufacturing of later exports, and is confident that this advice, if followed, "will turn to the profit of the kingdom in the balance of trade, and thereby also enable the King to lay up the more treasure." Mun recognizes that non-commodity items affect the direction and amount of the balance of trade paid in bullion, and specifically lists "the expences of travelers, the gifts to Ambassadors and Strangers, the fraud of some rich goods not entered into the Custom-house, the gain which is made here by Strangers by change and re-change, Interest of money, insurance upon Englishmen's goods and their lives."

In reproducing Mun's treatise, which follows, the editor has taken the liberty of modernizing the spelling of such words as might be confusing to the reader. However, the original spelling and capitalization have been retained where there can be no question of the meaning.

ENGLAND'S TREASURE
BY FOREIGN TRADE

1. *The means to enrich this Kingdom, and to increase our Treasure*

ALTHOUGH a Kingdom may be enriched by gifts received, or by purchase taken from some other Nations, yet these are things uncertain and of small consideration when they happen. The ordinary means therefore to increase our wealth and treasure is by *Foreign Trade,* wherein we must ever observe this rule; to sell more to strangers yearly than we consume of theirs in value. For suppose that when this Kingdom is plentifully served with the Cloth, Lead, Tin, Iron, Fish and other native commodities, we do yearly export the overplus to foreign Countries to the value of twenty two hundred thousand pounds; by which means we are enabled beyond the Seas to buy and bring in foreign wares for our use and Consumptions, to the value of twenty hundred thousand pounds; By this order duly kept in our trading, we may rest assured that the Kingdom shall be enriched yearly two hundred thousand pounds, which must be brought to us in so much Treasure; because that part of our stock which is not returned to us in wares must necessarily be brought home in treasure.

For in this case it cometh to pass in the stock of a Kingdom, as in the estate of a private man; who is supposed to have one thousand pounds yearly revenue and two thousand pounds of ready money in his Chest: If such a man through excess shall spend one thousand five hundred pounds *per annum,* all his ready money will be gone in four years; and in the like time his said money will be doubled if he take a Frugal course to spend but five hundred pounds *per annum;* which rule never faileth likewise in the Commonwealth, but in some cases (of no great moment) which I will hereafter declare, when I shall show by whom and in what manner this balance of the Kingdom's account ought to be drawn up yearly, or so often as it shall please the State to discover how much we gain or lose by trade with foreign Nations. But first I will say something concerning those ways and means which will increase our exportations and diminish our importations of wares; which being done,

I will then set down some other arguments both affirmative and negative to strengthen that which is here declared, and thereby to show that all the other means which are commonly supposed to enrich the Kingdom with Treasure are altogether insufficient and mere fallacies.

2. The particular ways and means to increase the exportation of our commodities, and to decrease our Consumption of foreign wares

The revenue or stock of a Kingdom by which it is provided of foreign wares is either *Natural* or *Artificial*. The Natural wealth is so much only as can be spared from our own use and necessities to be exported unto strangers. The Artificial consists in our manufactures and industrious trading with foreign commodities, concerning which I will set down such particulars as may serve for the cause we have in hand.

1. First, although this Realm be already exceeding rich by nature, yet might it be much increased by laying the waste grounds (which are infinite) into such employments as should no way hinder the present revenues of other manured lands, but hereby to supply our selves and prevent the importations of Hemp, Flax, Cordage, Tobacco, and divers other things which now we fetch from strangers to our great impoverishing.

2. We may likewise diminish our importations, if we would soberly refrain from excessive consumption of foreign wares in our diet and raiment, with such often change of fashions as is used, so much the more to increase the waste and charge; which vices at this present are more notorious amongst us than in former ages. Yet might they easily be amended by enforcing the observation of such good laws as are strictly practised in other Countries against the said excesses; where likewise by commanding their own manufactures to be used, they prevent the coming in of others, without prohibition, or offence to strangers in their mutual commerce.

3. In our exportations we must not only regard our own superfluities, but also we must consider our neighbours' necessities, that so upon the wares which they cannot want, nor yet be furnished thereof elsewhere, we may (besides the vent of the Materials) gain so much of the manufacture as we can, and also endeavour to sell them dear, so far forth as the high price cause not a less vent in the quantity. But the superfluity of our commodities which strangers use, and may also have the same from other Nations, or may abate their vent by the use of some such like wares from other places, and with little inconvenience; we must in this case strive to sell as cheap as possible we can, rather than to lose the utterance of such wares. For we have found of late years by good experience, that

being able to sell our Cloth cheap in Turkey, we have greatly increased the vent thereof, and the *Venetians* have lost as much in the utterance of theirs in those Countries, because it is dearer. And on the other side a few years past, when by the excessive price of Wools our Cloth was exceeding dear, we lost at the least half our clothing for foreign parts, which since is no otherwise (well near) recovered again than by the great fall of price for Wools and Cloth. We find that twenty five in the hundred less in the price of these and some other Wares, to the loss of private men's revenues, may raise above fifty upon the hundred in the quantity vented to the benefit of the public. For when Cloth is dear, other Nations do presently practise clothing, and we know they want neither art nor materials to this performance. But when by cheapness we drive them from this employment, and so in time obtain our dear price again, then do they also use their former remedy. So that by these alterations we learn, that it is in vain to expect a greater revenue of our wares than their condition will afford, but rather it concerns us to apply our endeavours to the times with care and diligence to help our selves the best we may, by making our cloth and other manufactures without deceit, which will increase their estimation and use.

4. The value of our exportations likewise may be much advanced when we perform it our selves in our own Ships, for then we get only not the price of our wares as they are worth here, but also the Merchants' gains, the charges of insurance, and freight to carry them beyond the seas. As for example, if the *Italian* Merchants should come hither in their own shipping to fetch our Corn, our red Herrings or the like, in this case the Kingdom should have ordinarily but 25s. for a quarter of Wheat, and 20s. for a barrel of red herrings, whereas if we carry these wares our selves into *Italy* upon the said rates, it is likely that we shall obtain fifty shillings for the first, and forty shillings for the last, which is a great difference in the utterance or vent of the Kingdom's stock. And although it is true that the commerce ought to be free to strangers to bring in and carry out at their pleasure, yet nevertheless in many places the exportation of victuals and munition are either prohibited, or at least limited to be done only by the people and Shipping of those places where they abound.

5. The frugal expending likewise of our own natural wealth might advance much yearly to be exported unto strangers; and if in our raiment we will be prodigal, yet let this be done with our own materials and manufactures, as Cloth, Lace, Embroideries, Cutworks and the like, where the excess of the rich may be the employment of the poor, whose labours notwithstanding of this kind, would be more profitable for the Commonwealth, if they were done to the use of strangers.

6. The Fishing in his Majesty's seas of *England, Scotland* and *Ireland* is our natural wealth, and would cost nothing but labour, which the

Dutch bestow willingly, and thereby draw yearly a very great profit to themselves by serving many places of Christendom with our Fish, for which they return and supply their wants both of foreign Wares and Money, besides the multitude of Mariners and Shipping, which hereby are maintain'd, whereof a long discourse might be made to show the particular manage of this important business. Our Fishing plantation likewise in *New-England, Virginia, Greenland,* the *Summer Islands* and the *New-found-land,* are of the like nature, affording much wealth and employments to maintain a great number of poor, and to increase our decaying trade.

7. A Staple or Magazine for foreign Corn, Indigo, Spices, Raw-silks, Cotton wool or any other commodity whatsoever, to be imported will increase Shipping, Trade, Treasure, and the King's customs, by exporting them again where need shall require, which course of Trading, hath been the chief means to raise *Venice, Genoa,* the *low-Countries,* with some others; and for such a purpose *England* stands most commodiously, wanting nothing to this performance but our own diligence and endeavour.

8. Also we ought to esteem and cherish those trades which we have in remote or far Countries, for besides the increase of Shipping and Mariners thereby, the wares also sent thither and receiv'd from thence are far more profitable unto the kingdom than by our trades near at hand; As for example; suppose Pepper to be worth here two Shillings the pound constantly, if then it be brought from the *Dutch* at *Amsterdam,* the Merchant may give there twenty pence the pound, and gain well by the bargain; but if he fetch this Pepper from the *East-indies,* he must not give above three pence the pound at the most, which is a mighty advantage, not only in that part which serveth for our own use, but also for that great quantity which (from hence) we transport yearly unto divers other Nations to be sold at a higher price: whereby it is plain, that we make a far greater stock by gain upon these *Indian* Commodities, than those Nations do where they grow, and to whom they properly appertain, being the natural wealth of their Countries. But for the better understanding of this particular, we must ever distinguish between the gain of the Kingdom, and the profit of the Merchant; for although the Kingdom payeth no more for this Pepper than is before supposed, nor for any other commodity bought in foreign parts more than the stranger receiveth from us for the same, yet the Merchant payeth not only that price, but also the freight, insurance, customs and other charges which are exceeding great in these long voyages; but yet all these in the Kingdom's account are but commutations among ourselves, and no Privation of the Kingdom's stock, which being duly considered, together with the support also of our other trades in our best Shipping to *Italy, France, Turkey,* the *East Countries* and other places, by transporting and venting the wares which

we bring yearly from the *East Indies;* It may well stir up our utmost endeavours to maintain and enlarge this great and noble business, so much importing the Public wealth, Strength, and Happiness. Neither is there less honour and judgment by growing rich (in this manner) upon the stock of other Nations, than by an industrious increase of our own means, especially when this latter is advanced by the benefit of the former, as we have found in the *East Indies* by sale of much of our Tin, Cloth, Lead and other Commodities, the vent whereof doth daily increase in those Countries which formerly had no use of our wares.

9. It would be very beneficial to export money as well as wares, being done in trade only, it would increase our Treasure; but of this I write more largely in the next Chapter to prove it plainly.

10. It were policy and profit for the State to suffer manufactures made of foreign Materials to be exported custom-free, as Velvets and all other wrought Silks, Fustians, thrown Silks and the like, it would employ very many poor people, and much increase the value of our stock yearly issued into other Countries, and it would (for this purpose) cause the more foreign Materials to be brought in, to the improvement of His Majesty's Customs. I will here remember a notable increase in our manufacture of winding and twisting only of foreign raw Silk, which within 35 years to my knowledge did not employ more than 300 people in the City and suburbs of London, where at this present time it doth set on work above fourteen thousand souls, as upon diligent enquiry hath been credibly reported unto His Majesty's Commissioners for Trade. And it is certain, that if the said foreign Commodities might be exported from hence, free of custom, this manufacture would yet increase very much, and decrease as fast in *Italy* and in the *Netherlands.* But if any man allege the *Dutch* proverb, *Live and let others live;* I answer, that the Dutchmen notwithstanding their own Proverb, do not only in these Kingdoms, encroach upon our livings, but also in other foreign parts of our trade (where they have power) they do hinder and destroy us in our lawful course of living, hereby taking the bread out of our mouth, which we shall never prevent by plucking the pot from their nose, as of late years too many of us do practise to the great hurt and dishonour of this famous Nation; We ought rather to imitate former times in taking sober and worthy courses more pleasing to God and suitable to our ancient reputation.

11. It is needful also not to charge the native commodities with too great customs, lest by endearing them to the stranger's use, it hinder their vent. And especially foreign wares brought in to be transported again should be favoured, for otherwise that manner of trading (so much importing the good of the Commonwealth) cannot prosper nor subsist. But the Consumption of such foreign wares in the Realm may be the

more charged, which will turn to the profit of the kingdom in the *Balance of the Trade,* and thereby also enable the King to lay up the more Treasure out of his yearly incomes.

12. Lastly, in all things we must endeavour to make the most we can of our own, whether it be *Natural* or *Artificial;* And forasmuch as the people which live by the Arts are far more in number than they who are masters of the fruits, we ought the more carefully to maintain those endeavours of the multitude, in whom doth consist the greatest strength and riches both of King and Kingdom: for where the people are many, and the arts good, there the traffic must be great, and the Country rich. The *Italians* employ a greater number of people, and get more money by their industry and manufactures of the raw Silks of the Kingdom of *Cicilia,* than the King of *Spain* and his Subjects have by the revenue of this rich commodity. But what need we fetch the example so far, when we know that our own natural wares do not yield us so much profit as our industry? For Iron ore in the Mines is of no great worth, when it is compared with the employment and advantage it yields being digged, tried, transported, bought, sold, cast into Ordnance, Muskets, and many other instruments of war for offence and defence, wrought into Anchors, bolts, spikes, nails and the like, for the use of Ships, Houses, Carts, Coaches, Ploughs, and other instruments for Tillage. Compare our Fleece-wools with our Cloth, which requires shearing, washing, carding, spinning, Weaving, fulling, dying, dressing and other trimmings, and we shall find these Arts more profitable than the natural wealth, whereof I might instance other examples, but I will not be more tedious, for if I would amplify upon this and the other particulars before written, I might find matter sufficient to make a large volume, but my desire in all is only to prove what I propound with brevity and plainness.

3. The Exportation of our Moneys in Trade of Merchandize is a means to increase our Treasure

This Position is so contrary to the common opinion, that it will require many and strong arguments to prove it before it can be accepted of the Multitude, who bitterly exclaim when they see any monies carried out of the Realm; affirming thereupon that we have absolutely lost so much Treasure, and that this is an act directly against the long continued laws made and confirmed by the wisdom of this Kingdom in the High Court of Parliament, and that many places, nay *Spain* it self which is the Fountain of Money, forbids the exportation thereof, some cases only excepted. To all which I might answer, that *Venice, Florence, Genoa,* the *Low Countries* and divers other places permit it, their people applaud it, and find great benefit by it; but all this makes a noise and proves nothing, we must therefore come to those reasons which concern the business in question.

First, I will take that for granted which no man of judgment will deny, that we have no other means to get Treasure but by foreign trade, for Mines we have none which do afford it, and how this money is gotten in the managing of our said Trade I have already showed, that it is done by making our commodities which are exported yearly to over balance in value the foreign wares which we consume; so that it resteth only to show how our moneys may be added to our commodities, and being jointly exported may so much the more increase our Treasure.

We have already supposed our yearly consumptions of foreign wares to be for the value of twenty hundred thousand pounds, and our exportations to exceed that two hundred thousand pounds, which sum we have thereupon affirmed is brought to us in treasure to balance the account. But now if we add three hundred thousand pounds more in ready money unto our former exportations in wares, what profit can we have (will some men say) although by this means we should bring in so much ready money more than we did before, seeing that we have carried out the like value.

To this the answer is, that when we have prepared our exportations of wares, and sent out as much of every thing as we can spare or vent abroad: It is not therefore said that then we should add our money thereunto to fetch in the more money immediately, but rather first to enlarge our trade by enabling us to bring in more foreign wares, which being sent out again will in due time much increase our Treasure.

For although in this manner we do yearly multiply our importations to the maintenance of more Shipping and Mariners, improvement of His Majesty's Customs and other benefits: yet our consumption of those foreign wares is no more than it was before; so that all the said increase of commodities brought in by the means of our ready money sent out as is afore written, doth in the end become an exportation unto us of a far greater value than our said moneys were, which is proved by three several examples following.

1. For I suppose that 100000. *l.* being sent in our Shipping to the East Countries, will buy there one hundred thousand quarters of wheat clear aboard the Ships, which being after brought into *England* and housed, to export the same at the best time for vent thereof in *Spain* or *Italy,* it cannot yield less in those parts than two hundred thousand pounds to make the Merchant but a saver, yet by this reckoning we see the Kingdom hath doubled that Treasure.

2. Again this profit will be far greater when we trade thus in remote Countries, as for example, if we send one hundred thousand pounds into

the *East-Indies* to buy Pepper there, and bring it hither, and from hence send it for *Italy* or *Turkey,* it must yield seven hundred thousand pounds at least in those places, in regard of the excessive charge which the Merchant disburseth in those long voyages in Shipping, Wages, Victuals, Insurance, Interest, Customs, Imposts, and the like, all which notwithstanding the King and the Kingdom gets.

3. But where the voyages are short & the wares rich, which therefore will not employ much Shipping, the profit will be far less. As when another hundred thousand pounds shall be employed in *Turkey* in raw Silks, and brought hither to be after transported from hence into *France,* the *Low Countries,* or *Germany,* the Merchant shall have good gain, although he sell it there but for one hundred and fifty thousand pounds: and thus take the voyages altogether in their *Medium,* the moneys exported will be returned unto us more than Trebled. But if any man will yet object, that these returns come to us in wares, and not really in money as they were issued out,

The answer is (keeping our first ground) that if our consumption of foreign wares be no more yearly than is already supposed, and that our exportations be so mightily increased by this manner of Trading with ready money as is before declared: It is not then possible but that all the over-balance or difference should return either in money or in such wares as we must export again, which, as is already plainly showed will be still a greater means to increase our Treasure.

For it is in the stock of the Kingdom as in the estates of private men, who having store of wares, do not therefore say that they will not venture out or trade with their money (for this were ridiculous) but do also turn that into wares, whereby they multiply their Money, and so by a continual and orderly change of one into the other grow rich, and when they please turn all their estates into Treasure; for they that have Wares cannot want money.

Neither is it said that Money is the Life of Trade, as if it could not subsist without the same; for we know that there was great trading by way of commutation or barter when there was little money stirring in the world. The *Italians* and some other Nations have such remedies against this want, that it can neither decay nor hinder their trade, for they transfer bills of debt, and have Banks both public and private, wherein they do assign their credits from one to another daily for very great sums with ease and satisfaction by writings only, whilst in the mean time the Mass of Treasure which gave foundation to these credits is employed in Foreign Trade as a Merchandize, and by the said means they have little other use of money in those countries more than for their ordinary expences. It is not therefore the keeping of our money in the Kingdom, but the necessity and use of our wares in foreign Countries, and our want of their commodities that causeth the vent and consumption on all sides, which makes a quick and ample Trade. If we were once poor, and now having gained some store of money by trade with resolution to keep it still in the Realm; shall this cause other Nations to spend more of our commodities than formerly they have done, whereby we might say that our trade is Quickened and Enlarged? no verily, it will produce no such good effect: but rather according to the alteration of times by their true causes we may expect the contrary; for all men do consent that plenty of money in a Kingdom doth make the native commodities dearer, which as it is to the profit of some private men in their revenues, so is it directly against the benefit of the Public in the quantity of the trade; for as plenty of money makes wares dearer, so dear wares decline their use and consumption, as hath been already plainly showed in the last Chapter upon that particular of our cloth; And although this is a very hard lesson for some great landed men to learn, yet I am sure it is a true lesson for all the land to observe, lest when we have gained some store of money by trade, we lose it again by not trading with our money. I knew a Prince in *Italy* (of famous memory) *Ferdinando the first,* great Duke of *Tuscanie,* who being very rich in Treasure, endeavoured therewith to enlarge his trade by issuing out to his Merchants great sums of money for very small profit; I my self had forty thousand crowns of him *gratis* for a whole year, although he knew that I would presently send it away in *Specie* for the parts of *Turkey* to be employed in wares for his Countries, he being well assured that in this course of trade it would return again (according to the old saying) with a Duck in the mouth: This noble and industrious Prince by his care and diligence to countenance and favour Merchants in their affairs, did so increase the practice thereof, but there is scarce a Nobleman or Gentleman in all his dominions that doth not Merchandize either by himself or in partnership with others, whereby within these thirty years the trade to his port of *Leghorn* is so much increased, that of a poor little town (as I my self knew it) it is now become a fair and strong City, being one of the most famous places for trade in all Christendom. And yet it is worthy our observation, that the multitude of Ships and wares which come thither from *England,* the *Low Countries,* and other places have little or no means to make their returns from thence but only in ready money, which they may and do carry away freely at all times, to the incredible advantage of the said great Duke of *Tuscanie* and his subjects, who are much enriched by the continual great concourse of Merchants from all the States of the neighbour Princes, bringing them plenty of money daily to supply their wants of the said wares. And thus we see that the current of Merchandize which carries away their Treasure, becomes a flowing stream to fill them again in a greater measure with money.

There is yet an objection or two as weak as all the rest: that is, if we trade with our Money we shall issue out the less wares; as if a man should say, those Countries which heretofore had occasion to consume our Cloth, Lead, Tin, Iron, Fish, and the like, shall now make use of our monies in the place of those necessaries, which were most absurd to affirm, or that the Merchant had not rather carry out wares by which there is ever some gains expected, than to export money which is still but the same without any increase.

But on the contrary there are many Countries which may yield us very profitable trade for our money, which otherwise afford us no trade at all, because they have no use of our wares, as namely the *East-Indies* for one in the first beginning thereof, although since by industry in our commerce with those Nations we have brought them into the use of much of our Lead, Cloth, Tin, and other things, which is a good addition to the former vent of our commodities.

Again, some men have alleged that those Countries which permit money to be carried out, do it because they have few or no wares to trade withal: but we have great store of commodities, and therefore their action ought not to be our example.

To this the answer is briefly, that if we have such a quantity of wares as doth fully provide us of all things needful from beyond the seas: why should we then doubt that our moneys sent out in trade, must not necessarily come back again in treasure; together with the great gains which it may procure in such manner as is before set down? And on the other side, if those Nations which send out their monies do it because they have but few wares of their own, how come they then to have so much Treasure as we ever see in those places which suffer it freely to be exported at all times and by whomsoever? I answer, *Even by trading with their Moneys;* for by what other means can they get it, having no Mines of Gold or Silver?

Thus may we plainly see, that when this weighty business is duly considered in his end as all our humane actions ought well to be weighed, it is found much contrary to that which most men esteem thereof, because they search no further than the beginning of the work, which misinforms their judgments, and leads them into error: For if we only behold the actions of the husbandman in the seed-time when he casteth away much good corn into the ground, we will rather account him a mad man than a husbandman: but when we consider his labours in the harvest which is the end of his endeavours, we find the worth and plentiful increase of his actions.

4. Foreign Trade is the only means to improve the price of our Lands

It is a common saying, that plenty or scarcity of money makes all things dear or good or cheap; and this money is either gotten or lost in foreign trade by the over or under-balancing of the same, as I have already showed. It resteth now that I distinguish the seeming plenties of money from that which is only substantial and able to perform the work: For there are divers ways and means whereby to procure plenty of money into a Kingdom, which do not enrich but rather impoverish the same by the several inconveniences which ever accompany such alterations.

As first, if we melt down our plate into Coin (which suits not with the Majesty of so great a Kingdom, except in cases of great extremity) it would cause Plenty of money for a time, yet should we be nothing the richer, but rather this treasure being thus altered is made the more apt to be carried out of the Kingdom, if we exceed our means by excess in foreign wares, or maintain a war by Sea or Land, where we do not feed and clothe the Soldier and supply the armies with our own native provisions, by which disorders our treasure will soon be exhausted.

Again, if we think to bring in store of money by suffering foreign Coins to pass current at higher rates than their intrinsic value compared with our Standard, or by debasing or by enhancing our own moneys, all these have their several inconveniences and difficulties, but admitting that by this means plenty of money might be brought into the Realm, yet should we be nothing the richer, neither can such treasure so gotten long remain with us. For if the stranger or the English Merchants bring in this money, it must be done upon a valuable consideration, either for wares carried out already, or after to be exported, which helps us nothing except the evil occasions of excess or war aforenamed be removed which do exhaust our treasure: for otherwise, what one man bringeth for gain, another man shall be forced to carry out for necessity; because there shall ever be a necessity to balance our Accounts with strangers, although it should be done with loss upon the rate of the money, and Confiscation also if it be intercepted by the Law.

The conclusion of this business is briefly thus. That as the treasure which is brought into the Realm by the balance of our foreign trade is that money which only doth abide with us, and by which we are enriched: so by this plenty of money thus gotten (and no otherwise) do our Lands improve. For when the Merchant hath a good dispatch beyond the Seas for his Cloth and other wares, he doth presently return to buy up the greater quantity, which raiseth the price of our Wools and other commodities, and consequently doth improve the Landlords' Rents as the Leases expire daily: And also by this means money being gained, and brought more abundantly into the Kingdom, it doth enable many men to buy Lands, which will make them the dearer. But if our foreign trade come to a stop or declination by neglect at home or injuries abroad, whereby the Merchants are impoverished, and thereby the wares of the Realm less issued, then do all the said benefits cease, and our Lands fall of price daily.

5. The diversity of gain by Foreign Trade

In the course of foreign trade there are three sorts of gain, the first is that of the Commonwealth, which may be done when the Merchant (who is the principal Agent therein) shall lose. The second is the gain of the Merchant, which he doth sometimes justly and worthily effect, although the Commonwealth be a loser. The third is the gain of the King, whereof he is ever certain, even when the Commonwealth and the Merchant shall be both losers.

Concerning the first of these, we have already sufficiently showed the ways and means whereby a Commonwealth may be enriched in the course of trade, whereof it is needless here to make any repetition, only I do in this place affirm, that such happiness may be in the Commonwealth, when the Merchant in his particular shall have no occasion to rejoice. As for example, suppose the *East-India* Company send out one hundred thousand pounds into the *East-Indies,* and receive home for the same the full value of three hundred thousand pounds; Hereby it is evident that this part of the Commonwealth is trebled, and yet I may boldly say that which I can well prove, that the said Company of Merchants shall lose at least fifty thousand pounds by such an adventure if the returns be made in *Spice, Indigo, Calicoes, Benjamin, refined Saltpeter,* and such other bulky wares in their several proportions according to their vent and use in these parts of *Europe.* For the freight of Shipping, the insurance of the adventure, the charges of Factors abroad and Officers at home, the forbearance of the Stock, His Majesty's Customs and Imposts, with other petty charges incident, cannot be less than two hundred and fifty thousand pounds, which being added to the principal produceth the said loss. And thus we see, that not only the Kingdom but also the King by his Customs and Imposts may get notoriously, even when the Merchant notwithstanding shall lose grievously; which giveth us good occasion here to consider, how much more the Realm is enriched by this noble Trade, when all things pass so happily that the Merchant is a gainer also with the King and Kingdom.

In the next place I affirm, that a Merchant by his laudable endeavours may both carry out and bring in wares to his advantage by selling them and buying them to good profit, which is the end of his labours; when nevertheless the Commonwealth shall decline and grow poor by a disorder in the people, when through Pride and other Excesses they do consume more foreign wares in value than the wealth of the Kingdom can satisfy and pay by the exportation of our own commodities, which is the very quality of an unthrift who spends beyond his means.

Lastly, the King is ever sure to get by trade, when both the Commonwealth and Merchant shall lose severally as afore-written, or jointly, as it may and doth sometimes happen, when at one and the same time our Commodities are over-balanced by foreign wares consumed, and that the Merchants success prove no better than is before declared.

But here we must not take the King's gain in this large sense, for so we might say that His Majesty should get, although half the trade of the Kingdom were lost; we will rather suppose that whereas the whole trade of the Realm for Exportations and Importations is now found for to be about the yearly value of four millions and a half pounds; it may be yet increased two hundred thousand pounds *per annum* more by the importation and consumption of foreign wares. By this means we know that the King shall be a gainer near twenty thousand pounds, but the Commonwealth shall lose the whole two hundred thousand pounds thus spent in excess. And the Merchant may be a loser also when the trade shall in this manner be increased to the profit of the King; who notwithstanding shall be sure in the end to have the greatest loss, if he prevent not such unthrifty courses as do impoverish his Subjects.

6. *The observation of the Statute of Employments to be made by strangers, cannot increase, nor yet preserve our Treasure*

To keep our money in the Kingdom is a work of no less skill and difficulty than to augment our Treasure: for the causes of their preservation and production are the same in nature. The statute for employment of stranger's wares into our commodities seemeth at the first to be a good and a lawful way leading to those ends; but upon th' examination of the particulars, we shall find that it cannot produce such good effects.

For as the use of foreign trade is alike unto all Nations, so may we easily perceive what will be done therein by strangers, when we do but observe our own proceedings in this weighty business, by which we do not only seek with the vent of our own commodities to supply our wants of foreign wares, but also to enrich ourselves with treasure: all which is done by a different manner of trading according to our own occasions and the nature of the places whereunto we do trade; as namely in some Countries we sell our commodities and bring away their wares, or part in money; in other Countries we sell our goods and take their money, because they have little or no wares that fits our turns: again in some places we have need of their commodities, but they have little use of ours; so they take our money which we get in other Countries: And thus by a course of traffic (which changeth according to the occurrence of time) the particular members do accommodate each other, and all accomplish the whole body of the trade, which will ever languish if the harmony of her health be distempered by the diseases of excess at home, violence abroad, charges and restrictions at home or abroad: but in this place I have occasion to speak only of restriction, which I will perform briefly.

There are three ways by which a Merchant may make the returns of his wares from beyond the Seas, that is to say in money, in commodities, or by Exchange. But the Statute of employment doth not only restrain money (in which there is a seeming providence and Justice) but also the use of the Exchange by bills, which doth violate the Law of Commerce, and is indeed an Act without example in any place of the world where we have trade, and therefore to be considered, that whatsoever (in this kind) we shall impose upon strangers here, will presently be made a Law for us in their Countries, especially where we have our greatest trade with our vigilant neighbours, who omit no care nor occasion to support their traffic in equal privileges with other Nations. And thus in the first place we should be deprived of that freedom and means which now we have to bring Treasure into the Kingdom, and therewith likewise we should lose the vent of much wares which we carry to divers places, whereby our trade and our Treasure would decay together.

Secondly, if by the said Statute we thrust the exportation of our wares (more than ordinary) upon the stranger, we must then take it from the *English,* which were injurious to our Merchants, Mariners and Shipping, besides the hurt to the Commonwealth in venting the Kingdom's stock to the stranger at far lower rates here than we must do if we sold it to them in their own Countries.

Thirdly, whereas we have already sufficiently showed, that if our commodities be over balanced in value by foreign wares, our money must be carried out. How is it possible to prevent this by tying the Stranger's hands, and leaving the English loose? shall not the same reasons and advantage cause that to be done by them now, that was done by the other before? or if we will make a statute (without example) to prevent both alike, shall we not then overthrow all at once? the King in his customs and the Kingdom in her profits; for such a restriction must of necessity destroy much trade, because the diversity of occasions and places which make an ample trade require that some men should both export and import wares; some export only, others import, some deliver out their monies by exchange, others take it up; some carry out money, others bring it in, and this in a greater or lesser quantity according to the good husbandry or excess in the Kingdom, over which only if we keep a strict law, it will rule all the rest, and without this all other Statutes are no rules either to keep or procure us Treasure.

Lastly, to leave no Objection unanswered, if it should be said that a Statute comprehending the English as well as the stranger must needs keep our money in the Kingdom. What shall we get by this, if it hinder the coming in of money by the decay of that ample Trade which we enjoyed in the freedom thereof? is not the Remedy far worse than the Disease? shall we not live more like Irishmen than Englishmen, when the King's revenues, our Merchants, Mariners, Shipping, Arts, Lands, Riches, and all decay together with our Trade?

Yea but, say some men, we have better hopes than so; for th' intent of the Statute is, that as all the foreign wares which are brought in shall be employed in our commodities, thereby to keep our money in the Kingdom: So we doubt not but to send out a sufficient quantity of our own wares over and above to bring in the value thereof in ready money.

Although this is absolutely denied by the reasons afore written, yet now we will grant it, because we desire to end the dispute: For if this be true, that other Nations will vent more of our commodities than we consume of theirs in value, then I affirm that the overplus must necessarily return unto us in treasure without the use of the Statute, which is therefore not only fruitless but hurtful, as some other like restrictions are found to be when they are fully discovered.

7. *It will not increase our treasure to enjoin the Merchant that exporteth Fish, Corn or Munition, to return all or part of the value in Money*

Victuals and Munition for war are so precious in a Commonwealth, that either it seemeth necessary to restrain the exportation altogether, or (if the plenty permits it) to require the return thereof in so much treasure; which appeareth to be reasonable and without difficulty, because *Spain* and other Countries do willingly part with their money for such wares, although in other occasions of trade they straightly prohibit the exportation thereof: all which I grant to be true, yet notwithstanding we must consider that all the ways and means which (in course of trade) force treasure into the Kingdom, do not therefore make it ours: for this can be done only by a lawful gain, and this gain is no way to be accomplished but by the overbalance of our trade, and this overbalance is made less by restrictions: therefore such restrictions do hinder the increase of our treasure. The Argument is plain, and needs no other reasons to strengthen it, except any man be so vain to think that restrictions would not cause the less wares to be exported. But if this likewise should be granted, yet to enjoin the Merchant to bring in money for Victuals and Munition carried out, will not cause us to have one penny the more in the Kingdom at the year's end; for whatsoever is forced in one way must out again another way: because only so much will remain and abide with us as is gained and incorporated into the estate of the Kingdom by the overbalance of the trade.

This may be made plain by an example taken from an Englishman, who had occasion to buy and consume the wares of divers strangers for the value of six hundred pounds, and having wares of his own for the value of one thousand pounds, he sold them to the said strangers, and presently forced all the money from them into his own power; yet upon clearing of the reckoning between them there remained only four hundred pounds to the said Englishman for overbalance of the wares bought and sold; so the rest which he had received was returned back from whence he forced it. And this shall suffice to show that whatsoever courses we take to force money into the Kingdom, yet so much only will remain with us as we shall gain by the balance of our trade.

8. The undervaluing of our Money which is delivered or received by Bills of Exchange here or beyond the Seas, cannot decrease our treasure

The Merchants Exchange by Bills is a means and practice whereby they that have money in one Country may deliver the same to receive it again in another Country at certain times and rates agreed upon, whereby the lender and the borrower are accommodated without transporting of treasure from State to State.

These Exchanges thus made between man and man, are not contracted at the equal value of the moneys, according to their respective weights and fineness: First, because he that delivereth his money doth respect the venture of the debt, and the time of forbearance; but that which causeth an under or overvaluing of moneys by Exchange, is the plenty or scarcity thereof in those places where the Exchanges are made. For example, when here is plenty of money to be delivered for *Amsterdam,* then shall our money be undervalued in Exchange, because they who take up the money, seeing it so plentifully thrust upon them, do thereby make advantage to themselves in taking the same at an undervalue.

And contrariwise, when here is scarcity of money to be delivered for *Amsterdam,* the deliverer will make the same advantage by overvaluing our money which he delivereth. And thus we see that as plenty or scarcity of money in a Common-wealth doth make all things dear or good cheap: so in the course of exchange it hath ever a contrary work-ing; wherefore in the next place it is fit to set down the true causes of this effect.

As plenty or scarcity of money do make the price of the exchange high or low, so the over or under balance of our trade doth effectually cause the plenty or scarcity of money. And here we must understand, that the balance of our trade is either General or Particular. The Gen-eral is, when all our yearly traffic is jointly valued, as I have formerly showed; the particular is when our trade to *Italy, France, Turkey, Spain,* and other Countries are severally considered: and by this latter course we shall perfectly find out the places where our money is under or over-valued in Exchange: For although our general exportations of wares may be yearly more in value than that which is imported: whereby the dif-ference is made good to us in so much treasure; nevertheless the par-ticular trades do work diversely. For peradventure the *Low Countries* may bring us more in value than we sell them, which if it be so, then do the *Low Country* Merchants not only carry away our treasure to balance the account between us, but also by this means money being plentiful here to be delivered by exchange, it is therefore undervalued by the takers, as I have before declared; And contrariwise if we carry more wares to *Spain,* and other places than we consume of theirs, then do we bring away their treasure, and likewise in the Merchants exchange we overvalue our own money.

Yet still there are some who will seem to make this plain by Demon-stration, that the undervaluing of our money by Exchange doth carry it out of the Kingdom: for, say they, we see daily great store of our English Coins carried over, which pass current in the Low-Countries, and there is great advantage to carry them thither, to save the loss which the Low-Countrymen have in the Exchange; for if one hundred pounds sterling delivered here, is so much undervalued, that ninety pounds of the same sterling money carried over *in specie* shall be suffi-cient to make repayment and full satisfaction of the said hundred pounds at *Amsterdam:* Is it not then (say they) the undervaluing of our Money which causeth it to be carried out of the Realm?

To this Objection I will make a full and plain Answer, showing that it is not the undervaluing of our money in exchange, but the overbal-ancing of our trade that carrieth away our treasure. For suppose that our whole trade with the Low-Countries for wares brought into this Realm be performed only by the Dutch for the value of five hundred thousand pounds yearly; and that all our commodities transported into the said Low-Countries be performed only by the English for four hundred thou-sand pounds yearly: Is it not then manifest, that the Dutch can exchange only four hundred thousand pounds with the English upon the *Par pro*

Pari or equal value of the respective Standards? So the other hundred thousand pounds which is the overbalance of the trade, they must of necessity carry that away in money. And the self same loss of treasure must happen if there were no exchange at all permitted: for the *Dutch* carrying away our money for their wares, and we bringing in their foreign Coins for their [our] commodities, there will be still one hundred thousand pounds loss.

Now let us add another example grounded upon the aforesaid proportion of trade between us and the *Low Countries.* The *Dutch* (as aforewritten) may exchange with the *English* for four hundred thousand pounds and no more upon the equal value of the monies, because the *English* have no further means to satisfy. But now suppose that in respect of the plenty of money, which in this case will be here in the hands of the *Dutch* to deliver by exchange, our money (according to that which hath been already said) be undervalued ten *per cent.* then is it manifest that the *Dutch* must deliver four hundred and forty thousand pounds to have the Englishman's four hundred thousand pounds in the *Low Countries:* so that there will then remain but 60000 pounds for the *Dutch* to carry out of the Realm to balance the account between them and us. Whereby we may plainly perceive that the undervaluing of our money in exchange, will not carry it out of the Kingdom, as some men have supposed, but rather is a means to make a less quantity thereof to be exported, than would be done at the *Par pro pari.*

Further let us suppose that the English Merchant carrieth out as much wares in value as the Dutch Merchant bringeth in, whereby the means is equal between them to make their returns by exchange without carrying away of any money to the prejudice of either State. And yet notwithstanding the Dutch Merchant for his occasions or advantage will forsake this course of exchange, and will venture to send part of his returns in ready money.

To this the answer is, that hereupon it must follow of necessity, that the Dutch shall want just so much means in exchange with the English, who therefore shall be forced to bring in the like sum of money from beyond the Seas, as the *Dutch* carried out of this Realm; so that we may plainly perceive that the monies which are carried from us within the balance of our trade are not considerable, for they do return to us again: and we lose those monies only which are made of the over-balance of our general trade, that is to say, That which we spend more in value in foreign wares, than we utter of our own commodities. And the contrary of this is the only means by which we get our treasure. In vain therefore hath *Gerard Malines* laboured so long, and in so many printed books to make the world believe that the undervaluing of our money in exchange doth exhaust our treasure, which is a mere fallacy of the cause, attributing that to a Secondary means, whose effects are wrought by another Principal Efficient, and would also come to pass although the said Secondary means were not at all. As vainly also hath he propounded a remedy by keeping the price of Exchange by Bills at the *par pro pari* by public Authority, which were a new-found Office without example in any part of the world, being not only fruitless but also hurtful, as hath been sufficiently proved in this Chapter, and therefore I will proceed to the next.

9. *The order and means whereby we may draw up the balance of our Foreign Trade*

Now, that we have sufficiently proved the Balance of our Foreign Trade to be the true rule of our Treasure; It resteth that we show by whom and in what manner the said balance may be drawn up at all times, when it shall please the State to discover how we prosper or decline in this great and weighty business, wherein the Officers of his Majesty's Customs are the only Agents to be employed, because they have the accounts of all the wares which are issued out or brought into the Kingdom; and although (it is true) they cannot exactly set down the cost and charges of other men's goods bought here or beyond the seas; yet nevertheless, if they ground themselves upon the book of Rates, they shall be able to make such an estimate as may well satisfy this enquiry: for it is not expected that such an account can possibly be drawn up to a just balance, it will suffice only that the difference be not over great.

First therefore, concerning our Exportations, when we have valued their first cost, we must add twenty-five *per cent.* thereunto for the charges here, for freight of Ships, insurance of the *Adventure,* and the *Merchant's* Gains; and for our Fishing Trades, which pay no Custom to his Majesty, the value of such Exportations may be easily esteem'd by good observations which have been made, and may continually be made, according to the increase or decrease of those affairs, the present estate of this commodity being valued at one hundred and forty thousand pounds issued yearly. Also we must add to our Exportations all the moneys which are carried out in Trade by license from his Majesty.

Secondly, for our Importations of Foreign Wares, the Custom-books serve only to direct us concerning the quantity, for we must not value them as they are rated here, but as they cost us with all charges laden into our Ships beyond the Seas, in the respective places where they are bought: for the Merchant's gain, the charges of Insurance, Freight of Ships, Customs, Imposts, and other Duties here, which do greatly endear them unto our use and consumption, are notwithstanding but Commutations amongst our selves, for the Stranger hath no part thereof: wherefore our said Importations ought to be valued at twenty five *per cent.* less than they are rated to be worth here. And although this may seem to be too great allowance upon many rich Commodities, which come but from the *Low Countries* and other places near hand, yet will it be found reasonable, when we consider it in gross Commodities, and upon Wares laden in remote Countries, as our Pepper, which cost us, with charges, but four pence the pound in the *East Indies,* and it is here rated at twenty pence the pound: so that when all is brought into a *medium,* the valuation ought to be made as afore-written. And therefore, the order which hath been used to multiply the full rates upon wares inwards by twenty, would produce a very great error in the Balance, for in this manner the ten thousand bags of Pepper, which this year we have brought hither from the *East Indies,* should be valued at very near two hundred and fifty thousand pounds, whereas all this Pepper in the Kingdom's account, cost not above fifty thousand pounds, because the Indians have had no more of us, although we paid them extraordinary dear prices for the same. All the other charges (as I have said before) is but a change of effects amongst our selves, and from the Subject to the King, which cannot impoverish the Common-wealth. But it is true, that whereas nine thousand bags of the said Pepper are already shipped out for divers foreign parts; These and all other Wares, foreign or domestic, which are thus transported Outwards, ought to be cast up by the rates of his Majesty's Custom-money, multiplied by twenty, or rather by twenty five (as I conceive) which will come nearer the reckoning, when we consider all our Trades to bring them into a *medium.*

Thirdly, we must remember, that all Wares exported or imported by Strangers (in their shipping) be esteemed by themselves, for what they carry out, the Kingdom hath only the first cost and the custom: And what they bring in, we must rate it as it is worth here, the Custom, Impost, and petty charges only deducted.

Lastly, there must be good notice taken of all the great losses which we receive at Sea in our Shipping either outward or homeward bound: for the value of the one is to be deducted from our Exportations, and the value of the other is to be added to our Importations: for to lose and to consume doth produce one and the same reckoning. Likewise if it happen that His Majesty doth make over any great sums of money by Exchange to maintain a foreign war, where we do not feed and clothe the Soldiers, and Provide the armies, we must deduct all this charge out of our Exportations or add it to our Importations; for this expence doth either carry out or hinder the coming in of so much Treasure. And here we must remember the great collections of money which are supposed to be made throughout the Realm yearly from our Recusants by Priests and Jesuits, who secretly convey the same unto their Colleges, Cloisters and Nunneries beyond the Seas, from whence it never returns to us again in any kind; therefore if this mischief cannot be prevented, yet it must be esteemed and set down as a clear loss to the Kingdom, except (to balance this) we will imagine that as great a value may perhaps come in from foreign Princes to their Pensioners here for Favours or Intelligence, which some States account good Policy, to purchase with great Liberality; the receipt whereof notwithstanding is plain Treachery.

There are yet some other petty things which seem to have reference to this Balance, of which the said Officers of His Majesty's Customs can take no notice, to bring them into the account. As namely, the expences of travelers, the gifts to Ambassadors and Strangers, the fraud of some rich goods not entered into the Custom-house, the gain which is made here by Strangers by change and re-change, Interest of money, insurance upon English men's goods and their lives: which can be little when the charges of their living here is deducted; besides that the very like advantages are as amply ministered unto the English in foreign Countries, which doth counterpoize all these things, and therefore they are not considerable in the drawing up of the said Balance.

10. *The conclusion upon all that hath been said, concerning the Exportation or Importation of Treasure*

The sum of all that hath been spoken, concerning the enriching of the Kingdom, and th' increase of our treasure by commerce with strangers, is briefly thus. That it is a certain rule in our foreign trade, in those places where our commodities exported are overbalanced in value by foreign wares brought into this Realm, there our money is undervalued in exchange; and where the contrary of this is performed, there our money is overvalued. But let the Merchants exchange be at a high rate, or at a low rate, or at the *Par pro pari,* or put down altogether; Let Foreign Princes enhance their Coins, or debase their Standards, and let His Majesty do the like, or keep them constant as they now stand; Let foreign Coins pass current here in all payments at higher rates than they are worth at the Mint; Let the Statute for employments by Strangers stand in force or be repealed; Let the mere Exchanger do his worst; Let Princes oppress, Lawyers extort, Usurers bite, Prodigals waste, and lastly let Merchants carry out what money they shall have occasion to use in traffic. Yet all these actions can work no other effects in the course of trade than is declared in this discourse. For so much Treasure only will be brought in or carried out of a Commonwealth, as the ForeignTrade doth over or under balance in value. And this must come to pass by a Necessity beyond all resistance.

So that all other courses (which tend not to this end) howsoever they may seem to force money into a Kingdom for a time, yet are they (in the end) not only fruitless but also hurtful: they are like to violent floods which bear down their banks, and suddenly remain dry again for want of waters.

Behold then the true form and worth of foreign Trade, which is, *The great Revenue of the King, the honour of the Kingdom, The Noble profession of the Merchant, The School of our Arts, The supply of our wants, The employment of our poor, The improvement of our Lands, The Nursery of our Mariners, The walls of the Kingdoms, The Means of our Treasure, The Sinews of our wars, The terror of our Enemies.* For all which great and weighty reasons, do so many well governed States highly countenance the profession, and carefully cherish the action, not only with policy to increase it, but also with power to protect it from all foreign energies: because they know it is a Principal in Reason of State to maintain and defend which doth Support them and their estates.

REFLECTIONS ON
THE FORMATION AND
DISTRIBUTION OF WEALTH

by

ANNE ROBERT JACQUES TURGOT

CONTENTS

Reflections on the Formation and Distribution of Wealth

1. Impossibility of Commerce upon equal division of lands
2. The above hypothesis has never existed
3. The products of the land require preparations
4. The necessity of these preparations brings about the exchange of produce
5. Pre-eminence of the Husbandman
6. The wages of the Workman are limited
7. The Husbandman is the sole source of all wealth
8. First division of the society into two classes
9. Proprietor not distinguished from Cultivator
10. Progress of the society
11. The Proprietors throw labour upon hired Cultivators
12. Inequality in the division of properties
13. Consequence of this inequality
14. Division of the produce
15. New division of the Society into three classes
16. Resemblance between the two working classes
17. Essential difference between the two working classes
18. Productive & barren classes
19. Of capitals in general
20. Birth of Commerce
21. How the current value establishes itself
22. Commerce gives to each article current value
23. Each article can serve as the common measure
24. Different articles serve as ordinary money
25. The Metals more fit for this purpose
26. Gold & Silver are constituted money
27. All economic undertakings limited before gold & silver
28. The industrious man ready to share profits
29. The loan upon interest
30. Errors of the Schoolmen refuted
31. True foundation of the interest of money
32. No disposable revenue except net produce of lands
33. The land also furnishes moveable riches
34. Specie forms but small part of total of capitals

ANNE ROBERT JACQUES TURGOT

1727–1781

ANNE ROBERT JACQUES TURGOT, French statesman and economist
of the physiocratic school, was born in Paris in 1727 and came
from a Norman family which for generations had been supplying administrative officers to the state. He studied theology
and at the age of twenty-two was elected prior of the Sorbonne.
In that capacity he delivered in 1750 an address "On the Benefits which the Christian Religion has Conferred on Mankind,"
and in the same year an account of "The Historical Progress of
the Human Mind" in which he predicted as inevitable the
separation of the American colonies from the mother country.
A year later he turned from theological to legal studies and
decided to enter the administrative and judicial service. He
held successively the posts of deputy counselor to the *pro-
cureur général,* counselor to the Parlement de Paris, and *maître
des requêtes.* In 1755 and 1756 he accompanied his friend
Vincent de Gournay, then a minister of commerce under
Louis XV, on tours of inspection through rural France.

It may have been Gournay who first awakened Turgot's
interest in physiocratic doctrine. The favorite maxim of Gournay was *laisser faire, laisser passer.* Another of Turgot's intimate friends was François Quesnay, court physician and physiocratic enthusiast. Of French economic writers Quesnay was the
first to use the word "physiocracy," interpreted to mean "the
rule of nature." The physiocrats were generally known in
their own time as *économistes.*

The physiocratic doctrine was a reaction against mercan-
tilism. The mercantile policy, with its emphasis on nationalism
and protection of industry, had tended to centralize manufacture and to sacrifice the country to the towns. The new

doctrine was the very antithesis of the old one. It looked with
favor on internationalism and free trade, and it placed agriculture at the very center of its system. Only the land, according
to the physiocratic argument, was productive. Manufacturers
and "artificers" were unproductive. The physiocrats proposed
a tax on the "net produce" of land—a "single tax" that anticipated the doctrine of Henry George more than a hundred
years later.

In 1761 Turgot was appointed administrator of the district
of Limoges, which included some of the poorest and most
overtaxed parts of France. He held this office for thirteen
years, and tried to apply in a practical way some of his economic principles. He improved the system of tax collection,
constructed new roads, increased facilities for grain trading,
established a system of poor relief, and strengthened the
schools. During this period Turgot was writing articles for
the great liberal French Encyclopedia and was corresponding
with Voltaire and Benjamin Franklin. A congenial group in
Paris in the winter of 1765–66 included David Hume (then
secretary of the British Embassy) and Adam Smith, who was
traveling with the Duke of Buccleuch. In the quickening of
minds to which Turgot contributed when he visited Paris,
the physiocratic system was beginning to take literary form.

Ten years before the appearance of the *Wealth of Nations*
Turgot wrote his *Reflections on the Formation and Distribution of Wealth,* which, according to Condorcet, French *philos-
ophe* and political theorist, contained in germ the larger work.
This brief treatise was first published in Dupont de Nemours'
periodical, the *Ephémérides du Citoyen.* One of its purposes
had been to enlighten two Chinese students who had been
brought to France and educated by Jesuits and then sent back
to their native land with a royal annuity and the understanding that they were to keep their European patrons informed
regarding the state of literature and science in their country.
Turgot had drawn up a list of questions for these students to
answer, and prepared the *Reflections* in order to give them
a better understanding of his interrogations. Among the
fundamental themes which the treatise covers are: division
of labor, the origin and use of money, the improvement of
agriculture, the nature of capital and the different modes of its
employment, the legitimacy of interest and loans, and the
revenue from land.

In 1774, on the accession of Louis XVI, Turgot was appointed minister of marine. Later in the same year he became controller of finance. The country was in a desperate financial situation, and Turgot's first act was to submit to the King his guiding principles: "No bankruptcy, no increase of taxation, no borrowing." He proceeded to attempt to carry out on a national scale the reforms which he had initiated in the Limoges district. In six famous edicts he proposed to abolish the system of unpaid labor (the *corvées*) then prevailing throughout the country; to suppress various taxes and tolls upon corn, cattle, et cetera, in Paris; and also to suppress the trade guilds, or corporations, which were raising the prices of commodities beyond reasonable limits. It had been Turgot's hope that revolution might be averted by timely reforms; but his program was not accepted, and in 1776, as a result of the opposition of Parliament and of exasperated privileged groups, he was dismissed from office. Jacques Necker, the father of Madame de Staël, took his place in a France that was rapidly approaching the revolutionary abyss. It is worth recording that the legislatures of the French Revolution re-enacted the measures which Louis XVI and his ministers had rejected.

Turgot represented a rare combination of statesman and theorist. In the world of practical affairs he pointed the way to progressive legislation. In the domain of economic theory he helped to expose fallacies and opened the path to a new period signalized by the publication of Adam Smith's *Wealth of Nations*.

REFLECTIONS ON THE FORMATION AND DISTRIBUTION OF WEALTH

1. Impossibility of Commerce upon the supposition of an equal division of lands, wherein every man should possess only what was necessary for his own support

IF THE LAND were so distributed among all the inhabitants of a country that each of them had precisely the quantity of it necessary for his support and nothing more, it is evident that, all being equal, no one would be willing to work for others. No one, besides, would possess anything with which to pay for the labour of another; for each, having only as much land as he needed to produce his subsistence, would consume all that he had gathered, and would have nothing that he could exchange for the labour of the others.

2. The above hypothesis has never existed, & could not have continued. The diversity of soils & the multiplicity of wants lead to the exchange of the products of the land for other products

This hypothesis can never have existed, because the lands have been cultivated before they have been divided; that very cultivation having been the sole motive for division and for the law which assures to each his property. Now the first who have cultivated have probably cultivated as much ground as their forces permitted, and consequently more than was necessary for their support.

Even if this state could have existed, it could not possibly have been durable; each man, as he got from his field nothing but his subsistence, and had nothing wherewith to pay the labour of the others, could only supply his other wants in the way of shelter, clothing, etc., by his own labour; and this would be almost impossible; *every piece of land by no means producing everything.*

He whose land was only fit for grain and would produce neither cotton nor hemp would be without cloth wherewith to clothe himself. Another would have a piece of land fit for cotton which would not produce grain. A third would be without wood wherewith to warm himself, while a fourth would be without grain wherewith to feed himself. Experience would soon teach each what was the kind of product for which his land would be best adapted, and he would limit himself to the cultivation of that particular crop, in order to procure for himself the things he was devoid of by means of exchange with his neighbours; and these, having in their turn made the same reflections, would have cultivated the crop best suited to their field and abandoned the cultivation of all the others.

3. The products of the land require preparations long & difficult, in order to render them fit to satisfy the wants of man

The crops which the land produces to satisfy the different wants of man cannot serve that purpose, for the most part, in the state in which nature gives them; they must undergo various changes and be prepared by art. Wheat must be converted into flour and then into bread; hides must be tanned or dressed; wool and cotton must be spun; silk must be drawn from the cocoons; hemp and flax must be soaked, peeled, and spun; next, different textures must be made from them; and then they must be cut and sewn into garments, footgear, etc. If the man who causes his land to produce all these different things and uses them to supply his wants were himself obliged to put them through all these intermediate stages, it is certain that he would succeed very badly. The greater part of these preparations demand an amount of care, of attention, of long experience, such as are only to be acquired by working continuously and on a great quantity of materials. Take for example the preparation of hides; what labourer could attend to all the details necessary in this operation, which lasts several months and sometimes several years? If he could, would he be able to, for a single hide? What loss of time, of space, of material, which might have served either at the same time or successively to tan a great quantity of hides! But even should he succeed in tanning a single hide, he only needs one pair of shoes; what shall he do with the rest? Shall he kill an ox to have this pair of shoes? Shall he cut down a tree to make himself a pair of sabots? One might say the same thing concerning all the other wants of each man, who, if he were reduced to his own field and his own labour, would consume much time and trouble to be very badly equipped in every respect, and would cultivate his land very badly.

4. The necessity of these preparations brings about the exchange of produce for labour

The same motive which has established the exchange of crop for crop between the Cultivators of different kinds of soil must, then, have necessarily brought about the exchange of crop for labour between the Cultivators and another part of the society, which shall have preferred the occupation of preparing and working up the produce of the land to that of growing it. Everyone profited by this arrangement, for each by devoting himself to a single kind of work succeeded much better in it. The Husbandman obtained from his field the greatest amount of produce possible, and procured for himself much more easily all the other things he needed by the exchange of his surplus than he would have done by his own labour. The Shoemaker, by making shoes for the Husbandman, obtained for himself a part of the latter's harvest. Each workman laboured to satisfy the wants of the workmen of all the other kinds, who, on their side, all laboured for him.

5. Pre-eminence of the Husbandman who produces over the Artisan who works up materials. The Husbandman is the first mover in the circulation of labours; it is he who causes the land to produce the wages of all the Artisans

It must however be observed that the Husbandman, furnishing all with the most important and most considerable article of their consumption, (I mean their food and also the materials of almost every industry) has the advantage of a greater independence. His labour, in the sequence of the labours divided among the different members of the society, retains the same primacy, the same pre-eminence, as the labour which provided his own food had among the different kinds of labour which, when he worked alone, he was obliged to devote to his different kinds of wants. We have here neither a primacy of honour nor of dignity; it is one of *physical necessity*. The Husbandman, we may say in general terms, can get on without the labour of the other workmen, but no workman can labour if the Husbandman does not enable him to live. In this circulation, which, by the reciprocal exchange of wants, renders men necessary to one another and forms the bond of the society, it is, then, the labour of the Husbandman which imparts the first impulse. What his labour causes the land to produce beyond his personal wants is the only fund for the wages which all the other members of the society receive in exchange for their labour. The latter, in making use of the price of this exchange to buy in their turn the products of the Husbandman, only return to him exactly what they have received from him. We have here a very essential difference between these two kinds of labours, upon which it is necessary to lay stress in order to be well assured of the evidence on which it rests, before we accept the innumerable consequences which flow from it.

6. *The wages of the Workman are limited to his subsistence by the competition among the Workmen. He gets only his livelihood*

The mere Workman, who has only his arms and his industry, has nothing except in so far as he succeeds in selling his toil to others. He sells it more or less dear; but this price, more or less high as it may be, does not depend upon himself alone: it results from the agreement which he makes with him who pays his labour. The latter pays him as little as he can; as he has the choice among a great number of Workmen, he prefers the one who works cheapest. The Workmen are therefore obliged to lower the price, in competition with one another. In every kind of work it cannot fail to happen, and as a matter of fact it does happen, that the wages of the workman are limited to what is necessary to procure him his subsistence.

7. *The Husbandman is the only person whose labour produces something over and above the wages of the labour. He is therefore the sole source of all wealth*

The position of the Husbandman is very different. The land pays him directly the price of his labour, independently of any other man or any agreement. Nature does not bargain with him to oblige him to content himself with what is absolutely necessary. What she grants is proportioned neither to his wants, nor to a contractual valuation of the price of his days of labour. It is the physical result of the fertility of the soil, and of the wisdom, far more than of the laboriousness, of the means which he has employed to render it fertile. As soon as the labour of the Husbandman produces more than his wants, he can, with this superfluity that nature accords him as a pure gift, over and above the wages of his toil, buy the labour of the other members of the society. The latter, in selling to him, gain only their livelihood; but the Husbandman gathers, beyond his subsistence, a wealth which is independent and disposable, which he has not bought and which he sells. He is, therefore, the sole source of the riches, which, by their circulation, animate all the labours of the society; because he is the only one whose labour produces over and above the wages of the labour.

8. First division of the society into two classes: the one productive, or that of the Cultivators; the second stipendiary, or that of the Artisans

Here then we have the whole society divided, by a necessity founded on the nature of things, into two classes: equally industrious. But one of these by its labour produces, or rather draws from the land, riches which are continually springing up afresh, and which supply the whole society with its subsistence and with the materials for all its needs. The other, occupied in giving to materials thus produced the preparations and the forms which render them suitable for the use of men, sells its labour to the first class, and receives in exchange its subsistence. The first may be called the *productive* class, and the second the *stipendiary* class.

9. In the first ages the Proprietor cannot have been distinguished from the Cultivator

Up to this point we have not yet distinguished the Husbandman from the Proprietor of the lands; and in fact they were not originally distinct. It is by the labour of those who have been the first to till the fields, and who have enclosed them, in order to secure to themselves the harvest, that all the lands have ceased to be common to all, and that landed properties have been established. Until the societies have been consolidated, and the public force, or law, now become superior to individual force, has been able to guarantee to each man the tranquil possession of his property against all invasion from without, a man could retain the ownership of a field only in the way he had acquired it and by continuing to cultivate it. It would not have been safe to get his field cultivated by somebody else, who, having taken all the trouble, would have had difficulty in understanding that the whole harvest did not belong to him. Moreover, in this early time, as every industrious man would find as much land as he wished, he could not be tempted to till the soil for others. It was necessary that every proprietor should cultivate his field himself, or give it up altogether.

10. Progress of the society; all the lands have a master

But the land filled up, and was more and more cleared. The best lands at length came to be all occupied. There remained for the last comers only the sterile soils rejected by the first. But in the end all land found its master, and those who could not have properties had at first no other resource than that of exchanging the labour of their arms, in the employ-ments of the *stipendiary* class, for the superfluous portion of the crops of the cultivating Proprietor.

11.   The Proprietors begin to be able to throw the labour of cultivation upon hired Cultivators

But since the land returned, to the master who cultivated it, not only his subsistence, not only that wherewith to procure for himself by way of exchange the other things he needed, but also a considerable superfluity, he could, with this superfluity, pay men to cultivate his land; and for men who live on wages, it was as good to earn them in this business as in any other. Thus ownership could be separated from the labour of cultivation; and soon it was.

12.   Inequality in the division of properties: causes which render that inevitable

The original Proprietors at first occupied, as has been already said, as much of the ground as their forces permitted them to cultivate with their family. A man of greater strength, more industrious, more anxious about the future, took more of it than a man of a contrary character. He whose family was more numerous, as he had more needs and more hands at his disposal, extended his possessions further: here was already a first inequality. All pieces of ground are not equally fertile: two men, with the same extent of ground and the same labour, could obtain a very different produce from it: second source of inequality. Properties, in passing from fathers to children, are divided into portions more or less small, according as the families are more or less numerous; as generations succeed one another, sometimes the inheritances are still further subdivided, some-times they are reunited again by the extinction of some of the branches: third source of inequality. The contrast between the intelligence, the activity, and, above all, the economy of some and the indolence, inaction and dissipation of others, was a fourth principle of inequality and the most powerful of all. The negligent and improvident Proprietor, who cultivates badly, who, in abundant years, consumes the whole of his superfluity in frivolities, finds himself reduced, on the least accident, to request assist-ance from his neighbour who has been more prudent, and to live by borrowing. If, by new accidents, or through a continuance of his neglect, he finds himself not in a condition to repay, if he is obliged to have recourse to new loans, he will at last have no other resource than to abandon a part or even the whole of his estate to his creditor, who will take it as an equivalent; or to assign it to another, in exchange for other values wherewith he will discharge his obligation to his creditor.

13. Consequence of this inequality: the Cultivator distinguished from the Proprietor

Here, then, we have landed properties as objects of commerce, and bought and sold. The portion of the extravagant or unfortunate Proprietor serves for the increase of that of the Proprietor who has been more fortunate or more prudent; and, in this infinitely varied inequality of possessions, it is impossible but that many Proprietors should have more than they can cultivate. Besides, it is natural enough that a rich man should wish to enjoy his wealth in tranquillity, and that instead of employing his whole time in toilsome labours, he should prefer to give a part of his superfluity to people who will work for him.

14. Division of the produce between the Cultivator & the Proprietor. Net produce or revenue

By this new arrangement the produce of the land is divided into two parts. The one includes the subsistence and the profits of the Husbandman, which are the reward of his labour and the condition upon which he undertakes to cultivate the field of the Proprietor. What remains is that independent and disposable part which the land gives as a pure gift to him who cultivates it, over and above his advances and the wages of his trouble; and this is the portion of the Proprietor, or the revenue with which the latter can live without labour and which he carries where he will.

15. New division of the Society into three classes, of Cultivators, of Artisans & of Proprietors; or the productive class, the stipendiary class and the disposable class

Here then we have the Society divided into three classes; the class of Husbandmen, for which we may keep the name of productive class; the class of Artisans and others who receive stipends from the produce of the land; and the class of Proprietors, the only one which, not being bound by the need of subsistence to a particular labour, can be employed for the general needs of the Society, such as war and the administration of justice, either by a personal service, or by the payment of a part of their revenue with which the State or the Society may engage men to discharge these functions. The name which, for this reason, suits it the best is that of *disposable class*.

16. Resemblance between the two working or non-disposable classes

The two classes of the Cultivators and the Artisans resemble each other in many respects, and above all in this, that those who compose them possess no revenue and live equally on wages, which are paid them out of the produce of the land. Both have also this in common, that they get nothing but the price of their labour and of their advances, and this price is nearly the same in the two classes; the Proprietor bargaining with those who cultivate the land to yield to them as small a part of the produce as possible, in the same way as he chaffers with his Shoemaker to buy his shoes as cheaply as possible. In a word, the Cultivator and the Artisan receive, neither of them, more than the recompense of their labour.

17. Essential difference between the two working classes

But there is this difference between the two kinds of labours, that the labour of the Cultivator produces his own wages, and, in addition, the revenue which serves to pay the whole class of Artisans and other stipendiaries; while the Artisans receive simply their wages; that is to say their part of the produce of the land in exchange for their labour, and do not produce any revenue. The Proprietor has nothing except through the labour of the Cultivator; he receives from him his subsistence, and that wherewith he pays the labours of the other stipendiaries. He has need of the Cultivator through the necessity of the physical order, in virtue of which the land produces nothing without labour; but the Cultivator has need of the Proprietor only by virtue of the human conventions and the civil laws which have been obliged to guarantee to the first Cultivators and to their heirs the ownership of the grounds which they have occupied even after they ceased to cultivate them. But these laws could guarantee to the man who took no part in the work himself only that portion of the produce which the land gives over and above the recompense due to the Cultivators. The Proprietor is obliged to give up this latter, on pain of losing the whole. The Cultivator, confined though he is to the recompense of his labour, thus preserves that natural and physical primacy which renders him the first mover of the whole machine of the Society and which causes his own subsistence as well as the wealth of the Proprietor and the wages of all the other labours to depend upon his labour alone. The Artisan, on the contrary, receives his wages, whether it be from the Proprietor or from the Cultivator, and gives them, in exchange for his labour, only the equivalent of these wages and nothing more.

Thus, although neither the Cultivator nor the Artisan gains more than the recompense of his labour, the Cultivator causes, over and above that recompense, the revenue of the Proprietor to come into existence; and the Artisan causes no revenue to come into existence either for himself or for others.

18.   This difference justifies their being distinguished as productive & barren *class respectively*

We can then distinguish the two non-disposable classes as the *productive class,* which is that of the Cultivators, and the *barren class,* which includes all the other stipendiary members of the Society.

19.   Of capitals in general, & of the revenue of money

There is another way of being rich, without labouring and without possessing lands, of which I have not yet spoken. It is necessary to explain its origin and its connection with the rest of the system of the distribution of riches in the society, of which I have just drawn the outline. This way consists in living upon what is called the revenue of one's money, or upon the interest one draws from money placed on loan.

20.   Birth of Commerce. Principle of the valuation of commercial things

Reciprocal want has led to the exchange of what people have for what they have not. People exchange one kind of produce for another, or produce for labour. In these exchanges it is necessary that the two parties should agree both as to the quality and the quantity of each of the things exchanged. In this agreement it is natural that each should wish to receive as much and give as little as he can; and both being equally masters of what they have to give in the exchange, each has to balance the attachment he has for the commodity he gives against the desire he has for the commodity he wishes to receive, and to fix in accordance therewith the quantity of each of the things exchanged. If the parties are not in accord, it will be necessary that they should approach one another by yielding a little on one side and a little on the other, offering more and contenting themselves with less. I will suppose that one has need of corn, and the other of wine, and that they agree to exchange *one bushel of corn* for *six pints of wine*. It is evident that by each of them *one bushel of corn* and *six pints of wine* are looked upon as exactly equivalent, and that in this particular exchange the price of *a bushel* of corn is *six pints* of wine, and the price of *six pints* of wine is *a bushel* of corn. But in another exchange between other men this price will be different, according as one of them happens to have a more or less pressing need of the commodity belonging to the other; and *a bushel* of corn may possibly be exchanged for *eight pints* of wine, while *another bushel* will be exchanged for only *four pints*. Now it is evident that no one of these three prices can be regarded as the true price of a bushel of corn rather than the others; for with each of the contracting parties the wine he has received was the equivalent of the corn he has given: in a word, so long as we consider each exchange as isolated and standing by itself, the value of each of the things exchanged has no other measure than the need or the desire and the means of the contracting parties, balanced one against the other, and it is fixed by nothing but the agreement of their will.

21. *How the current value establishes itself in the exchange of commodities*

However, it happens sometimes that several Individuals have wine to offer to the man who has corn: if one is not willing to give more than *four pints* for *a bushel,* the Proprietor of the corn will not give him his corn, when he comes to learn that someone else will give him *six* or *eight pints* for the same *bushel*. If the former wishes to have corn, he will be obliged to raise the price to the level of him who offers more. The Sellers of wine profit on their side by the competition among the Sellers of corn: no one makes up his mind to part with his commodity until he has compared the different offers that are made to him of the commodity he is in need of, and he gives the preference to the highest offer. The value of corn and of wine is no longer debated between two isolated Individuals in relation to their relative wants and abilities; it is fixed by the balance of the wants and abilities of the whole body of the Sellers of corn with those of the whole body of the Sellers of wine. For he who would willingly give *eight pints* of wine for *a bushel* of corn will only give *four* when he learns that a Proprietor of corn consents to give *two bushels* of corn for *eight pints*. The price midway between the different offers and the different demands will become the current price, whereto all the Buyers and Sellers will conform in their exchanges; and it will be true to say that *six pints* of wine are the equivalent of *a bushel* of corn for everyone if that is the *mean* price, until a diminution of the offer on the one side or of the demand on the other causes this valuation to change.

22. *Commerce gives to each article of commerce a current value, with respect to every other article; whence it follows that every article of commerce is the equivalent of a certain quantity of every other article, & can be regarded as a pledge which represents it*

Corn is exchanged not only for wine, but for all other articles which the proprietors of corn may need; for wood, leather, wool, cotton, etc.: it is the same with wine and with every other kind of produce. If *one bushel* of corn is the equivalent of *six pints* of wine, and *one sheep* is the equivalent of *three bushels* of corn this same *sheep* will be the equivalent of *eighteen pints* of wine. He who having corn needs wine can, without inconvenience, exchange his corn for a sheep, in order afterward to exchange this sheep for the wine he stands in need of.

23. *Each article of commerce can serve as the scale or common measure wherewith to compare the value of all others*

It follows from this that in a country where Commerce is very brisk, where there is much production and much consumption, where there are many offers and demands for all kinds of commodities, each kind will have a current price relatively to each other kind; that is to say, a certain quantity of one will be equivalent to a certain quantity of each of the others. Thus the same quantity of corn that will be worth eighteen pints of wine will be worth also one sheep, one piece of dressed leather, a certain quantity of iron: and all those things will have in commerce an equal value. To express and make known the value of any particular thing, it is evident that it is sufficient to declare the quantity of any other known commodity which may be regarded as its equivalent. Thus, in order to make known the value of a piece of leather of a certain size, we may say indifferently that it is worth *three bushels of corn* or *eighteen pints of wine*. We may in the same way express the value of a certain quantity of wine by the number of sheep or bushels of corn that it is worth in Commerce.

We see by this that all the kinds of commodities that can be the object of Commerce measure one another, so to speak; that each may serve as a common measure or a scale of comparison to which to refer the values of all the others; and in like manner each commodity becomes in the hands of its possessor a means to procure all the others: a sort of universal pledge.

24. Different articles have been able to serve & have served as ordinary money

Many Nations have adopted as a common measure of value in their language and in their Commerce different substances more or less precious; there are even today certain Barbarous Peoples who employ a kind of little shell called *Caurits*. I remember to have seen at College apricot stones exchanged and passed as a kind of money among the Scholars, who made use of them to play at different games. I have already spoken of the reckoning by head of cattle. One finds traces of it in the Laws of the ancient German Nations who destroyed the Roman Empire. The early Romans, or at least the Latins their ancestors, also made use of it. It is said that the first coin struck in copper represented the value of a sheep, and bore the imprint of that animal, and that it is from this that the word *pecunia* has come, from *pecus*. This conjecture has a good deal of probability.

25. The Metals, and especially gold and silver, are more fit for this purpose than any other substance; & why

We have thus come to the introduction of the precious metals into Commerce. All the metals, as one after the other they have been discovered, have been admitted into the exchanges in proportion to their real utility. Their brilliancy has caused them to be sought for to serve as ornament; their ductility and solidity have rendered them fit to make vessels more durable and lighter than those of clay. But these substances could not be in Commerce without becoming almost immediately the universal Money; a piece of any metal, whatever it may be, has exactly the same qualities as another piece of the same metal, provided it is equally pure: moreover the facility with which a metal can, by various operations of Chemistry, be separated from others with which it may be alloyed, makes it possible always to reduce them to the degree of purity, or, as they call it, to *the title,* that one desires: and then the value of the metal can only vary according to its weight. In expressing, then, the value of each commodity by the weight of the metal one gives in exchange we have the clearest, the most convenient, and the most exact expression of all the values; and henceforth it is impossible that it should not in practice be preferred to every other. Nor are the metals less suitable than other commodities to become the universal pledge of all the values they can measure: as they are susceptible of all imaginable divisions, there is no article of Commerce whose value, great or small, cannot be exactly paid for by a certain quantity of metal. To this advantage of lending themselves to every kind of division, they add that of being unalterable: and those that are rare, like gold and silver, have a very great value in a very inconsiderable weight and bulk.

These two metals are, then, of all merchandise the most easy to verify as to their quality, to divide as to their quantity, to keep forever without alteration, and to transport to all places at the least expense. Everyone who has a surplus commodity, and has not at the moment any need of another commodity for use, will hasten to exchange it for money; with which he is more sure, than with anything else, to be able to procure the commodity he shall wish for at the moment he is in want of it.

26. *Gold & Silver are constituted, by the nature of things, money, & universal money; independently of all convention & of all law*

Thus, then, we come to the constitution of gold and silver as money and universal money, and that without any arbitrary convention among men, without the intervention of any law, but by the nature of things. They are not, as many people have imagined, signs of values; they have themselves a value. If they are susceptible of being the measure and the pledge of other values, they have this property in common with all the other articles that have a value in Commerce. They differ only because being at once more divisible, more unalterable, and more easy to transport than the other commodities, it is more convenient to employ them to measure and represent the values.

27. *All economic undertakings, particularly those of manufacture & commerce, could not fail to be extremely limited before the introduction of gold & silver in commerce*

It is hardly necessary to remark that undertakings of all kinds, but especially those of manufacture and still more those of commerce, must needs have been greatly limited before the introduction of gold and silver in commerce; since it was almost impossible to accumulate considerable capitals, and still more difficult to multiply and divide payments, as much as is necessary to facilitate and multiply exchanges to the extent which is demanded by a thriving commerce and circulation. Agriculture alone could maintain itself a little, because cattle are the principal object of the advances it requires; moreover, it is probable that there was then no other agricultural undertaker but the proprietor. As to crafts of all kinds, they must have languished greatly before the introduction of money. They were limited to the roughest kinds of occupations, for which the Proprietors furnished the advances by feeding the Workmen and by providing them with materials, or which they caused to be carried on at home by their Domestics.

28. Capitals being as necessary to all undertakings as labour and industry, the industrious man is ready to share the profits of his undertaking with the Capitalist who furnishes him with the funds of which he has need

Since capitals are the indispensable foundation of every undertaking, since also money is a principal means for economising from small gains, amassing profits, and growing rich, those who, though they have industry and the love of labour, have no capitals or not enough for the undertakings they wish to embark in, have no difficulty in making up their minds to give up to the Possessors of capitals or money, who are willing to trust them with it, a portion of the profits they expect to gain over and above the return of their advances.

29.   The loan upon interest. Nature of the loan

The Possessors of money balance the risk their capital may run if the enterprise does not succeed, with the advantage of enjoying a definite profit without labour; and they are influenced thereby to demand more or less profit or interest for their money, or to consent to lend it in return for the interest the Borrower offers them. Here, then, is another outlet open to the Possessor of money,—lending on interest, or the trade in money. For one must not make a mistake; lending on interest is nothing in the world but a commercial transaction in which the Lender is a man who sells the use of his money and the Borrower a man who buys it; precisely as the Proprietor of an estate and his Farmer sell and buy respectively the use of a piece of land which is let out. This is what is perfectly expressed by the name the Latins gave to the interest of money placed on loan,—*usura pecuniæ,* a word the French Rendering of which has become hateful in consequence of the false ideas which have been formed as to the interest of money.

30.   Errors of the Schoolmen refuted

It is for want of having looked at lending on interest in its true light that certain moralists, more rigid than enlightened, have endeavoured to make us regard it as a crime. The Scholastic theologians have concluded from the fact that money produces nothing by itself that it was unjust to demand interest for money placed on loan. Full of their prejudices, they have believed their doctrine was sanctioned by this passage of the Gospel: *Mutuum date, nihil inde sperantes.* Those theologians who have adopted more reasonable principles on the subject of interest have had to endure the harshest reproaches from writers of the opposite party.

Nevertheless it needs but little reflection to realise the frivolity of the pretexts which have been made use of to condemn the taking of interest. A loan is a reciprocal contract, free between the two parties, which they make only because it is advantageous to them. It is evident that, if the Lender finds it to his advantage to receive something as the hire of his money, the Borrower is equally interested in finding the money of which he stands in need; as is shown by his making up his mind to borrow and to pay the hire of the money: but on what principle can one imagine a crime in a contract which is advantageous to the two parties, with which both are content and which certainly does not injure anyone else. To say that the Lender takes advantage of the Borrower's need of money to demand interest for it is to talk as absurdly as if one should say that a Baker who demands money for the bread he sells takes advantage of the Purchaser's need of bread. If, in the latter case, the money is the equivalent of the bread the Purchaser receives, the money which the Borrower receives today is equally the equivalent of the capital and of the interest which he promises to return at the expiration of a certain time; for, in short, it is an advantage for the Borrower to have during this interval the money he stands in need of, and it is a disadvantage to the Lender to be deprived of it. This disadvantage is capable of being estimated, and it is estimated; the interest is the price of it. This price ought to be higher if the Lender runs a risk of losing his capital by the insolvency of the Borrower. The bargain, therefore, is perfectly equal on both sides, and consequently fair. Money considered as a physical substance, as a mass of metal, does not produce anything; but money employed in advances for enterprises in Agriculture, Manufacture, and Commerce procures a definite profit. With money one can purchase an estate, and thereby procure a revenue. The person, therefore, who lends his money does not merely give up the barren possession of that money; he deprives himself of the profit or of the revenue which he would have been able to procure by it; and the interest which indemnifies him for this privation cannot be regarded as unjust.

31. True foundation of the interest of money

A man, then, may let his money as properly as he may sell it; and the possessor of money may do either one or the other, not only because the money is the equivalent of a revenue and a means to procure a revenue, not only because the lender loses during the time of the loan the revenue he might have secured by it, not only because he risks his capital, not only because the borrower may employ it in advantageous purchases or in undertakings from which he will draw large profits: the Proprietor of money may properly draw the interest of it in accordance with a more general and more decisive principle. Even if all the foregoing were not the case, he would none the less have a right to require the interest of the loan, simply because his money is his own. Since it is his own, he is free to keep it; nothing makes it his duty to lend: if, then, he does lend, he may attach to his loan such a condition as he chooses. In this he does no wrong to the borrower, since the latter acquiesces in the condition, and has no sort of right to the sum lent. The profit that a man may obtain by the use of the money is doubtless one of the commonest motives influencing the borrower to borrow on interest; it is one of the sources of the ease he finds in paying this interest; but this is by no means what gives a right to the lender to require it; it is enough for him that his money is his own, and this right is inseparable from that of property.

32. There exists no truly disposable revenue in a State except the net produce of lands

We see, by what has been said, that the interest of money placed on loan is taken either from the revenue of lands or from the profits of undertakings in agriculture, industry or commerce. But as to these profits themselves, we have already shown that they were only a part of the produce of lands; that the produce of lands falls into two parts; that the one was set aside for the wages of the cultivator, for his profits, and for the return of his advances and the interest upon them: and that the other was the share of the proprietor, that is to say, the revenue the proprietor expended at his pleasure, and from which he contributed to the general expenses of the State. We have shown that all that the other classes of the Society receive is merely the wages and the profits that are paid either by the proprietor from his revenue, or by the agents of the productive class from the part which is set aside to satisfy their needs, for which they are obliged to purchase commodities from the industrial class. Whether these profits be distributed in wages to work-men, in profits to undertakers, or in interest upon advances, they do not change their nature, and do not increase the sum of the revenue produced by the productive class over and above the price of its labour,— in which sum the industrial class participates only to the extent of the price of its labour.

The proposition, then, remains unshaken that there is no revenue save the net produce of lands, and that all other annual profit is either paid by the revenue, or forms part of the expenditure which serves to produce the revenue.

33. The land has also furnished the whole amount of moveable riches, or capitals, in existence, & these are formed only by part of its produce being saved every year

Not only does there not exist nor can there exist any other revenue than the net produce of lands, but it is also the land which has furnished all the capitals which make up the sum of all the advances of agriculture and commerce. It was that which offered without tillage the first rude advances which were indispensable for the earliest labours; all the rest is the accumulated fruit of the economy of the centuries that have fol-lowed one another since man began to cultivate the earth. This econo-mizing has doubtless taken place not only out of the revenues of the proprietors, but also out of the profits of all the members of the working classes. It is even generally true that, although the proprietors have a greater superfluity, they save less because as they have more leisure, they have more desires and more passions; they regard themselves as more assured of their fortunes; they think more about enjoying it agreeably than about increasing it: luxury is their inheritance. The wage-receivers, and especially the undertakers of the other classes, who receive profits proportionate to their advances, to their talent and to their activity, although they have no revenue properly so called, have yet a superfluity beyond their subsistence; and almost all of them, devoted as they are to their undertakings, occupied in increasing their fortunes, removed by their labour from expensive amusements and passions, save all their superfluity to invest it again in their business and so increase it. Most of the undertakers in agriculture borrow little, and scarcely any of them seek to make a profitable employment of anything but their own funds. The undertakers in other employments, who wish to make their fortunes stable, also try to get into the same position; and, unless they have great ability, those who carry on their enterprises upon borrowed funds run great risk of failing. But, although capitals are partly formed by saving from the profits of the working classes, yet, as these profits always come from the earth,—inasmuch as they are all paid, either from the revenue, or as part of the expenditure which serves to produce the revenue,—it is evident that capitals come from the land just as much as the revenue does; or, rather, that they are nothing but the accumulation of the part of the values produced by the land that the proprietors of the revenue, or those who share it with them, can lay by every year without using it for the satisfaction of their wants.

34. Although money is the immediate subject of saving, and is, so to speak, the first material of capitals when they are being formed, specie forms but an almost inappreciable part of the sum total of capitals

We have seen that money plays scarcely any part in the sum total of existing capitals; but it plays a great part in the formation of capitals. In fact, almost all savings are made in nothing but money; it is in money that the revenues come to the proprietors, that the advances and the profits return to undertakers of every kind; it is, therefore, from money that they save, and the annual increase of capitals takes place in money: but none of the undertakers make any other use of it than to convert it *immediately* into the different kinds of effects upon which their undertaking depends; and thus this money returns to circulation, and the greater part of capitals exists only in effects of different kinds, as we have already explained above.

AN INQUIRY INTO
THE NATURE AND CAUSES OF
THE WEALTH OF NATIONS

by

ADAM SMITH

CONTENTS

The Wealth of Nations

Introduction and Plan of Work

Book One: Of the Causes of Improvement in the productive Powers of Labour, and of the Order according to which its Produce is naturally distributed
  I. Of the Division of Labour
  II. Of the Principle Which Gives Occasion to the Division of Labour
  III. That the Division of Labour Is Limited by the Extent of the Market
  IV. Of the Origin and Use of Money
  V. Of the Real and Nominal Price of Commodities
  VI. Of the Component Parts of the Price of Commodities
  VII. Of the Natural and Market Price of Commodities
  VIII. Of the Wages of Labour
  IX. Of the Profits of Stock
  X. Of the Rent of Land

Book Two: Of the Nature, Accumulation, and Employment of Stock
  Introduction
  I. Of the Division of Stock
  II. Of the Accumulation of Capital
  III. Of Stock Lent at Interest
  IV. Of the Different Employment of Capitals

Book Three: Of the different Progress of Opulence in different Nations
  Of the Natural Progress of Opulence

Book Four: Of Systems of political Economy
  Introduction
  I. Of the Principle of the Commercial or Mercantile System
  II. Of Restraints upon the Importation from Foreign Countries
  III. Conclusion of the Mercantile System
  IV. Of the Agricultural Systems

Book Five: Of the Revenue of the Sovereign or Commonwealth
  I. Of the Expences of the Sovereign or Commonwealth
  II. Of the Sources of the General or Public Revenue of the Society

ADAM SMITH

1723–1790

ADAM SMITH, author of what is often described as the greatest book on economics ever written, was born at the small seaport town of Kirkcaldy, Scotland, in 1723. His father was a controller of customs. He studied moral philosophy at the University of Glasgow under Francis Hutcheson, whom he called the "never-to-be-forgotten Hutcheson" and from whom he learned, he said, to esteem "natural liberty." In 1748 he lectured in Edinburgh on rhetoric and belles-lettres. At this time began his lifelong friendship with David Hume, Scottish philosopher, historian, and political economist. Adam Smith became successively professor of logic and professor of moral philosophy in the University of Glasgow from 1751 to 1763. His first book, *The Theory of Moral Sentiments,* which argues that sympathy, rather than utility or self-interest, is the basis of morals, was published in 1759. It brought him fame and led to his selection as tutor to the young Duke of Buccleuch, with whom he traveled on the continent of Europe. In France he met and highly esteemed François Quesnay and others of the French *"économistes,"* or physiocrats. Smith lived in France, chiefly in Paris and Toulouse, until the year 1766. Meanwhile, the ideas which he embodied in *The Wealth of Nations* were ripening in his mind. It was not until ten years later, however, that the book was actually published. There is no doubt that Smith was strongly influenced by David Hume, as well as by the French physiocrats, and the appearance of the book was greeted by Hume in an enthusiastic letter in which he said: "It has depth and solidity and acuteness, and is so much illustrated by curious facts that it must at last attract the public attention."

During the years that followed the publication of his magnum opus, Adam Smith was feted and courted. He was appointed one of the commissioners of customs for Scotland in 1778, and lived in Edinburgh with his mother and a maiden cousin. Benjamin Franklin had visited him, and when Smith went to London he entered the charmed circle of Samuel Johnson's friends. In 1787 he was elected Lord Rector of the University of Glasgow. *The Wealth of Nations* appeared in five editions during Smith's lifetime and has been published in scores of editions since his death in 1790. It has been translated into all the chief European languages. The full title of this famous work is actually *An Inquiry into the Nature and Causes of the Wealth of Nations,* but it is almost universally spoken of as *The Wealth of Nations.*

The fact that *The Wealth of Nations* and the American Declaration of Independence were promulgated in the same year is much more than a coincidence. Adam Smith may appropriately be regarded as the patron saint of the capitalist system in the sense in which Thomas Jefferson was the formulator of the political ideals on which this country is based. Both Smith and Jefferson expressed, in memorable fashion, the spirit of the times, and both pointed to the opening of a new era.

The originality of Adam Smith's point of view lies in the fact that, in contradistinction to both the mercantilists and the physiocrats, he finds the real source of a country's wealth in its annual labor. On the first page of *The Wealth of Nations* he says: "The annual labour of every nation is the fund which originally supplies it with all the necessaries and conveniences of life which it annually consumes, and which consist always either in the immediate produce of that labour, or in what is purchased with that produce from other nations."

Growing out of this attitude are the ideas of division of labor and exchange value. Smith calls attention, at the outset of his book, to the immense importance of division of labor (as illustrated in the complexities of pinmaking). Then he says that man is the only animal that trucks, barters, and exchanges one thing for another. He saw that the idea of exchange value furnished a suitable central and unifying principle for economic discussion.

The system of Adam Smith is mainly a theory of production, and it has been properly called an "industrial system," for human industry is its efficient principle; but it is based on

manufacture industry in the original sense of the word manufacture, and was formulated before the industrial revolution
had, to any great extent, substituted machine industry for
handwork. Viewing everything from the standpoint of production, Adam Smith reached the conclusion that "natural"
value belongs to whatever embodies labor; that labor is the
cause of value—the real "price" of things.

Distribution he also interpreted as a "natural" function,
accounting for the shares meted out to each by construing
them in terms of the "necessary" equivalence of effort and
effect in production. Nature, he contended, makes no mistakes
and is not wasteful. Therefore, under conditions of natural
competition, effect must be proportioned to effort, and vice
versa.

Adam Smith believed in free trade, and his arguments in
this connection were quoted in the British Parliament and
influenced the younger Pitt, King George the Third's prime
minister, in negotiating a reciprocal treaty of commerce with
France.

AN INQUIRY INTO
THE NATURE AND CAUSES OF
THE WEALTH OF NATIONS

Introduction and Plan of Work

THE annual labour of every nation is the fund which originally supplies it with all the necessaries and conveniences of life which it annually consumes, and which consist always either in the immediate produce of that labour, or in what is purchased with that produce from other nations.

According therefore, as this produce, or what is purchased with it, bears a greater or smaller proportion to the number of those who are to consume it, the nation will be better or worse supplied with all the necessaries and conveniences for which it has occasion.

But this proportion must in every nation be regulated by two different circumstances; first, by the skill, dexterity, and judgment with which its labour is generally applied; and, secondly, by the proportion between the number of those who are employed in useful labour, and that of those who are not so employed. Whatever be the soil, climate, or extent of territory of any particular nation, the abundance or scantiness of its annual supply must, in that particular situation, depend upon those two circumstances.

The abundance or scantiness of this supply too seems to depend more upon the former of those two circumstances than upon the latter. Among the savage nations of hunters and fishers, every individual who is able to work, is more or less employed in useful labour, and endeavours to provide, as well as he can, the necessaries and conveniences of life, for himself, or such of his family or tribe as are either too old, or too young, or too infirm to go a hunting and fishing. Such nations, however, are so miserably poor, that from mere want, they are frequently reduced, or, at least, think themselves reduced, to the necessity sometimes of directly destroying, and sometimes of abandoning their infants, their old people, and those afflicted with lingering diseases, to perish with hunger, or to be devoured by wild beasts. Among civilized and thriving nations, on the contrary, though a great number of people do not labour at all, many of whom consume the produce of ten times, frequently of a hundred times more labour than the greater part of those who work; yet the produce of the whole labour of the society is so great, that all are often abundantly supplied, and a workman, even of the lowest and poorest order, if he is frugal and industrious, may enjoy a greater share of the necessaries and conveniences of life than it is possible for any savage to acquire.

The causes of this improvement, in the productive powers of labour, and the order, according to which its produce is naturally distributed among the different ranks and conditions of men in the society, make the subject of the First Book of this Inquiry.

Whatever be the actual state of the skill, dexterity, and judgment with which labour is applied in any nation, the abundance or scantiness of its annual supply must depend, during the continuance of that state, upon the proportion between the number of those who are annually employed in useful labour, and that of those who are not so employed. The number of useful and productive labourers, it will hereafter appear, is every where in proportion to the quantity of capital stock which is employed in setting them to work, and to the particular way in which it is so employed. The Second Book, therefore, treats of the nature of capital stock, of the manner in which it is gradually accumulated, and of the different quantities of labour which it puts into motion, according to the different ways in which it is employed.

Nations tolerably well advanced as to skill, dexterity, and judgment, in the application of labour, have followed very different plans in the general conduct cr direction of it; and those plans have not all been equally favourable to the greatness of its produce. The policy of some nations has given extraordinary encouragement to the industry of the country; that of others to the industry of towns. Scarce any nation has dealt equally and impartially with every sort of industry. Since the downfall of the Roman empire, the policy of Europe has been more favourable to arts, manufactures, and commerce, the industry of towns; than to agriculture, the industry of the country. The circumstances which seem to have introduced and established this policy are explained in the Third Book.

Though those different plans were, perhaps, first introduced by the private interests and prejudices of particular orders of men, without any regard to, or foresight of, their consequences upon the general welfare of the society; yet they have given occasion to very different theories of political economy; of which some magnify the importance of that industry which is carried on in towns, others of that which is carried on in the country. Those theories have had a considerable influence, not only upon the opinions of men of learning, but upon the public conduct of princes and sovereign states. I have endeavoured, in the Fourth Book, to explain, as fully and distinctly as I can, those different theories, and the principal effects which they have produced in different ages and nations.

To explain in what has consisted the revenue of the great body of the people, or what has been the nature of those funds, which, in different ages and nations, have supplied their annual consumption, is the object of these Four first Books. The Fifth and last Book treats of the revenue of the sovereign, or commonwealth.

Book One: Of the Causes of Improvement in the productive Powers of Labour, and of the Order according to which its Produce is naturally distributed among the different Ranks of the People.

I. OF THE DIVISION OF LABOUR

THE greatest improvement in the productive powers of labour, and the greater part of the skill, dexterity, and judgment with which it is any where directed, or applied, seem to have been the effects of the division of labour.

The effects of the division of labour, in the general business of society, will be more easily understood, by considering in what manner it operates in some particular manufactures. It is commonly supposed to be carried furthest in some very trifling ones; not perhaps that it really is carried further in them than in others of more importance: but in those trifling manufactures which are destined to supply the small wants of but a small number of people, the whole number of workmen must necessarily be small; and those employed in every different branch of the work can often be collected into the same workhouse, and placed at once under the view of the spectator. In those great manufactures, on the contrary, which are destined to supply the great wants of the great body of the people, every different branch of the work employs so great a number of workmen, that it is impossible to collect them all into the same workhouse. We can seldom see more, at one time, than those employed in one single branch. Though in such manufactures, therefore, the work may really be divided into a much greater number of parts, than in those of a more trifling nature, the division is not near so obvious, and has accordingly been much less observed.

To take an example, therefore, from a very trifling manufacture; but one in which the division of labour has been very often taken notice of, the trade of the pinmaker; a workman not educated to this business (which the division of labour has rendered a distinct trade), nor acquainted with the use of the machinery employed in it (to the invention of which the same division of labour has probably given occasion), could scarce, perhaps, with his utmost industry, make one pin in a day, and certainly could not make twenty. But in the way in which this business is now carried on, not only the whole work is a peculiar trade, but it is divided into a number of branches, of which the greater part are likewise peculiar trades. One man draws out the wire, another straights it, a third cuts it, a fourth points it, a fifth grinds it at the top for receiving the head; to make the head requires two or three distinct operations; to put it on, is a peculiar business, to whiten the pins is another; it is even a trade by itself to put them into the paper; and the important business of making a pin is, in this manner, divided into about eighteen distinct operations, which, in some manufactories, are all performed by distinct hands, though in others the same man will sometimes perform two or three of them. I have seen a small manufactory of this kind where ten men only were employed, and where some of them consequently performed two or three distinct operations. But though they were very poor, and therefore but indifferently accommodated with the necessary machinery, they could, when they exerted themselves, make among them about twelve pounds of pins in a day. There are in a pound upwards of four thousand pins of a middling size. Those ten persons, therefore, could make among them upwards of forty-eight thousand pins in a day. Each person, therefore, making a tenth part of forty-eight thousand pins, might be considered as making four thousand eight hundred pins in a day. But if they had all wrought separately and independently, and without any of them having been educated to this peculiar business, they certainly could not each of them have made twenty, perhaps not one pin in a day; that is, certainly, not the two hundred and fortieth, perhaps not the four thousand eight hundredth part of what they are at present capable of performing, in consequence of a proper division and combination of their different operations.

In every other art and manufacture, the effects of the division of labour are similar to what they are in this very trifling one; though, in many of them, the labour can neither be so much subdivided, nor reduced to so great a simplicity of operation. The division of labour, however, so far as it can be introduced, occasions, in every art, a proportionable increase of the productive powers of labour. The separation of different trades and employments from one another, seems to have taken place, in consequence of this advantage. This separation too is generally carried furthest in those countries which enjoy the highest degree of industry and improvement; what is the work of one man in a rude state of society, being generally that of several in an improved one. In every improved society, the farmer is generally nothing but a farmer; the manufacturer, nothing but a manufacturer. The labour too which is necessary to produce any one complete manufacture, is almost always divided among a great number of hands. How many different trades are employed in each branch of the linen and woollen manufactures, from the growers of the flax and the wool, to the bleachers and smoothers of the linen, or to the dyers and dressers of the cloth! The nature of agriculture, indeed, does not admit of so many subdivisions of labour, nor of so complete a separation of one business from another, as manufactures. It is impossible to separate so entirely, the business of the grazier from that of the corn farmer, as the trade of the carpenter is commonly separated from that of the smith. The spinner is almost always a distinct person from the weaver; but the ploughman, the harrower, the sower of the seed, and the reaper of the corn, are often the same. The occasions for those different sorts of labour returning with the different seasons of the year, it is impossible that one man should be constantly employed in any one of them. This impossibility of making so complete and entire a separation of all the different branches of labour employed in agriculture, is perhaps the reason why the improvement of the productive powers of labour in this art, does not always keep pace with their improvement in manufactures. The most opulent nations, indeed, generally excel all their neighbours in agriculture as well as in manufactures; but they are commonly more distinguished by their superiority in the latter than in the former. Their lands are in general better cultivated, and having more labour and expence bestowed upon them, produce more in proportion to the extent and natural fertility of the ground. But this superiority of produce is seldom much more than in proportion to the superiority of labour and expence. In agriculture, the labour of the rich country is not always much more productive than that of the poor; or, at least, it is never so much more productive, as it commonly is in manufactures. The corn of the rich country, therefore, will not always, in the same degree of goodness, come cheaper to market than that of the poor. The corn of Poland, in the same degree of goodness, is as cheap as that of France, notwithstanding the superior opulence and improvement of the latter country. The corn of France is, in the corn provinces, fully as good, and in most years nearly about the same price with the corn of England, though, in opulence and improvement, France is perhaps inferior to England. The cornlands of England, however, are better cultivated than those of France, and the cornlands of France are said to be much better cultivated than those of Poland. But though the poor country, notwithstanding the inferiority of its cultivation, can, in some measure, rival the rich in the cheapness and goodness of its corn, it can pretend to no such competition in its manufactures; at least if those manufactures suit the soil, climate, and situation of the rich country. The silks of France are better and cheaper than those of England, because the silk manufacture, at least under the present high duties upon the importation of raw silk, does not so well suit the climate of England as that of France. But the hardware and the coarse woollens of England are beyond all comparison superior to those of France, and much cheaper too in the same degree of goodness. In Poland there are said to be scarce any manufactures of any kind, a few of those coarser household manufactures excepted, without which no country can well subsist.

This great increase of the quantity of work, which, in consequence of the division of labour, the same number of people are capable of performing, is owing to three different circumstances; first, to the increase of dexterity in every particular workman; secondly, to the saving of the time which is commonly lost in passing from one species of work to another; and lastly, to the invention of a great number of machines which facilitate and abridge labour, and enable one man to do the work of many.

First, the improvement of the dexterity of the workman necessarily increases the quantity of the work he can perform; and the division of labour, by reducing every man's business to some one simple operation, and by making this operation the sole employment of his life, necessarily increases very much the dexterity of the workman. A common smith, who, though accustomed to handle the hammer, has never been used to make nails, if upon some particular occasion he is obliged to attempt it, will scarce, I am assured, be able to make above two or three hundred nails in a day, and those too very bad ones. A smith who has been accustomed to make nails, but whose sole or principal business has not been that of a nailer, can seldom with his utmost diligence make more than eight hundred or a thousand nails in a day. I have seen several boys under twenty years of age who had never exercised any other trade but that of making nails, and who, when they exerted themselves, could make, each of them, upwards of two thousand three hundred nails in a day. The making of a nail, however, is by no means one of the simplest operations. The same person blows the bellows, stirs or mends the fire as there is occasion, heats the iron, and forges every part of the nail: In forging the head too he is obliged to change his tools. The different operations into which the making of a pin, or of a metal button, is subdivided, are all of them much more simple, and the dexterity of the person, of whose life it has been the sole business to perform them, is usually much greater. The rapidity with which some of the operations of those manufactures are performed, exceeds what the human hand could, by those who had never seen them, be supposed capable of acquiring.

Secondly, the advantage which is gained by saving the time commonly lost in passing from one sort of work to another, is much greater than we should at first view be apt to imagine it. It is impossible to pass very quickly from one kind of work to another, that is carried on in a different place, and with quite different tools. A country weaver, who cultivates a small farm, must lose a good deal of time in passing from his loom to the field, and from the field to his loom. When the two trades can be carried on in the same workhouse, the loss of time is no doubt much less. It is even in this case, however, very considerable. A man commonly saunters a little in turning his hand from one sort of employment to another. When he first begins the new work he is seldom very keen and hearty; his mind, as they say, does not go to it, and for some time he rather trifles than applies to good purpose. The habit of sauntering and of indolent careless application, which is naturally, or rather necessarily acquired by every country workman who is obliged to change his work and his tools every half hour, and to apply his hand in twenty different ways almost every day of his life; renders him almost always slothful and lazy, and incapable of any vigorous application even on the most pressing occasions. Independent, therefore, of his deficiency in point of dexterity, this cause alone must always reduce considerably the quantity of work which he is capable of performing.

Thirdly, and lastly, every body must be sensible how much labour is facilitated and abridged by the application of proper machinery. It is unnecessary to give any example. I shall only observe, therefore, that the invention of all those machines by which labour is so much facilitated and abridged, seems to have been originally owing to the division of labour. Men are much more likely to discover easier and readier methods of attaining any object, when the whole attention of their minds is directed towards that single object, than when it is dissipated among a great variety of things. But in consequence of the division of labour, the whole of every man's attention comes naturally to be directed towards some one very simple object. It is naturally to be expected, therefore, that some one or other of those who are employed in each particular branch of labour should soon find out easier and readier methods of performing their own particular work, wherever the nature of it admits of such improvement. A great part of the machines made use of in those manufactures in which labour is most subdivided, were originally the inventions of common workmen, who, being each of them employed in some very simple operation, naturally turned their thoughts towards finding out easier and readier methods of performing it. Whoever has been much accustomed to visit such manufactures, must frequently have been shewn very pretty machines, which were the inventions of such workmen, in order to facilitate and quicken their own particular part of the work. In the first fire engines, a boy was constantly employed to open and shut alternately the communication between the boiler and the cylinder, according as the piston either ascended or descended. One of those boys, who loved to play with his companions, observed that, by tying a string from the handle of the valve which opened this communication to another part of the machine, the valve would open and shut without his assistance, and leave him at liberty to divert himself with his playfellows. One of the greatest improvements that has been made upon this machine, since it was first invented, was in this manner the discovery of a boy who wanted to save his own labour.

All the improvements in machinery, however, have by no means been the inventions of those who had occasion to use the machines. Many improvements have been made by the ingenuity of the makers of the machines, when to make them became the business of a peculiar trade; and some by that of those who are called philosophers or men of speculation, whose trade it is not to do any thing, but to observe every thing; and who, upon that account, are often capable of combining together the powers of the most distant and dissimilar objects. In the progress of society, philosophy or speculation becomes, like every other employment, the principal or sole trade and occupation of a particular class of citizens. Like every other employment too, it is subdivided into a great number of different branches, each of which affords occupation to a peculiar tribe or class of philosophers; and this subdivision of employment in philosophy, as well as in every other business, improves dexterity, and saves time. Each individual becomes more expert in his own peculiar branch, more work is done upon the whole, and the quantity of science is considerably increased by it.

It is the great multiplication of the productions of all the different arts, in consequence of the division of labour, which occasions, in a well-governed society, that universal opulence which extends itself to the lowest ranks of the people. Every workman has a great quantity of his own work to dispose of beyond what he himself has occasion for; and every other workman being exactly in the same situation, he is enabled to exchange a great quantity of his own goods for a great quantity, or, what comes to the same thing, for the price of a great quantity of theirs. He supplies them abundantly with what they have occasion for, and they accommodate him as amply with what he has occasion for, and a general plenty diffuses itself through all the different ranks of the society.

Observe the accommodation of the most common artificer or day labourer in a civilized and thriving country, and you will perceive that the number of people of whose industry a part, though but a small part, has been employed in procuring him this accommodation, exceeds all computation. The woollen coat, for example, which covers the day labourer, as coarse and rough as it may appear, is the produce of the joint labour of a great multitude of workmen. The shepherd, the sorter of the wool, the wool comber or carder, the dyer, the scribbler, the spinner, the weaver, the fuller, the dresser, with many others, must all join their different arts in order to complete even this homely production. How many merchants and carriers, besides, must have been employed in transporting the materials from some of those workmen to others who often live in a very distant part of the country! How much commerce and navigation in particular, how many shipbuilders, sailors, sailmakers, ropemakers, must have been employed in order to bring together the different drugs made use of by the dyer, which often come from the remotest corners of the world! What a variety of labour too is necessary in order to produce the tools of the meanest of those workmen! To say nothing of such complicated machines as the ship of the sailor, the mill of the fuller, or even the loom of the weaver, let us consider only what a variety of labour is requisite in order to form that very simple machine, the shears with which the shepherd clips the wool. The miner, the builder of the furnace for smelting the ore, the feller of the timber, the burner of the charcoal to be made use of in the smelting house, the brickmaker, the bricklayer, the workmen who attend the furnace, the millwright, the forger, the smith, must all of them join their different arts in order to produce them. Were we to examine, in the same manner, all the different parts of his dress and household furniture, the coarse linen shirt which he wears next his skin, the shoes which cover his feet, the bed which he lies on, and all the different parts which compose it, the kitchen grate at which he prepares his victuals, the coals which he makes use of for that purpose, dug from the bowels of the earth, and brought to him perhaps by a long sea and a long land carriage, all the other utensils of his kitchen, all the furniture of his table, the knives and forks, the earthen or pewter plates upon which he serves up and divides his victuals, the different hands employed in preparing his bread and his beer, the glass window which lets in the heat and the light, and keeps out the wind and the rain, with all the knowledge and art requisite for preparing that beautiful and happy invention, without which these northern parts of the world could scarce have afforded a very comfortable habitation, together with the tools of all the different workmen employed in producing those different conveniences; if we examine, I say, all these things, and consider what a variety of labour is employed about each of them, we shall be sensible that without the assistance and co-operation of many thousands, the very meanest person in a civilised country could not be provided, even according to, what we very falsely imagine, the easy and simple manner in which he is commonly accommodated. Compared, indeed, with the more extravagant luxury of the great, his accommodation must no doubt appear extremely simple and easy; and yet it may be true, perhaps, that the accommodation of an European prince does not always so much exceed that of an industrious and frugal peasant, as the accommodation of the latter exceeds that of many an African king, the absolute master of the lives and liberties of ten thousand naked savages.

II. Of the Principle Which Gives Occasion to the Division of Labour

This division of labour, from which so many advantages are derived, is not originally the effect of any human wisdom, which foresees and intends that general opulence to which it gives occasion. It is the necessary, though very slow and gradual, consequence of a certain propensity in human nature which has in view no such extensive utility; the propensity to truck, barter, and exchange one thing for another.

Whether this propensity be one of those original principles in human nature, of which no further account can be given; or whether, as seems more probable, it be the necessary consequence of the faculties of reason and speech, it belongs not to our present subject to enquire. It is common to all men, and to be found in no other race of animals, which seem to know neither this nor any other species of contracts. Two greyhounds, in running down the same hare, have sometimes the appearance of acting in some sort of concert. Each turns her towards his companion, or endeavours to intercept her when his companion turns her towards himself. This, however, is not the effect of any contract, but of the accidental concurrence of their passions in the same object at that particular time. Nobody ever saw a dog make a fair and deliberate exchange of one bone for another with another dog. Nobody ever saw one animal by its gestures and natural cries signify to another, this is mine, that yours; I am willing to give this for that. When an animal wants to obtain something either of a man or of another animal, it has no other means of persuasion but to gain the favour of those whose service it requires. A puppy fawns upon its dam, and a spaniel endeavours by a thousand attractions to engage the attention of its master who is at dinner, when it wants to be fed by him. Man sometimes uses the same arts with his brethren, and when he has no other means of engaging them to act according to his inclinations, endeavours by every servile and fawning attention to obtain their good will. He has not time, however, to do this upon every occasion. In civilized society he stands at all times in need of the co-operation and assistance of great multitudes, while his whole life is scarce sufficient to gain the friendship of a few persons. In almost every other race of animals each individual, when it is grown up to maturity, is entirely independent, and in its natural state has occasion for the assistance of no other living creature. But man has almost constant occasion for the help of his brethren, and it is in vain for him to expect it from their benevolence only. He will be more likely to prevail if he can interest their self-love in his favour, and shew them that it is for their own advantage to do for him what he requires of them. Whoever offers to another a bargain of any kind, proposes to do this. Give me that which I want, and you shall have this which you want, is the meaning of every such offer; and it is in this manner that we obtain from one another the far greater part of those good offices which we stand in need of. It is not from the benevolence of the butcher, the brewer, or the baker, that we expect our dinner, but from their regard to their own interest. We address ourselves, not to their humanity but to their self-love, and never talk to them of our own necessities but of their advantages. Nobody but a beggar chooses to depend chiefly upon the benevolence of his fellow citizens. Even a beggar does not depend upon it entirely. The charity of well-disposed people, indeed, supplies him with the whole fund of his subsistence. But though this principle ultimately provides him with all the necessaries of life which he has occasion for, it neither does nor can provide him with them as he has occasion for them. The greater part of his occasional wants are supplied in the same manner as those of other people, by treaty, by barter, and by purchase. With the money which one man gives him he purchases food. The old clothes which another bestows upon him he exchanges for other old clothes which suit him better, or for lodging, or for food, or for money, with which he can buy either food, clothes, or lodging, as he has occasion.

As it is by treaty, by barter, and by purchase, that we obtain from one another the greater part of those mutual good offices which we stand in need of, so it is this same trucking disposition which originally gives occasion to the division of labour. In a tribe of hunters or shepherds a particular person makes bows and arrows, for example, with more readiness and dexterity than any other. He frequently exchanges them for cattle or for venison with his companions; and he finds at last that he can in this manner get more cattle and venison, than if he himself went to the field to catch them. From a regard to his own interest, therefore, the making of bows and arrows grows to be his chief business, and he becomes a sort of armourer. Another excels in making the frames and covers of their little huts or moveable houses. He is accustomed to be of use in this way to his neighbours, who reward him in the same manner with cattle and with venison, till at last he finds it his interest to dedicate himself entirely to this employment, and to become a sort of house carpenter. In the same manner a third becomes a smith or a brazier; a fourth a tanner or dresser of hides or skins, the principal part of the clothing of savages. And thus the certainty of being able to exchange all that surplus part of the produce of his own labour, which is over and above his own consumption, for such parts of the produce of other men's labour as he may have occasion for, encourages every man to apply himself to a particular occupation, and to cultivate and bring to perfection whatever talent or genius he may possess for that particular species of business.

The difference of natural talents in different men is, in reality, much less than we are aware of; and the very different genius which appears to distinguish men of different professions, when grown up to maturity, is not upon many occasions so much the cause, as the effect of the division of labour. The difference between the most dissimilar characters, between a philosopher and a common street porter, for example, seems to arise not so much from nature, as from habit, custom, and education. When they came into the world, and for the first six or eight years of their existence, they were, perhaps, very much alike, and neither their parents nor playfellows could perceive any remarkable difference. About that age, or soon after, they come to be employed in very different occupations. The difference of talents comes then to be taken notice of, and widens by degrees, till at last the vanity of the philosopher is willing to acknowledge scarce any resemblance. But without the disposition to truck, barter, and exchange, every man must have procured to himself every necessary and conveniency of life which he wanted. All must have had the same duties to perform, and the same work to do, and there could have been no such difference of employment as could alone give occasion to any great difference of talents.

As it is this disposition which forms that difference of talents, so remarkable among men of different professions, so it is this same disposition which renders that difference useful. Many tribes of animals acknowledged to be all of the same species, derive from nature a much more remarkable distinction of genius, than what, antecedent to custom and education, appears to take place among men. By nature a philosopher is not in genius and disposition half so different from a street porter, as a mastiff is from a greyhound, or a greyhound from a spaniel, or this last from a shepherd's dog. Those different tribes of animals, however, though all of the same species, are of scarce any use to one another. The strength of the mastiff is not in the least supported either by the swiftness of the greyhound, or by the sagacity of the spaniel, or by the docility of the shepherd's dog. The effects of those different geniuses and talents, for want of the power or disposition to barter and exchange, cannot be brought into a common stock, and do not in the least contribute to the better accommodation and conveniency of the species. Each animal is still obliged to support and defend itself, separately and independently, and derives no sort of advantage from that variety of talents with which nature has distinguished its fellows. Among men, on the contrary, the most dissimilar geniuses are of use to one another; the different produces of their respective talents, by the general disposition to truck, barter, and exchange, being brought, as it were, into a common stock, where every man may purchase whatever part of the produce of other men's talents he has occasion for.

III. That the Division of Labour Is Limited by the Extent of the Market

As it is the power of exchanging that gives occasion to the division of labour, so the extent of this division must always be limited by the extent of that power, or, in other words, by the extent of the market. When the market is very small, no person can have any encouragement to dedicate himself entirely to one employment, for want of the power to exchange all that surplus part of the produce of his own labour, which is over and above his own consumption, for such parts of the produce of other men's labour as he has occasion for.

There are some sorts of industry, even of the lowest kind, which can be carried on no where but in a great town. A porter, for example, can find employment and subsistence in no other place. A village is by much too narrow a sphere for him; even an ordinary market town is scarce large enough to afford him constant occupation. In the lone houses and very small villages which are scattered about in so desert a country as the Highlands of Scotland, every farmer must be butcher, baker, and brewer for his own family. In such situations we can scarce expect to find even a smith, a carpenter, or a mason, within less than twenty miles of another of the same trade. The scattered families that live at eight or ten miles distance from the nearest of them, must learn to perform themselves a great number of little pieces of work, for which, in more populous countries, they would call in the assistance of those workmen. Country workmen are almost every where obliged to apply themselves to all the different branches of industry that have so much affinity to one another as to be employed about the same sort of materials. A country carpenter deals in every sort of work that is made of wood: a country smith in every sort of work that is made of iron. The former is not only a carpenter, but a joiner, a cabinet maker, and even a carver in wood, as well as a wheelwright, a ploughwright, a cart and waggon maker.

As by means of water carriage a more extensive market is opened to every sort of industry than what land carriage alone can afford it, so it is upon the seacoast, and along the banks of navigable rivers, that industry of every kind naturally begins to subdivide and improve itself, and it is frequently not till a long time after that those improvements extend themselves to the inland parts of the country. The extent of their market, therefore, must for a long time be in proportion to the riches and populousness of that country, and consequently their improvement must always be posterior to the improvement of that country. In our North American colonies the plantations have constantly followed either the seacoast or the banks of navigable rivers, and have scarce any where extended themselves to any considerable distance from both.

The nations that, according to the best authenticated history, appear to have been first civilized, were those that dwelt round the coast of the Mediterranean Sea. That sea, by far the greatest inlet that is known in the world, having no tides, nor consequently any waves except such as are caused by the wind only, was, by the smoothness of its surface, as well as by the multitude of its islands, and the proximity of its neighbouring shores, extremely favourable to the infant navigation of the world; when, from their ignorance of the compass, men were afraid to quit the view of the coast, and from the imperfection of the art of shipbuilding, to abandon themselves to the boisterous waves of the ocean.

IV. OF THE ORIGIN AND USE OF MONEY

WHEN the division of labour has been once thoroughly established, it is but a very small part of a man's wants which the produce of his own labour can supply. He supplies the far greater part of them by exchanging that surplus part of the produce of his own labour, which is over and above his own consumption, for such parts of the produce of other men's labour as he has occasion for. Every man thus lives by exchanging, or becomes in some measure a merchant, and the society itself grows to be what is properly a commercial society.

But when the division of labour first began to take place, this power of exchanging must frequently have been very much clogged and embarrassed in its operations. One man, we shall suppose, has more of a certain commodity than he himself has occasion for, while another has less. The former consequently would be glad to dispose of, and the latter to purchase, a part of this superfluity. But if this latter should chance to have nothing that the former stands in need of, no exchange can be made between them. The butcher has more meat in his shop than he himself can consume, and the brewer and the baker would each of them be willing to purchase a part of it. But they have nothing to offer in exchange, except the different productions of their respective trades, and the butcher is already provided with all the bread and beer which he has immediate occasion for. No exchange can, in this case, be made between them. He cannot be their merchant, nor they his customers; and they are all of them thus mutually less serviceable to one another. In order to avoid the inconveniency of such situations, every prudent man in every period of society, after the first establishment of the division of labour, must naturally have endeavoured to manage his affairs in such a manner, as to have at all times by him, besides the peculiar produce of his own industry, a certain quantity of some one commodity or other, such as he imagined few people would be likely to refuse in exchange for the produce of their industry.

Many different commodities, it is probable, were successively both thought of and employed for this purpose. In the rude ages of society, cattle are said to have been the common instrument of commerce; and, though they must have been a most inconvenient one, yet in old times we find things were frequently valued according to the number of cattle which had been given in exchange for them. The armour of Diomede, says Homer, cost only nine oxen; but that of Glaucus cost an hundred oxen. Salt is said to be the common instrument of commerce and exchanges in Abyssinia; a species of shells in some parts of the coast of India; dried cod at Newfoundland; tobacco in Virginia; sugar in some of our West India colonies; hides or dressed leather in some other countries; and there is at this day a village in Scotland where it is not uncommon, I am told, for a workman to carry nails instead of money to the baker's shop or the alehouse.

In all countries, however, men seem at last to have been determined by irresistible reasons to give the preference, for this employment, to metals above every other commodity. Metals can not only be kept with as little loss as any other commodity, scarce any thing being less perishable than they are, but they can likewise, without any loss, be divided into any number of parts, as by fusion those parts can easily be reunited again; a quality which no other equally durable commodities possess, and which more than any other quality renders them fit to be the instruments of commerce and circulation. The man who wanted to buy salt, for example, and had nothing but cattle to give in exchange for it, must have been obliged to buy salt to the value of a whole ox, or a whole sheep, at a time. He could seldom buy less than this, because what he was to give for it could seldom be divided without loss; and if he had a mind to buy more, he must, for the same reasons, have been obliged to buy double or triple the quantity, the value, to wit, of two or three oxen, or of two or three sheep. If, on the contrary, instead of sheep or oxen, he had metals to give in exchange for it, he could easily proportion the quantity of the metal to the precise quantity of the commodity which he had immediate occasion for.

Different metals have been made use of by different nations for this purpose. Iron was the common instrument of commerce among the ancient Spartans; copper among the ancient Romans; and gold and silver among all rich and commercial nations.

Those metals seem originally to have been made use of for this purpose in rude bars, without any stamp or coinage. Thus we are told by Pliny, upon the authority of Timæus, an ancient historian, that, till the time of Servius Tullius, the Romans had no coined money, but made use of unstamped bars of copper, to purchase whatever they had occasion for. These rude bars, therefore, performed at this time the function of money.

The use of metals in this rude state was attended with two very considerable inconveniencies; first with the trouble of weighing; and, secondly, with that of assaying them. In the precious metals, where a small difference in the quantity makes a great difference in the value, even the business of weighing, with proper exactness, requires at least very accurate weights and scales. The weighing of gold in particular is an operation of some nicety. In the coarser metals, indeed, where a small error would be of little consequence, less accuracy would, no doubt, be necessary. Yet we should find it excessively troublesome, if every time a poor man had occasion either to buy or sell a farthing's worth of goods, he was obliged to weigh the farthing. The operation of assaying is still more difficult, still more tedious, and, unless a part of the metal is fairly melted in the crucible, with proper dissolvents, any conclusion that can be drawn from it, is extremely uncertain. Before the institution of coined money, however, unless they went through this tedious and difficult operation, people must always have been liable to the grossest frauds and impositions, and instead of a pound weight of pure silver, or pure copper, might receive in exchange for their goods, an adulterated composition of the coarsest and cheapest materials, which had, however, in their outward appearance, been made to resemble those metals. To prevent such abuses, to facilitate exchanges, and thereby to encourage all sorts of industry and commerce, it had been found necessary, in all countries that have made any considerable advances towards improvement, to affix a public stamp upon certain quantities of such particular metals, as were in those countries commonly made use of to purchase goods. Hence the origin of coined money, and of those public offices called mints; institutions exactly of the same nature with those of the aulnegers and stampmasters of woollen and linen cloth. All of them are equally meant to ascertain, by means of a public stamp, the quantity and uniform goodness of those different commodities when brought to market.

The first public stamps of this kind that were affixed to the current metals, seem in many cases to have been intended to ascertain, what it was both most difficult and most important to ascertain, the goodness or fineness of the metal, and to have resembled the sterling mark which is at present affixed to plate and bars of silver, or the Spanish mark which is sometimes affixed to ingots of gold, and which being struck only upon one side of the piece, and not covering the whole surface, ascertains the fineness, but not the weight of the metal. Abraham weighs to Ephron the four hundred shekels of silver which he had agreed to pay for the field of Machpelah. They are said however to be the current money of the merchant, and yet are received by weight and not by tale, in the same manner as ingots of gold and bars of silver are at present. The revenues of the ancient Saxon kings of England are said to have been paid, not in money but in kind, that is, in victuals and provisions of all sorts. William the Conqueror introduced the custom of paying them in money. This money, however, was, for a long time, received at the exchequer, by weight and not by tale.

The inconveniency and difficulty of weighing those metals with exactness gave occasion to the institution of coins, of which the stamp, covering entirely both sides of the piece and sometimes the edges too, was supposed to ascertain not only the fineness, but the weight of the metal. Such coins, therefore, were received by tale as at present, without the trouble of weighing.

It is in this manner that money has become in all civilized nations the universal instrument of commerce, by the intervention of which goods of all kinds are bought and sold, or exchanged for one another.

What are the rules which men naturally observe in exchanging them either for money or for one another, I shall now proceed to examine. These rules determine what may be called the relative or exchangeable value of goods.

The word VALUE, it is to be observed, has two different meanings, and sometimes expresses the utility of some particular object, and sometimes the power of purchasing other goods which the possession of that object conveys. The one may be called "value in use"; the other, "value in exchange." The things which have the greatest value in use have frequently little or no value in exchange; and on the contrary, those which have the greatest value in exchange have frequently little or no value in use. Nothing is more useful than water: but it will purchase scarce any thing; scarce any thing can be had in exchange for it. A diamond, on the contrary, has scarce any value in use; but a very great quantity of other goods may frequently be had in exchange for it.

In order to investigate the principles which regulate the exchangeable value of commodities, I shall endeavour to show,

First, what is the real measure of this exchangeable value; or, wherein consists the real price of all commodities.

Secondly, what are the different parts of which this real price is composed or made up.

And, lastly, what are the different circumstances which sometimes raise some or all of these different parts of price above, and sometimes sink them below their natural or ordinary rate; or, what are the causes which sometimes hinder the market price, that is, the actual price of commodities, from coinciding exactly with what may be called their natural price.

I shall endeavour to explain, as fully and distinctly as I can, those three subjects in the three following chapters.

V. OF THE REAL AND NOMINAL PRICE OF COMMODITIES, OR OF THEIR PRICE IN LABOUR, AND THEIR PRICE IN MONEY

EVERY MAN is rich or poor according to the degree in which he can afford to enjoy the necessaries, conveniencies, and amusements of human life. But after the division of labour has once thoroughly taken place, it is but a very small part of these with which a man's own labour can supply him. The far greater part of them he must derive from the labour of other people, and he must be rich or poor according to the quantity of that labour which he can command, or which he can afford to purchase. The value of any commodity, therefore, to the person who possesses it, and who means not to use or consume it himself, but to exchange it for other commodities, is equal to the quantity of labour which it enables him to purchase or command. Labour, therefore, is the real measure of the exchangeable value of all commodities.

The real price of every thing, what every thing really costs to the man who wants to acquire it, is the toil and trouble of acquiring it. What every thing is really worth to the man who has acquired it, and who wants to dispose of it or exchange it for something else, is the toil and trouble which it can save to himself, and which it can impose upon other people. What is bought with money or with goods is purchased by labour, as much as what we acquire by the toil of our own body. That money or those goods indeed save us this toil. They contain the value of a certain quantity of labour which we exchange for what is supposed at the time to contain the value of an equal quantity. Labour was the first price, the original purchase-money that was paid for all things. It was not by gold or by silver, but by labour, that all the wealth of the world was originally purchased; and its value, to those who possess it, and who want to exchange it for some new productions, is precisely equal to the quantity of labour which it can enable them to purchase or command.

Wealth, as Mr. Hobbes says, is power. But the person who either acquires, or succeeds to a great fortune, does not necessarily acquire or succeed to any political power, either civil or military. His fortune may, perhaps, afford him the means of acquiring both, but the mere possession of that fortune does not necessarily convey to him either. The power which that possession immediately and directly conveys to him, is the power of purchasing; a certain command over all the labour, or over all the produce of labour which is then in the market. His fortune is greater or less, precisely in proportion to the extent of this power; or to the quantity either of other men's labour, or, what is the same thing, of the produce of other men's labour, which it enables him to purchase or command. The exchangeable value of every thing must always be precisely equal to the extent of this power which it conveys to its owner.

But though labour be the real measure of the exchangeable value of all commodities, it is not that by which their value is commonly estimated. It is often difficult to ascertain the proportion between two different quantities of labour. The time spent in two different sorts of work will not always alone determine this proportion. The different degrees of hardship endured, and of ingenuity exercised, must likewise be taken into account. There may be more labour in an hour's hard work than in two hours' easy business; or in an hour's application to a trade which it cost ten years' labour to learn, than in a month's industry at an ordinary and obvious employment. But it is not easy to find any accurate measure either of hardship or ingenuity. In exchanging indeed the different productions of different sorts of labour for one another, some allowance is commonly made for both. It is adjusted, however, not by any accurate measure, but by the higgling and bargaining of the market, according to that sort of rough equality which, though not exact, is sufficient for carrying on the business of common life.

Every commodity besides, is more frequently exchanged for, and thereby compared with, other commodities than with labour. It is more natural therefore, to estimate its exchangeable value by the quantity of some other commodity than by that of the labour which it can purchase. The greater part of people too understand better what is meant by a quantity of a particular commodity, than by a quantity of labour. The one is a plain palpable object; the other an abstract notion, which, though it can be made sufficiently intelligible, is not altogether so natural and obvious.

But when barter ceases, and money has become the common in strument of commerce, every particular commodity is more frequently exchanged for money than for any other commodity. The butcher seldom carries his beef or his mutton to the baker, or the brewer, in order to exchange them for bread or for beer; but he carries them to the market, where he exchanges them for money, and afterwards exchanges that money for bread and for beer. The quantity of money which he gets for them regulates too the quantity of bread and beer which he can after-wards purchase. It is more natural and obvious to him, therefore, to esti-mate their value by the quantity of money, the commodity for which he immediately exchanges them, than by that of bread and beer, the com-modities for which he can exchange them only by the intervention of another commodity; and rather to say that his butcher's meat is worth threepence or fourpence a pound, than that it is worth three or four pounds of bread, or three or four quarts of small beer. Hence it comes to pass, that the exchangeable value of every commodity is more fre-quently estimated by the quantity of money, than by the quantity either of labour or of any other commodity which can be had in exchange for it.

Gold and silver, however, like every other commodity, vary in their value, are sometimes cheaper and sometimes dearer, sometimes of easier and sometimes of more difficult purchase. The quantity of labour which any particular quantity of them can purchase or command, or the quan-tity of other goods which it will exchange for, depends always upon the fertility or barrenness of the mines which happen to be known about the time when such exchanges are made. The discovery of the abundant mines of America reduced, in the sixteenth century, the value of gold and silver in Europe to about a third of what it had been before. As it cost less labour to bring those metals from the mine to the market, so when they were brought thither they could purchase or command less labour; and this revolution in their value, though perhaps the greatest, is by no means the only one of which history gives some account. But as a measure of quantity, such as the natural foot, fathom, or handful, which is continually varying in its own quantity, can never be an accurate measure of the quantity of other things; so a commodity which is itself continually varying in its own value, can never be an accurate measure of the value of other commodities. Equal quantities of labour, at all times and places, may be said to be of equal value to the labourer. In his ordinary state of health, strength and spirits; in the ordinary degree of his skill and dexterity, he must always lay down the same portion of his ease, his liberty, and his happiness. The price which he pays must always be the same, whatever may be the quantity of goods which he receives in return for it. Of these, indeed, it may sometimes purchase a greater and sometimes a smaller quantity; but it is their value which varies, not that of the labour which purchases them. At all times and places that is dear which it is difficult to come at, or which it costs much labour to acquire; and that cheap which is to be had easily, or with very little labour. Labour alone, therefore, never varying in its own value, is alone the ultimate and real standard by which the value of all commodities can at all times and places be estimated and compared. It is their real price; money is their nominal price only.

But though equal quantities of labour are always of equal value to the labourer, yet to the person who employs him they appear sometimes to be of greater and sometimes of smaller value. He purchases them sometimes with a greater and sometimes with a smaller quantity of goods, and to him the price of labour seems to vary like that of all other things. It appears to him dear in the one case, and cheap in the other. In reality, however, it is the goods which are cheap in the one case, and dear in the other.

In this popular sense, therefore, labour, like commodities, may be said to have a real and a nominal price. Its real price may be said to consist in the quantity of the necessaries and conveniencies of life which are given for it; its nominal price, in the quantity of money. The labourer is rich or poor, is well or ill rewarded, in proportion to the real, not to the nominal price of his labour.

The distinction between the real and the nominal price of commodities and labour, is not a matter of mere speculation, but may sometimes be of considerable use in practice. The same real price is always of the same value; but on account of the variations in the value of gold and silver, the same nominal price is sometimes of very different values. When a landed estate, therefore, is sold with a reservation of a perpetual rent, if it is intended that this rent should always be of the same value, it is of importance to the family in whose favour it is reserved, that it should not consist in a particular sum of money. Its value would in this case be liable to variations of two different kinds; first, to those which arise from the different quantities of gold and silver which are contained at different times in coin of the same denomination; and, secondly, to those which arise from the different values of equal quantities of gold and silver at different times.

Princes and sovereign states have frequently fancied that they had a temporary interest to diminish the quantity of pure metal contained in their coins; but they seldom have fancied that they had any to augment it. The quantity of metal contained in the coins, I believe of all nations, has, accordingly, been almost continually diminishing, and hardly ever augmenting. Such variations therefore tend almost always to diminish the value of a money rent.

The discovery of the mines of America diminished the value of gold and silver in Europe. This diminution, it is commonly supposed, though I apprehend without any certain proof, is still going on gradually, and is likely to continue to do so for a long time. Upon this supposition, therefore, such variations are more likely to diminish, than to augment the value of a money rent, even though it should be stipulated to be paid, not in such a quantity of coined money of such a denomination (in so many pounds sterling, for example), but in so many ounces either of pure silver, or of silver of a certain standard.

The rents which have been reserved in corn have preserved their value much better than those which have been reserved in money, even where the denomination of the coin has not been altered. By the 18th of Elizabeth it was enacted, That a third of the rent of all college leases should be reserved in corn, to be paid, either in kind, or according to the current prices at the nearest public market. The money arising from this corn rent, though originally but a third of the whole, is in the present times, according to Doctor Blackstone, commonly near double of what arises from the other two thirds. The old money rents of colleges must, according to this account, have sunk almost to a fourth part of their ancient value; or are worth little more than a fourth part of the corn which they were formerly worth. But since the reign of Philip and Mary the denomination of the English coin has undergone little or no alteration, and the same number of pounds, shillings, and pence have contained very nearly the same quantity of pure silver. This degradation, therefore, in the value of the money rents of colleges, has arisen altogether from the degradation in the value of silver.

When the degradation in the value of silver is combined with the diminution of the quantity of it contained in the coin of the same denomination, the loss is frequently still greater. In Scotland, where the denomination of the coin has undergone much greater alterations than it ever did in England, and in France, where it has undergone still greater than it ever did in Scotland, some ancient rents, originally of considerable value, have in this manner been reduced almost to nothing.

Equal quantities of labour will at distant times be purchased more nearly with equal quantities of corn, the subsistence of the labourer, than with equal quantities of gold and silver, or perhaps of any other commodity. Equal quantities of corn, therefore, will, at distant times, be more nearly of the same real value, or enable the possessor to purchase or command more nearly the same quantity of the labour of other people. They will do this, I say, more nearly than equal quantities of almost any other commodity; for even equal quantities of corn will not do it exactly. The subsistence of the labourer, or the real price of labour, as I shall endeavour to show hereafter, is very different upon different occasions; more liberal in a society advancing to opulence, than in one that is standing still; and in one that is standing still, than in one that is going backwards. Every other commodity, however, will at any particular time purchase a greater or smaller quantity of labour in proportion to the quantity of subsistence which it can purchase at that time. A rent therefore reserved in corn is liable only to the variations in the quantity of labour which a certain quantity of corn can purchase. But a rent reserved in any other commodity is liable, not only to the variations in the quantity of labour which any particular quantity of corn can purchase, but to the variations in the quantity of corn which can be purchased by any particular quantity of that commodity.

Though the real value of a corn rent, it is to be observed however, varies much less from century to century than that of a money rent, it varies much more from year to year. The money price of labour, as I shall endeavour to show hereafter, does not fluctuate from year to year with the money price of corn, but seems to be every where accommodated, not to the temporary or occasional, but to the average or ordinary price of that necessary of life. The average or ordinary price of corn again is regulated, as I shall likewise endeavour to show hereafter, by the value of silver, by the richness or barrenness of the mines which supply the market with that metal, or by the quantity of labour which must be employed, and consequently of corn which must be consumed, in order to bring any particular quantity of silver from the mine to the market. But the value of silver, though it sometimes varies greatly from century to century, seldom varies much from year to year, but frequently continues the same, or very nearly the same, for half a century or a century together. The ordinary or average money price of corn, therefore, may, during so long a period, continue the same or very nearly the same too, and along with it the money price of labour, provided, at least, the society continues, in other respects, in the same or nearly in the same condition. In the mean time the temporary and occasional price of corn may frequently be double, one year, of what it had been the year before, or fluctuate, for example, from five and twenty to fifty shillings the quarter. But when corn is at the latter price, not only the nominal, but the real value of a corn rent will be double of what it is when at the former, or will command double the quantity either of labour or of the greater part of other commodities; the money price of labour, and along with it that of most other things, continuing the same during all these fluctuations.

Labour, therefore, it appears evidently, is the only universal, as well as the only accurate measure of value, or the only standard by which we can compare the values of different commodities at all times and at all places. We cannot estimate, it is allowed, the real value of different commodities from century to century by the quantities of silver which were given for them. We cannot estimate it from year to year by the quantities of corn. By the quantities of labour we can, with the greatest accuracy, estimate it both from century to century and from year to year. From century to century, corn is a better measure than silver, because from century to century, equal quantities of corn will command the same quantity of labour more nearly than equal quantities of silver. From year to year, on the contrary, silver is a better measure than corn, because equal quantities of it will more nearly command the same quantity of labour.

But though in establishing perpetual rents, or even in letting very long leases, it may be of use to distinguish between real and nominal price; it is of none in buying and selling, the more common and ordinary transactions of human life.

At the same time and place the real and the nominal price of all commodities are exactly in proportion to one another. The more or less money you get for any commodity, in the London market, for example, the more or less labour it will at that time and place enable you to purchase or command. At the same time and place, therefore, money is the exact measure of the real exchangeable value of all commodities. It is so, however, at the same time and place only.

Though at distant places, there is no regular proportion between the real and the money price of commodities, yet the merchant who carries goods from the one to the other has nothing to consider but their money price, or the difference between the quantity of silver for which he buys them, and that for which he is likely to sell them. Half an ounce of silver at Canton in China may command a greater quantity both of labour and of the necessaries and conveniencies of life, than an ounce at London. A commodity, therefore, which sells for half an ounce of silver at Canton may there be really dearer, of more real importance to the man who possesses it there, than a commodity which sells for an ounce at London is to the man who possesses it at London. If a London merchant, however, can buy at Canton for half an ounce of silver, a commodity which he can afterwards sell at London for an ounce, he gains a hundred per cent. by the bargain, just as much as if an ounce of silver was at London exactly of the same value as at Canton. It is of no importance to him that half an ounce of silver at Canton would have given him the command of more labour and of a greater quantity of the necessaries and conveniencies of life than an ounce can do at London. An ounce at London will always give him the command of double the quantity of all these, which half an ounce could have done there, and this is precisely what he wants.

As it is the nominal or money price of goods, therefore, which finally determines the prudence or imprudence of all purchases and sales, and thereby regulates almost the whole business of common life in which price is concerned, we cannot wonder that it should have been so much more attended to than the real price.

VI. Of the Component Parts of the Price of Commodities

In that early and rude state of society which precedes both the accumulation of stock and the appropriation of land, the proportion between the quantities of labour necessary for acquiring different objects seems to be the only circumstance which can afford any rule for exchanging them for one another. If among a nation of hunters, for example, it usually costs twice the labour to kill a beaver which it does to kill a deer, one beaver should naturally exchange for or be worth two deer. It is natural that what is usually the produce of two days' or two hours' labour, should be worth double of what is usually the produce of one day's or one hour's labour.

If the one species of labour should be more severe than the other, some allowance will naturally be made for this superior hardship; and the produce of one hour's labour in the one way may frequently exchange for that of two hours' labour in the other.

Or if the one species of labour requires an uncommon degree of dexterity and ingenuity, the esteem which men have for such talents, will naturally give a value to their produce, superior to what would be due to the time employed about it. Such talents can seldom be acquired but in consequence of long application, and the superior value of their produce may frequently be no more than a reasonable compensation for the time and labour which must be spent in acquiring them. In the advanced state of society, allowances of this kind, for superior hardship and superior skill, are commonly made in the wages of labour; and something of the same kind must probably have taken place in its earliest and rudest period.

In this state of things, the whole produce of labour belongs to the labourer; and the quantity of labour commonly employed in acquiring or producing any commodity, is the only circumstance which can regulate the quantity of labour which it ought commonly to purchase, command, or exchange for.

As soon as stock has accumulated in the hands of particular persons, some of them will naturally employ it in setting to work industrious people, whom they will supply with materials and subsistence, in order to make a profit by the sale of their work, or by what their labour adds to the value of the materials. In exchanging the complete manufacture either for money, for labour, or for other goods, over and above what may be sufficient to pay the price of the materials, and the wages of the workmen, something must be given for the profits of the undertaker of the work who hazards his stock in this adventure. The value which the workmen add to the materials, therefore, resolves itself in this case into two parts, of which the one pays their wages, the other the profits of their employer upon the whole stock of materials and wages which he advanced. He could have no interest to employ them, unless he expected from the sale of their work something more than what was sufficient to replace his stock to him; and he could have no interest to employ a great stock rather than a small one, unless his profits were to bear some proportion to the extent of his stock.

The profits of stock, it may perhaps be thought, are only a different name for the wages of a particular sort of labour, the labour of inspection and direction. They are, however, altogether different, are regulated by quite sufficient principles, and bear no proportion to the quantity, the hardship, or the ingenuity of this supposed labour of inspection and direction. They are regulated altogether by the value of the stock employed, and are greater or smaller in proportion to the extent of this stock. Let us suppose, for example, that in some particular place, where the common annual profits of manufacturing stock are ten per cent. there are two different manufactures, in each of which twenty workmen are employed at the rate of fifteen pounds a year each, or at the expence of three hundred a year in each manufactory. Let us suppose too, that the coarse materials annually wrought up in the one cost only seven hundred pounds, while the finer materials in the other cost seven thousand. The capital annually employed in the one will in this case amount only to one thousand pounds; whereas that employed in the other will amount to seven thousand three hundred pounds. At the rate of ten per cent. therefore, the undertaker of the one will expect an yearly profit of about one hundred pounds only; while that of the other will expect about seven hundred and thirty pounds. But though their profits are so very different, their labour of inspection and direction may be either altogether or very nearly the same. In many great works, almost the whole labour of this kind is committed to some principal clerk. His wages properly express the value of this labour of inspection and direction. Though in settling them some regard is had commonly, not only to his labour and skill, but to the trust which is reposed in him, yet they never bear any regular proportion to the capital of which he oversees the management; and the owner of this capital, though he is thus discharged of almost all labour, still expects that his profits should bear a regular proportion to his capital. In the price of commodities, therefore, the profits of stock constitute a component part altogether different from the wages of labour, and regulated by quite different principles.

In this state of things, the whole produce of labour does not always belong to the labourer. He must in most cases share it with the owner of the stock which employs him. Neither is the quantity of labour commonly employed in acquiring or producing any commodity, the only circumstance which can regulate the quantity which it ought commonly to purchase, command, or exchange for. An additional quantity, it is evident, must be due for the profits of the stock which advanced the wages and furnished the materials of that labour.

As soon as the land of any country has all become private property, the landlords, like all other men, love to reap where they never sowed, and demand a rent even for its natural produce. The wood of the forest, the grass of the field, and all the natural fruits of the earth, which, when land was in common, cost the labourer only the trouble of gathering them, come, even to him, to have an additional price fixed upon them. He must give up to the landlord a portion of what his labour either collects or produces. This portion, or, what comes to the same thing, the price of this portion, constitutes the rent of land, and in the price of the greater part of commodities makes a third component part.

The real value of all the different component parts of price, it must be observed, is measured by the quantity of labour which they can, each of them, purchase or command. Labour measures the value not only of that part of price which resolves itself into labour, but of that which resolves itself into rent, and of that which resolves itself into profit.

In every society the price of every commodity finally resolves itself into some one or other, or all of those three parts; and in every improved society, all the three enter more or less, as component parts, into the price of the far greater part of commodities.

In the price of corn, for example, one part pays the rent of the landlord, another pays the wages or maintenance of the labourers and labouring cattle employed in producing it, and the third pays the profit of the farmer. These three parts seem either immediately or ultimately to make up the whole price of corn. A fourth part, it may perhaps be thought, is necessary for replacing the stock of the farmer, or for compensating the wear and tear of his labouring cattle, and other instruments of husbandry. But it must be considered that the price of any instrument of husbandry, such as a labouring horse, is itself made up of the same three parts; the rent of the land upon which he is reared, the labour of tending and rearing him, and the profits of the farmer who advances both the rent of this land, and the wages of this labour. Though the price of the corn, therefore, may pay the price as well as the maintenance of the horse, the whole price still resolves itself either immediately or ultimately into the same three parts of rent, labour, and profit.

VII. Of the Natural and Market Price of Commodities

There is in every society or neighbourhood an ordinary or average rate both of wages and profit in every different employment of labour and stock. This rate is naturally regulated, as I shall show hereafter, partly by the general circumstances of the society, their riches or poverty, their advancing, stationary, or declining condition; and partly by the particular nature of each employment.

There is likewise in every society or neighbourhood an ordinary or average rate of rent, which is regulated too, as I shall show hereafter, partly by the general circumstances of the society or neighbourhood in which the land is situated, and partly by the natural or improved fertility of the land.

These ordinary or average rates may be called the natural rates of wages, profit, and rent, at the time and place in which they commonly prevail.

When the price of any commodity is neither more nor less than what is sufficient to pay the rent of the land, the wages of the labour, and the profits of the stock employed in raising, preparing, and bringing it to market, according to their natural rates, the commodity is then sold for what may be called its natural price.

The commodity is then sold precisely for what it is worth, or for what it really costs the person who brings it to market; for though in common language what is called the prime cost of any commodity does not comprehend the profit of the person who is to sell it again, yet if he sells it at a price which does not allow him the ordinary rate of profit in his neighbourhood, he is evidently a loser by the trade; since by employing his stock in some other way he might have made that profit. His profit, besides, is his revenue, the proper fund of his subsistence. As, while he is preparing and bringing the goods to market, he advances to his workmen their wages, or their subsistence; so he advances to himself, in the same manner, his own subsistence, which is generally suitable to the profit which he may reasonably expect from the sale of his goods. Unless they yield him this profit, therefore, they do not repay him what they may very properly be said to have really cost him.

Though the price, therefore, which leaves him this profit, is not always the lowest at which a dealer may sometimes sell his goods, it is the lowest at which he is likely to sell them for any considerable time; at least where there is perfect liberty, or where he may change his trade as often as he pleases.

The actual price at which any commodity is commonly sold is called its market price. It may either be above, or below, or exactly the same with its natural price.

The market price of every particular commodity is regulated by the proportion between the quantity which is actually brought to market, and the demand of those who are willing to pay the natural price of the commodity, or the whole value of the rent, labour, and profit, which must be paid in order to bring it thither. Such people may be called the effectual demanders, and their demand the effectual demand; since it may be sufficient to effectuate the bringing of the commodity to market. It is different from the absolute demand. A very poor man may be said in some sense to have a demand for a coach and six; he might like to have it; but his demand is not an effectual demand, as the commodity can never be brought to market in order to satisfy it.

When the quantity of any commodity which is brought to market falls short of the effectual demand, all those who are willing to pay the whole value of the rent, wages, and profit, which must be paid in order to bring it thither, cannot be supplied with the quantity which they want. Rather than want it altogether, some of them will be willing to give more. A competition will immediately begin among them, and the market price will rise more or less above the natural price, according as either the greatness of the deficiency, or the wealth and wanton luxury of the competitors, happen to animate more or less the eagerness of the competition. Among competitors of equal wealth and luxury the same deficiency will generally occasion a more or less eager competition, according as the acquisition of the commodity happens to be of more or less importance to them. Hence the exorbitant price of the necessaries of life during the blockade of a town or in a famine.

When the quantity brought to market exceeds the effectual demand, it cannot be all sold to those who are willing to pay the whole value of the rent, wages and profit, which must be paid in order to bring it thither. Some part must be sold to those who are willing to pay less, and the low price which they give for it must reduce the price of the whole. The market price will sink more or less below the natural price, according as the greatness of the excess increases more or less the competition of the sellers, or according as it happens to be more or less important to them to get immediately rid of the commodity. The same excess in the importation of perishable, will occasion a much greater competition than in that of durable commodities; in the importation of oranges, for example, than in that of old iron.

When the quantity brought to market is just sufficient to supply the effectual demand and no more, the market price naturally comes to be either exactly, or as nearly as can be judged of, the same with the natural price. The whole quantity upon hand can be disposed of for this price, and cannot be disposed of for more. The competition of the different dealers obliges them all to accept of this price, but does not oblige them to accept of less.

The quantity of every commodity brought to market naturally suits itself to the effectual demand. It is the interest of all those who employ their land, labour, or stock, in bringing any commodity to market, that the quantity never should exceed the effectual demand; and it is the interest of all other people that it never should fall short of that demand.

If at any time it exceeds the effectual demand, some of the component parts of its price must be paid below their natural rate. If it is rent, the interest of the landlords will immediately prompt them to withdraw a part of their land; and if it is wages or profit, the interest of the labourers in the one case, and of their employers in the other, will prompt them to withdraw a part of their labour or stock from this employment. The quantity brought to market will soon be no more than sufficient to supply the effectual demand. All the different parts of its price will rise to their natural rate, and the whole price to its natural price.

If, on the contrary, the quantity brought to market should at any time fall short of the effectual demand, some of the component parts of its price must rise above their natural rate. If it is rent, the interest of all other landlords will naturally prompt them to prepare more land for the raising of this commodity; if it is wages or profit, the interest of all other labourers and dealers will soon prompt them to employ more labour and stock in preparing and bringing it to market. The quantity brought thither will soon be sufficient to supply the effectual demand. All the different parts of its price will soon sink to their natural rate, and the whole price to its natural price.

The natural price, therefore, is, as it were, the central price, to which the prices of all commodities are continually gravitating. Different accidents may sometimes keep them suspended a good deal above it, and sometimes force them down even somewhat below it. But whatever may be the obstacles which hinder them from settling in this center of repose and continuance, they are constantly tending towards it.

But though the market price of every particular commodity is in this manner continually gravitating, if one may say so, towards the natural price, yet sometimes particular accidents, sometimes natural causes, and sometimes particular regulations of police, may, in many commodities, keep up the market price, for a long time together, a good deal above the natural price.

VIII. OF THE WAGES OF LABOUR

THE PRODUCE of labour constitutes the natural recompence or wages of labour.

In that original state of things, which precedes both the appropriation of land and the accumulation of stock, the whole produce of labour belongs to the labourer. He has neither landlord nor master to share with him.

Had this state continued, the wages of labour would have augmented with all those improvements in its productive powers, to which the division of labour gives occasion. All things would gradually have become cheaper. They would have been produced by a smaller quantity of labour; and as the commodities produced by equal quantities of labour would naturally in this state of things be exchanged for one another, they would have been purchased likewise with the produce of a smaller quantity.

But this original state of things, in which the labourer enjoyed the whole produce of his own labour, could not last beyond the first introduction of the appropriation of land and the accumulation of stock. It was at an end, therefore, long before the most considerable improvements were made in the productive powers of labour, and it would be to no purpose to trace further what might have been its effect upon the recompence or wages of labour. As soon as land becomes private property, the landlord demands a share of almost all the produce which the labourer can either raise, or collect from it. His rent makes the first deduction from the produce of the labour which is employed upon land.

It seldom happens that the person who tills the ground has wherewithal to maintain himself till he reaps the harvest. His maintenance is generally advanced to him from the stock of a master, the farmer who employs him, and who would have no interest to employ him, unless he was to share in the produce of his labour, or unless his stock was to be replaced to him with a profit. This profit makes a second deduction from the produce of the labour which is employed upon land.

The produce of almost all other labour is liable to the like deduction of profit. In all arts and manufactures the greater part of the workmen stand in need of a master to advance them the materials of their work, and their wages and maintenance till it be completed. He shares in the produce of their labour, or in the value which it adds to the materials upon which it is bestowed; and in this share consists his profit.

It sometimes happens, indeed, that a single independent workman has stock sufficient both to purchase the materials of his work, and to maintain himself till it be completed. He is both master and workman, and enjoys the whole produce of his own labour, or the whole value which it adds to the materials upon which it is bestowed. It includes what are usually two distinct revenues, belonging to two distinct persons, the profits of stock, and the wages of labour.

Such cases, however, are not very frequent, and in every part of Europe, twenty workmen serve under a master for one that is independent; and the wages of labour are every where understood to be, what they usually are, when the labourer is one person, and the owner of the stock which employs him another.

What are the common wages of labour, depends every where upon the contract usually made between those two parties, whose interests are by no means the same. The workmen desire to get as much, the masters to give as little as possible. The former are disposed to combine in order to raise, the latter in order to lower the wages of labour.

It is not, however, difficult to foresee which of the two parties must, upon all ordinary occasions, have the advantage in the dispute, and force the other into a compliance with their terms. The masters, being fewer in number, can combine much more easily; and the law, besides, authorises, or at least does not prohibit their combinations, while it prohibits those of the workmen. We have no acts of parliament against combining to lower the price of work; but many against combining to raise it. In all such disputes the masters can hold out much longer. A landlord, a farmer, a master manufacturer, or merchant, though they did not employ a single workman, could generally live a year or two upon the stocks which they have already acquired. Many workmen could not subsist a week, few could subsist a month, and scarce any a year without employment. In the long run the workman may be as necessary to his master as his master is to him, but the necessity is not so immediate.

We rarely hear, it has been said, of the combinations of masters, though frequently of those of workmen. But whoever imagines, upon this account, that masters rarely combine, is as ignorant of the world as of the subject. Masters are always and every where in a sort of tacit, but constant and uniform combination, not to raise the wages of labour above their actual rate. To violate this combination is every where a most unpopular action, and a sort of reproach to a master among his neighbours and equals. We seldom, indeed, hear of this combination, because it is the usual, and one may say, the natural state of things which nobody ever hears of. Masters too sometimes enter into particular combinations to sink the wages of labour even below this rate. These are always conducted with the utmost silence and secrecy, till the moment of execution, and when the workmen yield, as they sometimes do, without resistance, though severely felt by them, they are never heard of by other people. Such combinations, however, are frequently resisted by a contrary defensive combination of the workmen; who sometimes too, without any provocation of this kind, combine of their own accord to raise the price of their labour. Their usual pretences are, sometimes the high price of provisions; sometimes the great profit which their masters make by their work. But whether their combinations be offensive or defensive, they are always abundantly heard of. In order to bring the point to a speedy decision, they have always recourse to the loudest clamour, and sometimes to the most shocking violence and outrage. They are desperate, and act with the folly and extravagance of desperate men, who must either starve, or frighten their masters into an immediate compliance with their demands. The masters upon these occasions are just as clamorous upon the other side, and never cease to call aloud for the assistance of the civil magistrate, and the rigorous execution of those laws which have been enacted with so much severity against the combinations of servants, labourers, and journeymen. The workmen, accordingly, very seldom derive any advantage from the violence of those tumultuous combinations, which, partly from the interposition of the civil magistrate, partly from the superior steadiness of the masters, partly from the necessity which the greater part of the workmen are under of submitting for the sake of present subsistence, generally end in nothing, but the punishment or ruin of the ringleaders.

But though in disputes with their workmen, masters must generally have the advantage, there is however a certain rate below which it seems impossible to reduce, for any considerable time, the ordinary wages even of the lowest species of labour.

A man must always live by his work, and his wages must at least be sufficient to maintain him. They must even upon most occasions be somewhat more; otherwise it would be impossible for him to bring up a family, and the race of such workmen could not last beyond the first generation. Mr. Cantillon seems, upon this account, to suppose that the lowest species of common labourers must every where earn at least double their own maintenance, in order that one with another they may be enabled to bring up two children; the labour of the wife, on account of her necessary attendance on the children, being supposed no more than sufficient to provide for herself. But one half the children born, it is computed, die before the age of manhood. The poorest labourers, therefore, according to this account, must, one with another, attempt to rear at least four children, in order that two may have an equal chance of living to that age. But the necessary maintenance of four children, it is supposed, may be nearly equal to that of one man. The labour of an able-bodied slave, the same author adds, is computed to be worth double his maintenance; and that of the meanest labourer, he thinks, cannot be worth less than that of an able-bodied slave. Thus far at least seems certain, that, in order to bring up a family, the labour of the husband and wife together must, even in the lowest species of common labour, be able to earn something more than what is precisely necessary for their own maintenance; but in what proportion, whether in that above mentioned, or in any other, I shall not take upon me to determine.

There are certain circumstances, however, which sometimes give the labourers an advantage, and enable them to raise their wages considerably above this rate; evidently the lowest which is consistent with common humanity.

When in any country the demand for those who live by wages; labourers, journeymen, servants of every kind, is continually increasing;

when every year furnishes employment for a greater number than had been employed the year before, the workmen have no occasion to combine in order to raise their wages. The scarcity of hands occasions a competition among masters, who bid against one another, in order to get workmen, and thus voluntarily break through the natural combination of masters not to raise wages.

The demand for those who live by wages, it is evident, cannot increase but in proportion to the increase of the funds which are destined for the payment of wages. These funds are of two kinds; first, the revenue which is over and above what is necessary for the maintenance; and, secondly, the stock which is over and above what is necessary for the employment of their masters.

When the landlord, annuitant, or monied man, has a greater revenue than what he judges sufficient to maintain his own family, he employs either the whole or a part of the surplus in maintaining one or more menial servants. Increase this surplus, and he will naturally increase the number of those servants.

When an independent workman, such as a weaver or shoemaker, has got more stock than what is sufficient to purchase the materials of his own work, and to maintain himself till he can dispose of it, he naturally employs one or more journeymen with the surplus, in order to make a profit by their work. Increase this surplus, and he will naturally increase the number of his journeymen.

The demand for those who live by wages, therefore, necessarily increases with the increase of the revenue and stock of every country, and cannot possibly increase without it. The increase of revenue and stock is the increase of national wealth. The demand for those who live by wages, therefore, naturally increases with the increase of national wealth, and cannot possibly increase without it.

It is not the actual greatness of national wealth, but its continual increase, which occasions a rise in the wages of labour. It is not, accordingly, in the richest countries, but in the most thriving, or in those which are growing rich the fastest, that the wages of labour are highest. England is certainly, in the present times, a much richer country than any part of North America. The wages of labour, however, are much higher in North America than in any part of England.

Though North America is not yet so rich as England, it is much more thriving, and advancing with much greater rapidity to the further acquisition of riches. The most decisive mark of the prosperity of any country is the increase of the number of its inhabitants. In Great Britain, and most other European countries, they are not supposed to double in less than five hundred years. In the British colonies in North America, it has been found, that they double in twenty or five-and-twenty years. Nor in the present times is this increase principally owing to the continual importation of new inhabitants, but to the great multiplication of the species. Those who live to old age, it is said, frequently see there from fifty to a hundred, and sometimes many more, descendants from their own body. Labour is there so well rewarded that a numerous family of children, instead of being a burthen is a source of opulence and prosperity to the parents. The labour of each child, before it can leave their house, is computed to be worth a hundred pounds clear gain to them. A young widow with four or five young children, who, among the middling or inferior ranks of people in Europe, would have so little chance for a second husband, is there frequently courted as a sort of fortune. The value of children is the greatest of all encouragements to marriage. We cannot, therefore, wonder that the people in North America should generally marry very young. Notwithstanding the great increase occasioned by such early marriages, there is a continual complaint of the scarcity of hands in North America. The demand for labourers, the funds destined for maintaining them, increase, it seems, still faster than they can find labourers to employ.

Though the wealth of a country should be very great, yet if it has been long stationary, we must not expect to find the wages of labour very high in it. The funds destined for the payment of wages, the revenue and stock of its inhabitants, may be of the greatest extent; but if they have continued for several centuries of the same, or very nearly of the same extent, the number of labourers employed every year could easily supply, and even more than supply, the number wanted the following year. There could seldom be any scarcity of hands, nor could the masters be obliged to bid against one another in order to get them. The hands, on the contrary, would, in this case, naturally multiply beyond their employment. There would be a constant scarcity of employment, and the labourers would be obliged to bid against one another in order to get it. If in such a country the wages of labour had ever been more than sufficient to maintain the labourer, and to enable him to bring up a family, the competition of the labourers and the interest of the masters would soon reduce them to this lowest rate which is consistent with common humanity. China has been long one of the richest, that is, one of the most fertile, best cultivated, most industrious, and most populous countries in the world. It seems, however, to have been long stationary. Marco Polo, who visited it more than five hundred years ago, describes its cultivation, industry, and populousness, almost in the same terms in which they are described by travellers in the present times. It had perhaps, even long before his time, acquired that full complement of riches which the nature of its laws and institutions permits it to acquire. The accounts of all travellers, inconsistent in many other respects, agree in the low wages of labour, and in the difficulty which a labourer finds in bringing up a family in China. If by digging the ground a whole day he can get what will purchase a small quantity of rice in the evening, he is contented. The condition of artificers is, if possible, still worse. Instead of waiting indolently in their workhouses, for the calls of their customers, as in Europe, they are continually running about the streets with the tools of their respective trades, offering their service, and as it were begging employment. The poverty of the lower ranks of people in China far surpasses that of the most beggarly nations in Europe. In the neighbourhood of Canton many hundred, it is commonly said, many thousand families have no habitation on the land, but live constantly in little fishing boats upon the rivers and canals. The subsistence which they find there is so scanty that they are eager to fish up the nastiest garbage thrown overboard from any European ship. Any carrion, the carcase of a dead dog or cat, for example, though half putrid and stinking, is as welcome to them as the most wholesome food to the people of other countries. Marriage is encouraged in China, not by the profitableness of children, but by the liberty of destroying them. In all great towns several are every night exposed in the street, or drowned like puppies in the water. The performance of this horrid office is even said to be the avowed business by which some people earn their subsistence.

China, however, though it may perhaps stand still, does not seem to go backwards. Its towns are nowhere deserted by their inhabitants. The lands which had once been cultivated are nowhere neglected. The same or very nearly the same annual labour must therefore continue to be performed, and the funds destined for maintaining it must not, consequently, be sensibly diminished. The lowest class of labourers, therefore, notwithstanding their scanty subsistence, must some way or another make shift to continue their race so far as to keep up their usual numbers.

But it would be otherwise in a country where the funds destined for the maintenance of labour were sensibly decaying. Every year the demand for servants and labourers would, in all the different classes of employments, be less than it had been the year before. Many who had been bred in the superior classes, not being able to find employment in their own business, would be glad to seek it in the lowest. The lowest class being not only overstocked with its own workmen, but with the overflowings of all the other classes, the competition for employment would be so great in it, as to reduce the wages of labour to the most miserable and scanty subsistence of the labourer. Many would not be able to find employment even upon these hard terms, but would either starve, or be driven to seek a subsistence either by begging, or by the perpetration perhaps of the greatest enormities. Want, famine, and mortality would immediately prevail in that class, and from thence extend themselves to all the superior classes, till the number of inhabitants in the country was reduced to what could easily be maintained by the revenue and stock which remained in it, and which had escaped either the tyranny or calamity which had destroyed the rest. This perhaps is nearly the present state of Bengal, and of some other of the English settlements in the East Indies. In a fertile country which had before been much depopulated, where subsistence, consequently, should not be very difficult, and where, notwithstanding, three or four hundred thousand people die of hunger in one year, we may be assured that the funds destined for the maintenance of the labouring poor are fast decaying. The difference between the genius of the British constitution which protects and governs North America, and that of the mercantile company which oppresses and domineers in the East Indies, cannot perhaps be better illustrated than by the different state of those countries.

The liberal reward of labour, therefore, as it is the necessary effect, so it is the natural symptom of increasing national wealth. The scanty maintenance of the labouring poor, on the other hand, is the natural symptom that things are at a stand, and their starving condition that they are going fast backwards.

In Great Britain the wages of labour seem, in the present times, to be evidently more than what is precisely necessary to enable the labourer to bring up a family. In order to satisfy ourselves upon this point it will not be necessary to enter into any tedious or doubtful calculation of what may be the lowest sum upon which it is possible to do this. There are many plain symptoms that the wages of labour are nowhere in this country regulated by this lowest rate which is consistent with common humanity.

First, in almost every part of Great Britain there is a distinction, even in the lowest species of labour, between summer and winter wages. Summer wages are always highest. But on account of the extraordinary expence of fuel, the maintenance of a family is most expensive in winter. Wages, therefore, being highest when this expence is lowest, it seems evident that they are not regulated by what is necessary for this expence; but by the quantity and supposed value of the work. A labourer, it may be said indeed, ought to save part of his summer wages in order to defray his winter expence; and that through the whole year they do not exceed what is necessary to maintain his family through the whole year. A slave, however, or one absolutely dependent on us for immediate subsistence, would not be treated in this manner. His daily subsistence would be proportioned to his daily necessities.

Secondly, the wages of labour do not in Great Britain fluctuate with the price of provisions. These vary everywhere from year to year, frequently from month to month. But in many places the money price of labour remains uniformly the same sometimes for half a century together. If in these places, therefore, the labouring poor can maintain their families in dear years, they must be at their ease in times of moderate plenty, and in affluence in those of extraordinary cheapness. The high price of provisions during these ten years past has not in many parts of the kingdom been accompanied with any sensible rise in the money price of labour. It has, indeed, in some; owing probably more to the increase of the demand for labour than to that of the price of provisions.

Thirdly, as the price of provisions varies more from year to year than the wages of labour, so, on the other hand, the wages of labour vary more from place to place than the price of provisions. The prices of bread and butcher's meat are generally the same or very nearly the same through the greater part of the united kingdom. These and most other things which are sold by retail, the way in which the labouring poor buy all things, are generally fully as cheap or cheaper in great towns than in the remoter parts of the country, for reasons which I shall have occasion to explain hereafter. But the wages of labour in a great town and its neighbourhood are frequently a fourth or a fifth part, twenty or five-and-twenty per cent. higher than at a few miles distance.

Fourthly, the variations in the price of labour not only do not correspond either in place or time with those in the price of provisions, but they are frequently quite opposite.

Grain, the food of the common people, is dearer in Scotland than in England, whence Scotland receives almost every year very large supplies. But English corn must be sold dearer in Scotland, the country to which it is brought, than in England, the country from which it comes; and in proportion to its quality it cannot be sold dearer in Scotland than the Scotch corn that comes to the same market in competition with it. The quality of grain depends chiefly upon the quantity of flour or meal which it yields at the mill, and in this respect English grain is so much superior to the Scotch, that, though often dearer in appearance, or in proportion to the measure of its bulk, it is generally cheaper in reality, or in proportion to its quality, or even to the measure of its weight. The price of labour, on the contrary, is dearer in England than in Scotland. If the labouring poor, therefore, can maintain their families in the one part of the united kingdom, they must be in affluence in the other. Oatmeal indeed supplies the common people in Scotland with the greatest and the best part of their food, which is in general much inferior to that of their neighbours of the same rank in England. This difference, however, in the mode of their subsistence is not the cause, but the effect, of the difference in their wages; though, by a strange misapprehension, I have frequently heard it represented as the cause. It is not because one man keeps a coach while his neighbour walks a-foot, that the one is rich and the other poor; but because the one is rich he keeps a coach, and because the other is poor he walks a-foot.

But though it is certain that in both parts of the united kingdom grain was somewhat dearer in the last century than in the present, it is equally certain that labour was much cheaper. If the labouring poor, therefore, could bring up their families then, they must be much more at their ease now. In England the improvements of agriculture, manufactures and commerce began much earlier than in Scotland. The demand for labour, and consequently its price, must necessarily have increased with those improvements. In the last century, accordingly, as well as in the present, the wages of labour were higher in England than in Scotland. They have risen too considerably since that time, though, on account of the greater variety of wages paid there in different places, it is more difficult to ascertain how much. The price of labour, it must be observed, cannot be ascertained very accurately any where, different prices being often paid at the same place and for the same sort of labour, not only according to the different abilities of the workmen, but according to the easiness or hardness of the masters. Where wages are not regulated by law, all that we can pretend to determine is what are the most usual; and experience seems to show that law can never regulate them properly, though it has often pretended to do so.

The real recompence of labour, the real quantity of the necessaries and conveniencies of life which it can procure to the labourer, has, during the course of the present century, increased perhaps in a still greater proportion than its money price. Not only grain has become somewhat cheaper, but many other things, from which the industrious poor derive an agreeable and wholesome variety of food, have become a great deal cheaper. Potatoes, for example, do not at present, through the greater part of the kingdom, cost half the price which they used to do thirty or forty years ago. The same thing may be said of turnips, carrots, cabbages; things which were formerly never raised but by the spade, but which are now commonly raised by the plough. All sort of garden stuff too has become cheaper. The greater part of the apples and even of the onions consumed in Great Britain were in the last century imported from Flanders. The great improvements in the coarser manufactures of both linen and woollen cloth furnish the labourers with cheaper and better clothing; and those in the manufactures of the coarser metals, with cheaper and better instruments of trade, as well as with many agreeable and convenient pieces of household furniture. Soap, salt, candles, leather, and fermented liquors, have, indeed, become a good deal dearer; chiefly from the taxes which have been laid upon them. The quantity of these, however, which the labouring poor are under any necessity of consuming, is so very small, that the increase in their price does not compensate the diminution in that of so many other things. The common complaint that luxury extends itself even to the lowest ranks of the people, and that the labouring poor will not now be contented with the same food, clothing and lodging which satisfied them in former times, may convince us that it is not the money price of labour only, but its real recompence, which has augmented.

Is this improvement in the circumstances of the lower ranks of the people to be regarded as an advantage or as an inconveniency to the society? The answer seems at first sight abundantly plain. Servants, labourers and workmen of different kinds, make up the far greater part of every great political society. But what improves the circumstances of the greater part can never be regarded as an inconveniency to the whole. No society can surely be flourishing and happy, of which the far greater part of the members are poor and miserable. It is but equity, besides, that they who feed, clothe and lodge the whole body of the people, should have such a share of the produce of their own labour as to be themselves tolerably well fed, clothed and lodged.

Poverty, though it no doubt discourages, does not always prevent marriage. It seems even to be favourable to generation. A half-starved Highland woman frequently bears more than twenty children, while a pampered fine lady is often incapable of bearing any, and is generally exhausted by two or three. Barrenness, so frequent among women of fashion, is very rare among those of inferior station. Luxury in the fair sex, while it inflames perhaps the passion for enjoyment, seems always to weaken, and frequently to destroy altogether, the powers of generation.

But poverty, though it does not prevent the generation, is extremely unfavourable to the rearing of children. The tender plant is produced, but in so cold a soil, and so severe a climate, soon withers and dies. It is not uncommon, I have been frequently told, in the Highlands of Scotland for a mother who has borne twenty children not to have two alive. Several officers of great experience have assured me, that so far from recruiting their regiment, they have never been able to supply it with drums and fifes from all the soldiers' children that were born in it. A greater number of fine children, however, is seldom seen any where than about a barrack of soldiers. Very few of them, it seems, arrive at the age of thirteen or fourteen. In some places one half the children born die before they are four years of age; in many places before they are seven; and in almost all places before they are nine or ten. This great mortality, however, will every where be found chiefly among the children of the common people, who cannot afford to tend them with the same care as those of better station. Though their marriages are generally more fruitful than those of people of fashion, a smaller proportion of their children arrive at maturity. In foundling hospitals, and among the children brought up by parish charities, the mortality is still greater than among those of the common people.

Every species of animals naturally multiplies in proportion to the means of their subsistence, and no species can ever multiply beyond it. But in civilized society it is only among the inferior ranks of people that the scantiness of subsistence can set limits to the further multiplication of the human species; and it can do so in no other way than by destroying a great part of the children which their fruitful marriages produce.

The liberal reward of labour, by enabling them to provide better for their children, and consequently to bring up a greater number, naturally tends to widen and extend those limits. It deserves to be remarked too, that it necessarily does this as nearly as possible in the proportion which the demand for labour requires. If this demand is continually increasing, the reward of labour must necessarily encourage in such a manner the marriage and multiplication of labourers, as may enable them to supply that continually increasing demand by a continually increasing population. If the reward should at any time be less than what was requisite for this purpose, the deficiency of hands would soon raise it; and if it should at any time be more, their excessive multiplication would soon lower it to this necessary rate. The market would be so much understocked with labour in the one case, and so much overstocked in the other, as would soon force back its price to that proper rate which the circumstances of the society required. It is in this manner that the demand for men, like that for any other commodity, necessarily regulates the production of men; quickens it when it goes on too slowly, and stops it when it advances too fast. It is this demand which regulates and determines the state of propagation in all the different countries of the world, in North America, in Europe, and in China; which renders it rapidly progressive in the first, slow and gradual in the second, and altogether stationary in the last.

The wear and tear of a slave, it has been said, is at the expence of his master; but that of a free servant is at his own expence. The wear and tear of the latter, however, is, in reality, as much at the expence of his master as that of the former. The wages paid to journeymen and servants of every kind must be such as may enable them, one with another, to continue the race of journeymen and servants, according as the increasing, diminishing, or stationary demand of the society may happen to require. But though the wear and tear of a free servant be equally at the expence of his master, it generally costs him much less than that of a slave. The fund destined for replacing or repairing, if I may say so, the wear and tear of the slave, is commonly managed by a negligent master or careless overseer. That destined for performing the same office with regard to the free man, is managed by the free man himself. The disorders which generally prevail in the economy of the rich, naturally introduce themselves into the management of the former: the strict frugality and parsimonious attention of the poor as naturally establish themselves in that of the latter. Under such different management, the same purpose must require very different degrees of expence to execute it. It appears, accordingly, from the experience of all ages and nations, I believe, that the work done by freemen comes cheaper in the end than that performed by slaves. It is found to do so even at Boston, New York, and Philadelphia, where the wages of common labour are so very high.

The liberal reward of labour, therefore, as it is the effect of increasing wealth, so it is the cause of increasing population. To complain of it, is to lament over the necessary effect and cause of the greatest public prosperity.

It deserves to be remarked, perhaps, that it is in the progressive state, while the society is advancing to the further acquisition, rather than when it has acquired its full complement of riches, that the condition of the labouring poor, of the great body of the people, seems to be the happiest and the most comfortable. It is hard in the stationary, and miserable in the declining state. The progressive state is in reality the cheerful and the hearty state to all the different orders of the society. The stationary is dull; the declining melancholy.

The liberal reward of labour, as it encourages the propagation, so it increases the industry of the common people. The wages of labour are the encouragement of industry, which, like every other human quality, improves in proportion to the encouragement it receives. A plentiful subsistence increases the bodily strength of the labourer, and the comfortable hope of bettering his condition, and of ending his days perhaps in ease and plenty, animates him to exert that strength to the utmost. Where wages are high, accordingly, we shall always find the workmen more active, diligent, and expeditious, than where they are low; in England, for example, than in Scotland; in the neighbourhood of great towns, than in remote country places.

The increase in the wages of labour necessarily increases the price of many commodities, by increasing that part of it which resolves itself into wages, and so far tends to diminish their consumption both at home and abroad. The same cause, however, which raises the wages of labour, the increase of stock, tends to increase its productive powers, and to make a smaller quantity of labour produce a greater quantity of work. The owner of the stock which employs a great number of labourers, necessarily endeavours, for his own advantage, to make such a proper division and distribution of employment, that they may be enabled to produce the greatest quantity of work possible. For the same reason, he endeavours to supply them with the best machinery which either he or they can think of. What takes place among the labourers in a particular workhouse, takes place, for the same reason, among those of a great society. The greater their number, the more they naturally divide themselves into different classes and subdivisions of employment. More heads are occupied in inventing the most proper machinery for executing the work of each, and it is, therefore, more likely to be invented. There are many commodities, therefore, which, in consequence of these improvements, come to be produced by so much less labour than before, that the increase of its price is more than compensated by the diminution of its quantity.

IX. Of the Profits of Stock

The rise and fall in the profits of stock depend upon the same causes with the rise and fall in the wages of labour, the increasing or declining state of the wealth of the society; but those causes affect the one and the other very differently.

The increase of stock, which raises wages, tends to lower profit. When the stocks of many rich merchants are turned into the same trade, their mutual competition naturally tends to lower its profit; and when there is a like increase of stock in all the different trades carried on in the same society, the same competition must produce the same effect in them all.

It is not easy, it has already been observed, to ascertain what are the average wages of labour even in a particular place, and at a particular time. We can, even in this case, seldom determine more than what are the most usual wages. But even this can seldom be done with regard to the profits of stock. Profit is so very fluctuating, that the person who carries on a particular trade cannot always tell you himself what is the average of his annual profit. It is affected, not only by every variation of price in the commodities which he deals in, but by the good or bad fortune both of his rivals and of his customers, and by a thousand other accidents to which goods when carried either by sea or by land, or even when stored in a warehouse, are liable. It varies, therefore, not only from year to year, but from day to day, and almost from hour to hour. To ascertain what is the average profit of all the different trades carried on in a great kingdom, must be much more difficult; and to judge of what it may have been formerly, or in remote periods of time, with any degree of precision, must be altogether impossible.

But though it may be impossible to determine with any degree of precision, what are or were the average profits of stock, either in the present, or in ancient times, some notion may be formed of them from the interest of money. It may be laid down as a maxim, that wherever a great deal can be made by the use of money, a great deal will commonly be given for the use of it; and that wherever little can be made by it, less will commonly be given for it. According, therefore, as the usual market rate of interest varies in any country, we may be assured that the ordinary profits of stock must vary with it, must sink as it sinks, and rise as it rises. The progress of interest, therefore, may lead us to form some notion of the progress of profit.

By the 37th of Henry VIII all interest above ten per cent. was declared unlawful. More, it seems, had sometimes been taken before that. In the reign of Edward VI religious zeal prohibited all interest. This prohibition, however, like all others of the same kind, is said to have produced no effect, and probably rather increased than diminished the evil of usury. The statute of Henry VIII was revived by the 13th of Elizabeth, cap. 8. and ten per cent. continued to be the legal rate of interest till the 21st of James I when it was restricted to eight per cent. It was reduced to six per cent. soon after the restoration, and by the 12th of Queen Anne, to five per cent. All these different statutory regulations seem to have been made with great propriety. They seem to have followed and not to have gone before the market rate of interest, or the rate at which people of good credit usually borrowed. Since the time of Queen Anne, five per cent. seems to have been rather above than below the market rate.

Since the time of Henry VIII the wealth and revenue of the country have been continually advancing, and, in the course of their progress, their pace seems rather to have been gradually accelerated than retarded. They seem, not only to have been going on, but to have been going on faster and faster. The wages of labour have been continually increasing during the same period, and in the greater part of the different branches of trade and manufactures the profits of stock have been diminishing.

It generally requires a greater stock to carry on any sort of trade in a great town than in a country village. The great stocks employed in every branch of trade, and the number of rich competitors, generally reduce the rate of profit in the former below what it is in the latter. But the wages of labour are generally higher in a great town than in a country village. In a thriving town the people who have great stocks to employ, frequently cannot get the number of workmen they want, and therefore bid against one another in order to get as many as they can, which raises the wages of labour, and lowers the profits of stock. In the remote parts of the country there is frequently not stock sufficient to employ all the people, who therefore bid against one another in order to get employment, which lowers the wages of labour, and raises the profits of stock.

In Scotland, though the legal rate of interest is the same as in England, the market rate is rather higher. There are few trades which cannot be carried on with a smaller stock in Scotland than in England. The common rate of profit, therefore, must be somewhat greater. The wages of labour, it has already been observed, are lower in Scotland than in England. The country too is not only much poorer, but the steps by which it advances to a better condition, for it is evidently advancing, seem to be much slower and more tardy.

France is perhaps in the present times not so rich a country as England; and though the legal rate of interest has in France frequently been lower than in England, the market rate has generally been higher; for there, as in other countries, they have several very safe and easy methods of evading the law. The profits of trade, I have been assured by British merchants who had traded in both countries, are higher in France than in England; and it is no doubt upon this account that many British subjects choose rather to employ their capitals in a country where trade is in disgrace, than in one where it is highly respected. The wages of labour are lower in France than in England. When you go from Scotland to England, the difference which you may remark between the dress and countenance of the common people in the one country and in the other, sufficiently indicates the difference in their condition. The contrast is still greater when you return from France. France, though no doubt a richer country than Scotland, seems not to be going forward so fast.

The province of Holland, on the other hand, in proportion to the extent of its territory and the number of its people, is a richer country than England. The government there borrows at two per cent., and private people of good credit at three. The wages of labour are said to be higher in Holland than in England, and the Dutch, it is well known, trade upon lower profits than any people in Europe. The trade of Holland, it has been pretended by some people, is decaying, and it may perhaps be true that some particular branches of it are so. But these symptoms seem to indicate sufficiently that there is no general decay. When profit diminishes, merchants are very apt to complain that trade decays; though the diminution of profits is the natural effect of its prosperity, or of a greater stock being employed in it than before.

In our North American and West Indian colonies, not only the wages of labour, but the interest of money, and consequently the profits of stock, are higher than in England. In the different colonies both the legal and the market rate of interest run from six to eight per cent. High wages of labour and high profits of stock, however, are things, perhaps, which scarce ever go together, except in the peculiar circumstances of new colonies. A new colony must always for some time be more understocked in proportion to the extent of its territory, and more underpeopled in proportion to the extent of its stock, than the greater part of other countries. They have more land than they have stock to cultivate. What they have, therefore, is applied to the cultivation only of what is most fertile and most favourably situated, the land near the seashore, and along the banks of navigable rivers. Such land too is frequently purchased at a price below the value even of its natural produce. Stock employed in the purchase and improvement of such lands must yield a very large profit, and consequently afford to pay a very large interest. Its rapid accumulation in so profitable an employment enables the planter to increase the number of his hands faster than he can find them in a new settlement. Those whom he can find, therefore, are very liberally rewarded. As the colony increases, the profits of stock gradually diminish. When the most fertile and best situated lands have been all occupied, less profit can be made by the cultivation of what is inferior both in soil and situation, and less interest can be afforded for the stock which is so employed. In the greater part of our colonies, accordingly, both the legal and the market rate of interest have been considerably reduced during the course of the present century. As riches, improvement, and population have increased, interest has declined. The wages of labour do not sink with the profits of stock. The demand for labour increases with the increase of stock whatever be its profits.

The acquisition of new territory, or of new branches of trade, may sometimes raise the profits of stock, and with them the interest of money, even in a country which is fast advancing in the acquisition of riches. The stock of the country not being sufficient for the whole accession of business, which such acquisitions present to the different people among whom it is divided, is applied to those particular branches only which afford the greatest profit. Part of what had before been employed in other trades, is necessarily withdrawn from them, and turned into some of the new and more profitable ones. In all those old trades, therefore, the competition comes to be less than before. The market comes to be less fully supplied with many different sorts of goods. Their price necessarily rises more or less, and yields a greater profit to those who deal in them, who can, therefore, afford to borrow at a higher interest.

The diminution of the capital stock of the society, or of the funds destined for the maintenance of industry, however, as it lowers the wages of labour, so it raises the profits of stock, and consequently the interest of money. By the wages of labour being lowered, the owners of what stock remains in the society can bring their goods at less expence to market than before, and less stock being employed in supplying the market than before, they can sell them dearer. Their goods cost them less, and they get more for them. Their profits, therefore, being augmented at both ends, can well afford a large interest. The great fortunes so suddenly and so easily acquired in Bengal and the other British settlements in the East Indies, may satisfy us that, as the wages of labour are very low, so the profits of stock are very high in those ruined countries. The interest of money is proportionably so. In Bengal, money is frequently lent to the farmers at forty, fifty, and sixty per cent. and the succeeding crop is mortgaged for the payment. As the profits which can afford such an interest must eat up almost the whole rent of the landlord, so such enormous usury must in its turn eat up the greater part of those profits. Before the fall of the Roman republic, a usury of the same kind seems to have been common in the provinces, under the ruinous administration of their proconsuls. The virtuous Brutus lent money in Cyprus at eight-and-forty per cent. as we learn from the letters of Cicero.

In a country which had acquired that full complement of riches which the nature of its soil and climate, and its situation with respect to other countries, allowed it to acquire; which could, therefore, advance no further, and which was not going backwards, both the wages of labour and the profits of stock would probably be very low. In a country fully peopled in proportion to what either its territory could maintain or its stock employ, the competition for employment would necessarily be so great as to reduce the wages of labour to what was barely sufficient to keep up the number of labourers, and, the country being already fully peopled, that number could never be augmented. In a country fully stocked in proportion to all the business it had to transact, as great a quantity of stock would be employed in every particular branch as the nature and extent of the trade would admit. The competition, therefore, would everywhere be as great, and consequently the ordinary profit as low as possible.

But perhaps no country has ever yet arrived at this degree of opulence. China seems to have been long stationary, and had probably long ago acquired that full complement of riches which is consistent with the nature of its laws and institutions. But this complement may be much inferior to what, with other laws and institutions, the nature of its soil, climate, and situation might admit of. A country which neglects or despises foreign commerce, and which admits the vessels of foreign nations into one or two of its ports only, cannot transact the same quantity of business which it might do with different laws and institutions. In a country too, where, though the rich or the owners of large capitals enjoy a good deal of security, the poor or the owners of small capitals enjoy scarce any, but are liable, under the pretence of justice, to be pillaged and plundered at any time by the inferior mandarines, the quantity of stock employed in all the different branches of business transacted within it, can never be equal to what the nature and extent of that business might admit. In every different branch, the oppression of the poor must establish the monopoly of the rich, who, by engrossing the whole trade to themselves, will be able to make very large profits. Twelve per cent. accordingly is said to be the common interest of money in China, and the ordinary profits of stock must be sufficient to afford this large interest.

A defect in the law may sometimes raise the rate of interest considerably above what the condition of the country, as to wealth or poverty, would require. When the law does not enforce the performance of contracts, it puts all borrowers nearly upon the same footing with bankrupts or people of doubtful credit in better regulated countries. The uncertainty of recovering his money makes the lender exact the same usurious interest which is usually required from bankrupts. Among the barbarous nations who overran the western provinces of the Roman empire, the performance of contracts was left for many ages to the faith of the contracting parties. The courts of justice of their kings seldom intermeddled in it. The high rate of interest which took place in those ancient times may perhaps be partly accounted for from this cause.

When the law prohibits interest altogether, it does not prevent it. Many people must borrow, and nobody will lend without such a consideration for the use of their money as is suitable, not only to what can be made by the use of it, but to the difficulty and danger of evading the law. The high rate of interest among all Mahometan nations is accounted for by Mr. Montesquieu, not from their poverty, but partly from this, and partly from the difficulty of recovering the money.

The lowest ordinary rate of profit must always be something more than what is sufficient to compensate the occasional losses to which every employment of stock is exposed. It is this surplus only which is neat or clear profit. What is called gross profit comprehends frequently, not only this surplus, but what is retained for compensating such extraordinary losses. The interest which the borrower can afford to pay is in proportion to the clear profit only.

The lowest ordinary rate of interest must, in the same manner, be something more than sufficient to compensate the occasional losses to which lending, even with tolerable prudence, is exposed. Were it not more, charity or friendship could be the only motives for lending.

In a country which had acquired its full complement of riches, where in every particular branch of business there was the greatest quantity of stock that could be employed in it, as the ordinary rate of clear profit would be very small, so the usual market rate of interest which could be afforded out of it, would be so low as to render it impossible for any but the very wealthiest people to live upon the interest of their money. All people of small or middling fortunes would be obliged to superintend themselves the employment of their own stocks. It would be necessary that almost every man should be a man of business, or engage in some sort of trade. The province of Holland seems to be approaching near to this state. It is there unfashionable not to be a man of business. Necessity makes it usual for almost every man to be so, and custom every where regulates fashion. As it is ridiculous not to dress, so is it, in some measure, not to be employed, like other people. As a man of a civil profession seems awkward in a camp or a garrison, and is even in some danger of being despised there, so does an idle man among men of business.

X. OF THE RENT OF LAND

RENT, considered as the price paid for the use of land, is naturally the highest which the tenant can afford to pay in the actual circumstances of the land. In adjusting the terms of the lease, the landlord endeavours to leave him no greater share of the produce than what is sufficient to keep up the stock from which he furnishes the seed, pays the labour, and purchases and maintains the cattle and other instruments of husbandry, together with the ordinary profits of farming stock in the neighbourhood. This is evidently the smallest share with which the tenant can content himself without being a loser, and the landlord seldom means to leave him any more. Whatever part of the produce, or, what is the same thing, whatever part of its price, is over and above this share, he naturally endeavours to reserve to himself as the rent of his land, which is evidently the highest the tenant can afford to pay in the actual circumstances of the land. Sometimes, indeed, the liberality, more frequently the ignorance, of the landlord, makes him accept of somewhat less than this portion; and sometimes too, though more rarely, the ignorance of the tenant makes him undertake to pay somewhat more, or to content himself with somewhat less, than the ordinary profits of farming stock in the neighbourhood. This portion, however, may still be considered as the natural rent of land, or the rent for which it is naturally meant that land should for the most part be let.

The rent of land, it may be thought, is frequently no more than a reasonable profit or interest for the stock laid out by the landlord upon its improvement. This, no doubt, may be partly the case upon some occasions; for it can scarce ever be more than partly the case. The landlord demands a rent even for unimproved land, and the supposed interest or profit upon the expence of improvement is generally an addition to this original rent. Those improvements, besides, are not always made by the stock of the landlord, but sometimes by that of the tenant. When the lease comes to be renewed, however, the landlord commonly demands the same augmentation of rent, as if they had been all made by his own.

He sometimes demands rent for what is altogether incapable of human improvement. Kelp is a species of seaweed, which, when burnt, yields an alkaline salt, useful for making glass, soap, and for several other purposes. It grows in several parts of Great Britain, particularly in Scotland, upon such rocks only as lie within the high water mark, which are twice every day covered with the sea, and of which the produce, therefore, was never augmented by human industry. The landlord, however, whose estate is bounded by a kelp shore of this kind, demands a rent for it as much as for his corn fields.

The sea in the neighbourhood of the islands of Shetland is more than commonly abundant in fish, which make a great part of the subsistence of their inhabitants. But in order to profit by the produce of the water, they must have a habitation upon the neighbouring land. The rent of the landlord is in proportion, not to what the farmer can make by the land, but to what he can make both by the land and by the water. It is partly paid in sea fish; and one of the very few instances in which rent makes a part of the price of that commodity, is to be found in that country.

The rent of land, therefore, considered as the price paid for the use of the land, is naturally a monopoly price. It is not at all proportioned to what the landlord may have laid out upon the improvement of the land, or to what he can afford to take; but to what the farmer can afford to give.

Such parts only of the produce of land can commonly be brought to market of which the ordinary price is sufficient to replace the stock which must be employed in bringing them thither, together with its ordinary profits. If the ordinary price is more than this, the surplus part of it will naturally go to the rent of the land. If it is not more, though the commodity may be brought to market, it can afford no rent to the landlord. Whether the price is, or is not more, depends upon the demand.

There are some parts of the produce of land for which the demand must always be such as to afford a greater price than what is sufficient to bring them to market; and there are others for which it either may or may not be such as to afford this greater price. The former must always afford a rent to that landlord. The latter sometimes may, and sometimes may not, according to different circumstances.

Rent, it is to be observed, therefore, enters into the composition of the price of commodities in a different way from wages and profit. High or low wages and profit, are the causes of high or low price; high or low rent is the effect of it. It is because high or low wages and profit must be paid, in order to bring a particular commodity to market, that its price is high or low. But it is because its price is high or low; a great deal more, or very little more, or no more, than what is sufficient to pay those wages and profit, that it affords a high rent, or a low rent, or no rent at all.

The particular consideration, first, of those parts of the produce of land which always afford some rent; secondly, of those which sometimes may and sometimes may not afford rent; and, thirdly, of the variations which, in the different periods of improvement, naturally take place, in the relative value of those two different sorts of rude produce, when compared both with one another and with manufactured commodities, will divide this chapter into three parts.

PART ONE: Of the Produce of Land which always affords Rent

As men, like all other animals, naturally multiply in proportion to the means of their subsistence, food is always, more or less, in demand. It can always purchase or command a greater or smaller quantity of labour, and somebody can always be found who is willing to do something in order to obtain it. The quantity of labour, indeed, which it can purchase, is not always equal to what it could maintain, if managed in the most economical manner, on account of the high wages which are sometimes given to labour. But it can always purchase such a quantity of labour as it can maintain, according to the rate at which that sort of labour is commonly maintained in the neighbourhood.

But land, in almost any situation, produces a greater quantity of food than what is sufficient to maintain all the labour necessary for bringing it to market, in the most liberal way in which that labour is ever maintained. The surplus too is always more than sufficient to replace the stock which employed that labour, together with its profits. Something, therefore, always remains for a rent to the landlord.

The most desert moors in Norway and Scotland produce some sort of pasture for cattle, of which the milk and the increase are always more than sufficient, not only to maintain all the labour necessary for tending them, and to pay the ordinary profit to the farmer or owner of the herd or flock; but to afford some small rent to the landlord. The rent increases in proportion to the goodness of the pasture. The same extent of ground not only maintains a greater number of cattle, but as they are brought within a smaller compass, less labour becomes requisite to tend them, and to collect their produce. The landlord gains both ways; by the increase of the produce, and by the diminution of the labour which must be maintained out of it.

The rent of land not only varies with its fertility, whatever be its produce, but with its situation, whatever be its fertility. Land in the neighbourhood of a town gives a greater rent than land equally fertile in a distant part of the country. Though it may cost no more labour to cultivate the one than the other, it must always cost more to bring the produce of the distant land to market. A greater quantity of labour, therefore, must be maintained out of it; and the surplus, from which are drawn both the profit of the farmer and the rent of the landlord, must be diminished. But in remote parts of the country the rate of profits, as has already been shown, is generally higher than in the neighbourhood of a large town. A smaller proportion of this diminished surplus, therefore, must belong to the landlord.

Good roads, canals, and navigable rivers, by diminishing the expence of carriage, put the remote parts of the country more nearly upon a level with those in the neighbourhood of the town. They are upon that account the greatest of all improvements. They encourage the cultivation of the remote, which must always be the most extensive circle of the country. They are advantageous to the town, by breaking down the monopoly of the country in its neighbourhood. They are advantageous even to that part of the country. Though they introduce some rival commodities into the old market, they open many new markets to its produce. Monopoly, besides, is a great enemy to good management, which can never be universally established but in consequence of that free and universal competition which forces everybody to have recourse to it for the sake of self-defence.

PART TWO: Of the Produce of Land which sometimes does, and sometimes does not, afford Rent

Human food seems to be the only produce of land which always and necessarily affords some rent to the landlord. Other sorts of produce sometimes may and sometimes may not, according to different circumstances.

After food, clothing and lodging are the two great wants of mankind.

Land in its original rude state can afford the materials of clothing and lodging to a much greater number of people than it can feed. In its improved state it can sometimes feed a greater number of people than it can supply with those materials; at least in the way in which they require them, and are willing to pay for them. In the one state, therefore, there is always a superabundance of those materials, which are frequently, upon that account, of little or no value. In the other there is often a scarcity, which necessarily augments their value. In the one state a great part of them is thrown away as useless, and the price of what is used is considered as equal only to the labour and expence of fitting it for use, and can, therefore, afford no rent to the landlord. In the other they are all made use of, and there is frequently a demand for more than can be had. Somebody is always willing to give more for every part of them than what is sufficient to pay the expence of bringing them to market. Their price, therefore, can always afford some rent to the landlord.

The skins of the larger animals were the original materials of clothing. Among nations of hunters and shepherds, therefore, whose food consists chiefly in the flesh of those animals, every man, by providing himself with food, provides himself with the materials of more clothing than he can wear. If there was no foreign commerce, the greater part of them would be thrown away as things of no value. This was probably the case among the hunting nations of North America, before their country was discovered by the Europeans, with whom they now exchange their surplus peltry, for blankets, firearms, and brandy, which gives it some value. In the present commercial state of the known world, the most barbarous nations, I believe, among whom land property is established, have some foreign commerce of this kind, and find among their wealthier neighbours such a demand for all the materials of clothing, which their land produces, and which can neither be wrought up nor consumed at home, as raises their price above what it costs to send them to those wealthier neighbours. It affords, therefore, some rent to the landlord. When the greater part of the highland cattle were consumed on their own hills, the exportation of their hides made the most considerable article of the commerce of that country, and what they were exchanged for afforded some addition to the rent of the highland estates. The wool of England, which in old times could neither be consumed nor wrought up at home, found a market in the then wealthier and more industrious country of Flanders, and its price afforded something to the rent of the land which produced it. In countries not better cultivated than England was then, or than the highlands of Scotland are now, and which had no foreign commerce, the materials of clothing would evidently be so superabundant, that a great part of them would be thrown away as useless, and no part could afford any rent to the landlord.

The materials of lodging cannot always be transported to so great a distance as those of clothing, and do not so readily become an object of foreign commerce. When they are superabundant in the country which produces them, it frequently happens, even in the present commercial state of the world, that they are of no value to the landlord. A good stone quarry in the neighbourhood of London would afford a considerable rent. In many parts of Scotland and Wales it affords none. Barren timber for building is of great value in a populous and well-cultivated country, and the land which produces it affords a considerable rent. But in many parts of North America the landlord would be much obliged to any body who would carry away the greater part of his large trees. In some parts of the highlands of Scotland the bark is the only part of the wood which, for want of roads and water carriage, can be sent to market. The timber is left to rot upon the ground. When the materials of lodging are so superabundant, the part made use of is worth only the labour and expence of fitting it for that use. It affords no rent to the landlord, who generally grants the use of it to whoever takes the trouble of asking it. The demand of wealthier nations, however, sometimes enables him to get a rent for it. The paving of the streets of London has enabled the owners of some barren rocks on the coast of Scotland to draw a rent from what never afforded any before. The woods of Norway and of the coasts of the Baltic, find a market in many parts of Great Britain which they could not find at home, and thereby afford some rent to their proprietors.

Countries are populous, not in proportion to the number of people whom their produce can clothe and lodge, but in proportion to that of those whom it can feed. When food is provided, it is easy to find the necessary clothing and lodging. But though these are at hand, it may often be difficult to find food. In some parts even of the British dominions what is called A House, may be built by one day's labour of one man. The simplest species of clothing, the skins of animals, require somewhat more labour to dress and prepare them for use. They do not, however, require a great deal. Among savage and barbarous nations, a hundredth or little more than a hundredth part of the labour of the whole year, will be sufficient to provide them with such clothing and lodging as satisfy the greater part of the people. All the other ninety-nine parts are frequently no more than enough to provide them with food.

But when by the improvement and cultivation of land the labour of one family can provide food for two, the labour of half the society becomes sufficient to provide food for the whole. The other half, therefore, or at least the greater part of them, can be employed in providing other things, or in satisfying the other wants and fancies of mankind. Clothing and lodging, household furniture, and what is called Equipage, are the principal objects of the greater part of those wants and fancies. The rich man consumes no more food than his poor neighbour. In quality it may be very different, and to select and prepare it may require more labour and art; but in quantity it is very nearly the same. But compare the spacious palace and great wardrobe of the one, with the hovel and the few rags of the other, and you will be sensible that the difference between their clothing, lodging, and household furniture, is almost as great in quantity as it is in quality. The desire of food is limited in every man by the narrow capacity of the human stomach; but the desire of the conveniencies and ornaments of building, dress, equipage, and household furniture, seems to have no limit or certain boundary. Those, therefore, who have the command of more food than they themselves can consume, are always willing to exchange the surplus, or, what is the same thing, the price of it, for gratifications of this other kind. What is over and above satisfying the limited desire, is given for the amusement of those desires which cannot be satisfied, but seem to be altogether endless. The poor, in order to obtain food, exert themselves to gratify those fancies of the rich, and to obtain it more certainly, they vie with one another in the cheapness and perfection of their work.

Food is in this manner, not only the original source of rent, but every other part of the produce of land which afterwards affords rent, derives that part of its value from the improvement of the powers of labour in producing food by means of the improvement and cultivation of land.

PART THREE: Of the Variations in the Proportion between the respective Values of that Sort of Produce which always affords Rent, and of that which sometimes does and sometimes does not afford Rent

The increasing abundance of food, in consequence of increasing improvement and cultivation, must necessarily increase the demand for every part of the produce of land which is not food, and which can be applied either to use or to ornament. In the whole progress of improvement, it might therefore be expected, there should be only one variation in the comparative values of those two different sorts of produce. The value of that sort which sometimes does and sometimes does not afford rent, should constantly rise in proportion to that which always affords some rent. As art and industry advance, the materials of clothing and lodging, the useful fossils and minerals of the earth, the precious metals and the precious stones should gradually come to be more and more in demand, should gradually exchange for a greater and a greater quantity of food, or in other words, should gradually become dearer and dearer. This accordingly has been the case with most of these things upon most occasions, and would have been the case with all of them upon all occasions, if particular accidents had not upon some occasions increased the supply of some of them in a still greater proportion than the demand.

The value of a freestone quarry, for example, will necessarily increase with the increasing improvement and population of the country round about it; especially if it should be the only one in the neighbourhood. But the value of a silver mine, even though there should not be another within a thousand miles of it, will not necessarily increase with the improvement of the country in which it is situated. The market for the produce of a freestone quarry can seldom extend more than a few miles round about it, and the demand must generally be in proportion to the improvement and population of that small district. But the market for the produce of a silver mine may extend over the whole known world. Unless the world in general, therefore, be advancing in improvement and population, the demand for silver might not be at all increased by the improvement even of a large country in the neighbourhood of the mine.

Conclusion of the Chapter

I shall conclude this chapter with observing that every improvement in the circumstances of the society tends either directly or indirectly to raise the real rent of land, to increase the real wealth of the landlord, his power of purchasing the labour, or the produce of the labour of other people.

The extension of improvement and cultivation tends to raise it directly. The landlord's share of the produce necessarily increases with the increase of the produce.

That rise in the real price of those parts of the rude produce of land, which is first the effect of extended improvement and cultivation, and afterwards the cause of their being still further extended, the rise in the price of cattle, for example, tends too to raise the rent of land directly, and in a still greater proportion. The real value of the landlord's share, his real command of the labour of other people, not only rises with the real value of the produce, but the proportion of his share to the whole produce rises with it. That produce, after the rise in its real price, requires no more labour to collect it than before. A smaller proportion of it will, therefore, be sufficient to replace, with the ordinary profit, the stock which employs that labour. A greater proportion of it must, consequently, belong to the landlord.

The whole annual produce of the land and labour of every country, or what comes to the same thing, the whole price of that annual produce, naturally divides itself, it has already been observed, into three parts; the rent of land, the wages of labour, and the profits of stock; and constitutes a revenue to three different orders of people; to those who live by rent, to those who live by wages, and to those who live by profit. These are the three great, original and constituent orders of every civilized society, from whose revenue that of every other order is ultimately derived.

Book Two: Of the Nature, Accumulation, and Employment of Stock

INTRODUCTION

IN THAT rude state of society in which there is no division of labour, in which exchanges are seldom made, and in which every man provides every thing for himself, it is not necessary that any stock should be accumulated or stored up beforehand, in order to carry on the business of the society. Every man endeavours to supply by his own industry his own occasional wants as they occur. When he is hungry, he goes to the forest to hunt; when his coat is worn out, he clothes himself with the skin of the first large animal he kills: and when his hut begins to go to ruin, he repairs it, as well as he can, with the trees and the turf that are nearest it.

But when the division of labour has once been thoroughly introduced, the produce of a man's own labour can supply but a very small part of his occasional wants. The far greater part of them are supplied by the produce of other men's labour, which he purchases with the produce, or what is the same thing, with the price of the produce of his own. But this purchase cannot be made till such time as the produce of his own labour has not only been completed, but sold. A stock of goods of different kinds, therefore, must be stored up somewhere sufficient to maintain him, and to supply him with the materials and tools of his work, till such time, at least, as both these events can be brought about. A weaver cannot apply himself entirely to his peculiar business, unless there is beforehand stored up somewhere, either in his own possession or in that of some other person, a stock sufficient to maintain him, and to supply him with the materials and tools of his work, till he has not only completed but sold his web. This accumulation must, evidently, be previous to his applying his industry for so long a time to such a peculiar business.

As the accumulation of stock must, in the nature of things, be previous to the division of labour, so labour can be more and more subdivided in proportion only as stock is previously more and more accumulated. The quantity of materials which the same number of people can work up, increases in a great proportion as labour comes to be more and more subdivided; and as the operations of each workman are gradually reduced to a greater degree of simplicity, a variety of new machines come to be invented for facilitating and abridging those operations. As the division of labour advances, therefore, in order to give constant employment to an equal number of workmen, an equal stock of provisions, and a greater stock of materials and tools than what would have been necessary in a ruder state of things, must be accumulated beforehand. But the number of workmen in every branch of business generally increases with the division of labour in that branch, or rather it is the increase of their number which enables them to class and subdivide themselves in this manner.

As the accumulation of stock is previously necessary for carrying on this great improvement in the productive powers of labour, so that accumulation naturally leads to this improvement. The person who employs his stock in maintaining labour, necessarily wishes to employ it in such a manner as to produce as great a quantity of work as possible. He endeavours, therefore, both to make among his workmen the most proper distribution of employment, and to furnish them with the best machines which he can either invent or afford to purchase. His abilities in both these respects are generally in proportion to the extent of his stock, or to the number of people whom it can employ. The quantity of industry, therefore, not only increases in every country with the increase of the stock which employs it, but, in consequence of that increase, the same quantity of industry produces a much greater quantity of work.

Such are in general the effects of the increase of stock upon industry and its productive powers.

In the following book I have endeavoured to explain the nature of stock, the effects of its accumulation into capitals of different kinds, and the effects of the different employments of those capitals.

I. Of the Division of Stock

When the stock which a man possesses is no more than sufficient to maintain him for a few days or a few weeks, he seldom thinks of deriving any revenue from it. He consumes it as sparingly as he can, and endeavours by his labour to acquire something which may supply its place before it be consumed altogether. His revenue is, in this case, derived from his labour only. This is the state of the greater part of the labouring poor in all countries.

But when he possesses stock sufficient to maintain him for months or years, he naturally endeavours to derive a revenue from the greater part of it; reserving only so much for his immediate consumption as may maintain him till this revenue begins to come in. His whole stock, therefore, is distinguished into two parts. That part which, he expects, is to afford him this revenue, is called his capital. The other is that which supplies his immediate consumption; and which consists either, first, in that portion of his whole stock which was originally reserved for this purpose; or, secondly, in his revenue, from whatever source derived, as it gradually comes in; or, thirdly, in such things as had been purchased by either of these in former years, and which are not yet entirely consumed; such as a stock of clothes, household furniture, and the like. In one, or other, or all of these three articles, consists the stock which men commonly reserve for their own immediate consumption.

There are two different ways in which a capital may be employed so as to yield a revenue or profit to its employer.

First, it may be employed in raising, manufacturing, or purchasing goods, and selling them again with a profit. The capital employed in this manner yields no revenue or profit to its employer, while it either remains in his possession, or continues in the same shape. The goods of the merchant yield him no revenue or profit till he sells them for money, and the money yields him as little till it is again exchanged for goods. His capital is continually going from him in one shape, and returning to him in another, and it is only by means of such circulation, or successive exchanges, that it can yield him any profit. Such capitals, therefore, may very properly be called circulating capitals.

Secondly, it may be employed in the improvement of land, in the purchase of useful machines and instruments of trade, or in such-like things as yield a revenue or profit without changing masters, or circulating any further. Such capitals, therefore, may very properly be called fixed capitals.

Different occupations require very different proportions between the fixed and circulating capitals employed in them.

The capital of a merchant, for example, is altogether a circulating capital. He has occasion for no machines or instruments of trade, unless his shop, or warehouse, be considered as such.

Some part of the capital of every master artificer or manufacturer must be fixed in the instruments of his trade. This part, however, is very small in some, and very great in others. A master tailor requires no other instruments of trade but a parcel of needles. Those of the master shoemaker are a little, though but a very little, more expensive. Those of the weaver rise a good deal above those of the shoemaker. The far greater part of the capital of all such master artificers, however, is circulated, either in the wages of their workmen, or in the price of their materials, and repaid with a profit by the price of the work.

In other works a much greater fixed capital is required. In a great ironwork, for example, the furnace for melting the ore, the forge, the slitt mill, are instruments of trade which cannot be erected without a very great expense. In coal works, and mines of every kind, the machinery necessary both for drawing out the water and for other purposes, is frequently still more expensive.

That part of the capital of the farmer which is employed in the instruments of agriculture is a fixed; that which is employed in the wages and maintenance of his labouring servants, is a circulating capital. He makes a profit of the one by keeping it in his own possession, and of the other by parting with it. The price or value of his labouring cattle is a fixed capital in the same manner as that of the instruments of husbandry: Their maintenance is a circulating capital in the same manner as that of the labouring servants. The farmer makes his profit by keeping the labouring cattle, and by parting with their maintenance. Both the price and the maintenance of the cattle which are bought in and fattened, not for labour, but for sale, are a circulating capital. The farmer makes his profit by parting with them. A flock of sheep or a herd of cattle that, in a breeding country, is bought in, neither for labour, nor for sale, but in order to make a profit by their wool, by their milk, and by their increase, is a fixed capital. The profit is made by keeping them. Their maintenance is a circulating capital. The profit is made by parting with it; and it comes back with both its own profit, and the profit upon the whole price of the cattle, in the price of the wool, the milk, and the increase. The whole value of the seed too is properly a fixed capital. Though it goes backwards and forwards between the ground and the granary, it never changes masters, and therefore does not properly circulate. The farmer makes his profit, not by its sale, but by its increase.

The general stock of any country or society is the same with that of all its inhabitants or members, and therefore naturally divides itself into the same three portions, each of which has a distinct function or office.

The First, is that portion which is reserved for immediate consumption, and of which the characteristic is that it affords no revenue or profit. It consists in the stock of food, clothes, household furniture, &c., which have been purchased by their proper consumers, but which are not yet entirely consumed. The whole stock of mere dwelling houses too subsisting at any one time in the country, make a part of this first portion. The stock that is laid out in a house, if it is to be the dwelling house of the proprietor, ceases from that moment to serve in the function of a capital, or to afford any revenue to its owner. A dwelling house, as such, contributes nothing to the revenue of its inhabitant; and though it is, no doubt, extremely useful to him, it is as his clothes and household furniture are useful to him, which, however, make a part of his expence, and not of his revenue. If it is to be let to a tenant for rent, as the house itself can produce nothing, the tenant must always pay the rent out of some other revenue which he derives either from labour, or stock, or land. Though a house, therefore, may yield a revenue to its proprietor, and thereby serve in the function of a capital to him, it cannot yield any to the public, nor serve in the function of a capital to it, and the revenue of the whole body of the people can never be in the smallest degree increased by it. Clothes, and household furniture, in the same manner, sometimes yield a revenue, and thereby serve in the function of a capital to particular persons. In countries where masquerades are common, it is a trade to let out masquerade dresses for a night. Upholsterers frequently let furniture by the month or by the year. Undertakers let the furniture of funerals by the day and by the week. Many people let furnished houses, and get a rent, not only for the use of the house, but for that of the furniture. The revenue, however, which is derived from such things, must always be ultimately drawn from some other source of revenue. Of all parts of the stock, either of an individual, or of a society, reserved for immediate consumption, what is laid out in houses is most slowly consumed. A stock of clothes may last several years: a stock of furniture half a century or a century: but a stock of houses, well built and properly taken care of, may last many centuries. Though the period of their total consumption, however, is more distant, they are still as really a stock reserved for immediate consumption as either clothes or household furniture.

The Second of the three portions into which the general stock of the society divides itself, is the fixed capital; of which the characteristic is, that it affords a revenue or profit without circulating or changing masters. It consists chiefly of the four following articles:

First, of all useful machines and instruments of trade which facilitate and abridge labour:

Secondly, of all those profitable buildings which are the means of procuring a revenue, not only to their proprietor who lets them for a rent, but to the person who possesses them and pays that rent for them; such as shops, warehouses, workhouses, farmhouses, with all their necessary buildings; stables, granaries, &c. These are very different from mere dwelling houses. They are a sort of instruments of trade, and may be considered in the same light:

Thirdly, of the improvements of land, of what has been profitably laid out in clearing, draining, enclosing, manuring, and reducing it into the condition most proper for tillage and culture. An improved farm may very justly be regarded in the same light as those useful machines which facilitate and abridge labour, and by means of which, an equal circulating capital can afford a much greater revenue to its employer. An improved farm is equally advantageous and more durable than any of those machines, frequently requiring no other repairs than the most profitable application of the farmer's capital employed in cultivating it:

Fourthly, of the acquired and useful abilities of all the inhabitants or members of the society. The acquisition of such talents, by the maintenance of the acquirer during his education, study, or apprenticeship, always costs a real expence, which is a capital fixed and realized, as it were, in his person. Those talents, as they make a part of his fortune, so do they likewise of that of the society to which he belongs. The improved dexterity of a workman may be considered in the same light as a machine or instrument of trade which facilitates and abridges labour, and which, though it costs a certain expence, repays that expence with a profit.

The Third and last of the three portions into which the general stock of the society naturally divides itself, is the circulating capital; of which the characteristic is, that it affords a revenue only by circulating or changing masters. It is composed likewise of four parts:

First, of the money by means of which all the other three are circulated and distributed to their proper consumers:

Secondly, of the stock of provisions which are in the possession of the butcher, the grazier, the farmer, the corn merchant, the brewer, &c. and from the sale of which they expect to derive a profit:

Thirdly, of the materials, whether altogether rude, or more or less manufactured, of clothes, furniture and building, which are not yet made up into any of those three shapes, but which remain in the hands of the growers, the manufacturers, the mercers, and drapers, the timber merchants, the carpenters and joiners, the brickmakers, &c.

Fourthly, and lastly, of the work which is made up and completed, but which is still in the hands of the merchant or manufacturer, and not yet disposed of or distributed to the proper consumers; such as the finished work which we frequently find ready-made in the shops of the smith, the cabinet maker, the goldsmith, the jeweller, the china merchant, &c. The circulating capital consists in this manner, of the provisions, materials, and finished work of all kinds that are in the hands of their respective dealers, and of the money that is necessary for circulating and distributing them to those who are finally to use, or to consume them.

Of these four parts three, provisions, materials, and finished work, are, either annually, or in a longer or shorter period, regularly withdrawn from it, and placed either in the fixed capital or in the stock reserved for immediate consumption.

Every fixed capital is both originally derived from, and requires to be continually supported by a circulating capital. All useful machines and instruments of trade are originally derived from a circulating capital, which furnishes the materials of which they are made, and the maintenance of the workmen who make them. They require too a capital of the same kind to keep them in constant repair.

No fixed capital can yield any revenue but by means of a circulating capital. The most useful machines and instruments of trade will produce nothing without the circulating capital which affords the materials they are employed upon, and the maintenance of the workmen who employ them. Land, however improved, will yield no revenue without a circulating capital, which maintains the labourers who cultivate and collect its produce.

To maintain and augment the stock which may be reserved for immediate consumption, is the sole end and purpose both of the fixed and circulating capitals. It is this stock which feeds, clothes, and lodges the people. Their riches or poverty depends upon the abundant or sparing supplies which those two capitals can afford to the stock reserved for immediate consumption.

II. Of the Accumulation of Capital, or of Productive and Unproductive Labour

There is one sort of labour which adds to the value of the subject upon which it is bestowed: there is another which has no such effect. The former, as it produces a value, may be called productive; the latter, unproductive labour. Thus the labour of a manufacturer adds, generally, to the value of the materials which he works upon, that of his own maintenance, and of his master's profit. The labour of a menial servant, on the contrary, adds to the value of nothing. Though the manufacturer has his wages advanced to him by his master, he, in reality, costs him no expence, the value of those wages being generally restored, together with a profit, in the improved value of the subject upon which his labour is bestowed. But the maintenance of a menial servant never is restored. A man grows rich by employing a multitude of manufacturers: he grows poor, by maintaining a multitude of menial servants. The labour of the latter, however, has its value, and deserves its reward as well as that of the former. But the labour of the manufacturer fixes and realizes itself in some particular subject or vendible commodity, which lasts for some time at least after that labour is past. It is, as it were, a certain quantity of labour stocked and stored up to be employed, if necessary, upon some other occasion. That subject, or what is the same thing, the price of that subject, can afterwards, if necessary, put into motion a quantity of labour equal to that which had originally produced it. The labour of the menial servant, on the contrary, does not fix or realize itself in any particular subject or vendible commodity. His services generally perish in the very instant of their performance, and seldom leave any trace or value behind them, for which an equal quantity of service could afterwards be procured.

The labour of some of the most respectable orders in the society is, like that of menial servants, unproductive of any value, and does not fix or realize itself in any permanent subject, or vendible commodity, which endures after that labour is past, and for which an equal quantity of labour could afterwards be procured. The sovereign, for example, with all the officers both of justice and war who serve under him, the whole army and navy, are unproductive labourers. They are the servants of the public, and are maintained by a part of the annual produce of the industry of other people. Their service, how honourable, how useful, or how necessary soever, produces nothing for which an equal quantity of service can afterwards be procured. The protection, security, and defence of the commonwealth, the effect of their labour this year, will not purchase its protection, security, and defence for the year to come. In the same class must be ranked, some both of the gravest and most important, and some of the most frivolous professions: churchmen, lawyers, physicians, men of letters of all kinds; players, buffoons, musicians, opera singers, opera dancers, &c. The labour of the meanest of these has a certain value, regulated by the very same principles which regulate that of every other sort of labour; and that of the noblest and most useful, produces nothing which could afterwards purchase or procure an equal quantity of labour. Like the declamation of the actor, the harangue of the orator, or the tune of the musician, the work of all of them perishes in the very instant of its production.

Both productive and unproductive labourers, and those who do not labour at all, are all equally maintained by the annual produce of the land and labour of the country. This produce, how great soever, can never be infinite, but must have certain limits. According, therefore, as a smaller or greater proportion of it is in any one year employed in maintaining unproductive hands, the more in the one case and the less in the other will remain for the productive, and the next year's produce will be greater or smaller accordingly; the whole annual produce, if we except the spontaneous productions of the earth, being the effect of productive labour.

Parsimony, and not industry, is the immediate cause of the increase of capital. Industry, indeed, provides the subject which parsimony accumulates. But whatever industry might acquire, if parsimony did not save and store up, the capital would never be the greater.

Parsimony, by increasing the fund which is destined for the maintenance of productive hands, tends to increase the number of those hands whose labour adds to the value of the subject upon which it is bestowed. It tends therefore to increase the exchangeable value of the annual produce of the land and labour of the country. It puts into motion an additional quantity of industry, which gives an additional value to the annual produce.

What is annually saved is as regularly consumed as what is annually spent, and nearly in the same time too; but it is consumed by a different set of people. That portion of his revenue which a rich man annually spends, is in most cases consumed by idle guests, and menial servants, who leave nothing behind them in return for their consumption. That portion which he annually saves, as for the sake of the profit it is immediately employed as a capital, is consumed in the same manner, and nearly in the same time too, but by a different set of people, by labourers, manufacturers, and artificers, who reproduce with a profit the value of their annual consumption. His revenue, we shall suppose, is paid him in money. Had he spent the whole, the food, clothing, and lodging, which the whole could have purchased, would have been distributed among the former set of people. By saving a part of it, as that part is for the sake of the profit immediately employed as a capital either by himself or by some other person, the food, clothing, and lodging, which may be purchased with it, are necessarily reserved for the latter. The consumption is the same, but the consumers are different.

By what a frugal man annually saves, he not only affords maintenance to an additional number of productive hands, for that or the ensuing year, but, like the founder of a public workhouse, he establishes as it were a perpetual fund for the maintenance of an equal number in all times to come. The perpetual allotment and destination of this fund, indeed, is not always guarded by any positive law, by any trust right or deed of mortmain. It is always guarded, however, by a very powerful principle, the plain and evident interest of every individual to whom any share of it shall ever belong. No part of it can ever afterwards be employed to maintain any but productive hands, without an evident loss to the person who thus perverts it from its proper destination.

The prodigal perverts it in this manner. By not confining his expence within his income, he encroaches upon his capital. Like him who perverts the revenues of some pious foundation to profane purposes, he pays the wages of idleness with those funds which the frugality of his forefathers had, as it were, consecrated to the maintenance of industry. By diminishing the funds destined for the employment of productive labour, he necessarily diminishes, so far as it depends upon him, the quantity of that labour which adds a value to the subject upon which it is bestowed, and, consequently, the value of the annual produce of the land and labour of the whole country, the real wealth and revenue of its inhabitants. If the prodigality of some was not compensated by the frugality of others, the conduct of every prodigal, by feeding the idle with the bread of the industrious, tends not only to beggar himself, but to impoverish his country.

The annual produce of the land and labour of any nation can be increased in its value by no other means, but by increasing either the number of its productive labourers, or the productive powers of those labourers who had before been employed. The number of its productive labourers, it is evident, can never be much increased, but in consequence of an increase of capital, or of the funds destined for maintaining them. The productive powers of the same number of labourers cannot be increased, but in consequence either of some addition and improvement to those machines and instruments which facilitate and abridge labour; or of a more proper division and distribution of employment. In either case an additional capital is almost always required. It is by means of an additional capital only, that the undertaker of any work can either provide his workmen with better machinery, or make a more proper distribution of employment among them. When the work to be done consists of a number of parts, to keep every man constantly employed in one way, requires a much greater capital than where every man is occasionally employed in every different part of the work. When we compare, therefore, the state of a nation at two different periods, and find, that the annual produce of its land and labour is evidently greater at the latter than at the former, that its lands are better cultivated, its manufactures more numerous and more flourishing, and its trade more extensive, we may be assured that its capital must have increased during the interval between those two periods, and that more must have been added to it by the good conduct of some, than had been taken from it either by the private misconduct of others, or by the public extravagance of government. But we shall find this to have been the case of almost all nations, in all tolerably quiet and peaceful times, even of those who have not enjoyed the most prudent and parsimonious governments. To form a right judgment of it, indeed, we must compare the state of the country at periods somewhat distant from one another. The progress is frequently so gradual, that, at near periods, the improvement is not only not sensible, but from the declension either of certain branches of industry, or of certain districts of the country, things which sometimes happen though the country in general be in great prosperity, there frequently arises a suspicion, that the riches and industry of the whole are decaying.

III. OF STOCK LENT AT INTEREST

THE STOCK which is lent at interest is always considered as a capital by the lender. He expects that in due time it is to be restored to him, and that in the mean time the borrower is to pay him a certain annual rent for the use of it. The borrower may use it either as a capital, or as a stock reserved for immediate consumption. If he uses it as a capital, he employs it in the maintenance of productive labourers, who reproduce the value with a profit. He can, in this case, both restore the capital and pay the interest without alienating or encroaching upon any other source of revenue. If he uses it as a stock reserved for immediate consumption, he acts the part of a prodigal, and dissipates in the maintenance of the idle, what was destined for the support of the industrious. He can, in this case, neither restore the capital nor pay the interest, without either alienating or encroaching upon some other source of revenue, such as the property or the rent of land.

The stock which is lent at interest is, no doubt, occasionally employed in both these ways, but in the former much more frequently than in the latter. The man who borrows in order to spend will soon be ruined, and he who lends to him will generally have occasion to repent of his folly. To borrow or to lend for such a purpose, therefore, is in all cases, where gross usury is out of the question, contrary to the interest of both parties; and though it no doubt happens sometimes that people do both the one and the other; yet, from the regard that all men have for their own interest, we may be assured, that it cannot happen so very frequently as we are sometimes apt to imagine. Ask any rich man of common prudence, to which of the two sorts of people he has lent the greater part of his stock, to those who, he thinks, will employ it profitably, or to those who will spend it idly, and he will laugh at you for proposing the question. Even among borrowers, therefore, not the people in the world most famous for frugality, the number of the frugal and industrious surpasses considerably that of the prodigal and idle.

Almost all loans at interest are made in money, either of paper, or of gold and silver. But what the borrower really wants, and what the lender really supplies him with, is not the money, but the money's worth, or the goods which it can purchase. If he wants it as a stock for immediate consumption, it is those goods only which he can place in that stock. If he wants it as a capital for employing industry, it is from those goods only that the industrious can be furnished with the tools, materials, and maintenance, necessary for carrying on their work. By means of the loan, the lender, as it were, assigns to the borrower his right to a certain portion of the annual produce of the land and labour of the country, to be employed as the borrower pleases.

The quantity of stock, therefore, or, as it is commonly expressed, of money which can be lent at interest in any country, is not regulated by the value of the money, whether paper or coin, which serves as the instrument of the different loans made in that country, but by the value of that part of the annual produce which, as soon as it comes either from the ground, or from the hands of the productive labourers, is destined not only for replacing a capital, but such a capital as the owner does not care to be at the trouble of employing himself.

In some countries the interest of money has been prohibited by law. But as something can everywhere be made by the use of money, something ought everywhere to be paid for the use of it. This regulation, instead of preventing, has been found from experience to increase the evil of usury; the debtor being obliged to pay, not only for the use of the money, but for the risk which his creditor runs by accepting a compensation for that use. He is obliged, if one may say so, to insure his creditor from the penalties of usury.

In countries where interest is permitted, the law, in order to prevent the extortion of usury, generally fixes the highest rate which can be taken without incurring a penalty. This rate ought always to be somewhat above the lowest market price, or the price which is commonly paid for the use of money by those who can give the most undoubted security. If this legal rate should be fixed below the lowest market rate, the effects of this fixation must be nearly the same as those of a total prohibition of interest. The creditor will not lend his money for less than the use of it is worth, and the debtor must pay him for the risk which he runs by accepting the full value of that use. If it is fixed precisely at the lowest market price, it ruins with honest people, who respect the laws of their country, the credit of all those who cannot give the very best security, and obliges them to have recourse to exorbitant usurers. In a country, such as Great Britain, where money is lent to government at three per cent. and to private people upon good security at four, and four and a half, the present legal rate, five per cent., is perhaps, as proper as any.

IV. OF THE DIFFERENT EMPLOYMENT OF CAPITALS

THOUGH all capitals are destined for the maintenance of productive labour only, yet the quantity of that labour, which equal capitals are capable of putting into motion, varies extremely according to the diversity of their employment; as does likewise the value which that employment adds to the annual produce of the land and labour of the country.

A capital may be employed in four different ways: either, first, in procuring the rude produce annually required for the use and consumption of the society; or, secondly, in manufacturing and preparing that rude produce for immediate use and consumption; or, thirdly, in transporting either the rude or manufactured produce from the places where they abound to those where they are wanted; or, lastly, in dividing particular portions of either into such small parcels as suit the occasional demands of those who want them. In the first way are employed the capitals of all those who undertake the improvement or cultivation of lands, mines, or fisheries; in the second, those of all master manufacturers; in the third, those of all wholesale merchants; and in the fourth, those of all retailers. It is difficult to conceive that a capital should be employed in any way which may not be classed under some one or other of those four.

Each of those four methods of employing a capital is essentially necessary either to the existence or extension of the other three, or to the general conveniency of the society.

Unless a capital was employed in furnishing rude produce to a certain degree of abundance, neither manufactures nor trade of any kind could exist.

Unless a capital was employed in manufacturing that part of the rude produce which requires a good deal of preparation before it can be fit for use and consumption, it either would never be produced, because there could be no demand for it; or if it was produced spontaneously, it would be of no value in exchange, and could add nothing to the wealth of the society.

Unless a capital was employed in transporting, either the rude or manufactured produce, from the places where it abounds to those where it is wanted, no more of either could be produced than was necessary for the consumption of the neighbourhood. The capital of the merchant exchanges the surplus produce of one place for that of another, and thus encourages the industry and increases the enjoyments of both.

Unless a capital was employed in breaking and dividing certain portions either of the rude or manufactured produce, into such small parcels as suit the occasional demands of those who want them, every man would be obliged to purchase a greater quantity of the goods he wanted, than his immediate occasions required. If there was no such trade as a butcher, for example, every man would be obliged to purchase a whole ox or a whole sheep at a time. This would generally be inconvenient to the rich, and much more so to the poor. If a poor workman was obliged to purchase a month's or six months' provisions at a time, a great part of the stock which he employs as a capital in the instruments of his trade, or in the furniture of his shop, and which yields him a revenue, he would be forced to place in that part of his stock which is reserved for immediate consumption, and which yields him no revenue. Nothing can be more convenient for such a person than to be able to purchase his subsistence from day to day, or even from hour to hour, as he wants it. He is thereby enabled to employ almost his whole stock as a capital. He is thus enabled to furnish work to a greater value, and the profit, which he makes by it in this way, much more than compensates the additional price which the profit of the retailer imposes upon the goods. The prejudices of some political writers against shopkeepers and tradesmen, are altogether without foundation. So far is it from being necessary, either to tax them, or to restrict their numbers, that they can never be multiplied so as to hurt the publick, though they may so as to hurt one another. The quantity of grocery goods, for example, which can be sold in a particular town, is limited by the demand of that town and its neighbourhood. The capital, therefore, which can be employed in the grocery trade cannot exceed what is sufficient to purchase that quantity. If this capital is divided between two different grocers, their competition will tend to make both of them sell cheaper, than if it were in the hands of one only; and if it were divided among twenty, their competition would be just so much the greater, and the chance of their combining together, in order to raise the price, just so much the less. Their competition might perhaps ruin some of themselves; but to take care of this is the business of the parties concerned, and it may safely be trusted to their discretion. It can never hurt either the consumer, or the producer; on the contrary, it must tend to make the retailers both sell cheaper and buy dearer, than if the whole trade was monopolized by one or two persons.

The persons whose capitals are employed in any of those four ways are themselves productive labourers. Their labour, when properly directed, fixes and realizes itself in the subject or vendible commodity upon which it is bestowed, and generally adds to its price the value at least of their own maintenance and consumption. The profits of the farmer, of the manufacturer, of the merchant, and retailer, are all drawn from the price of the goods which the two first produce, and the two last buy and sell. Equal capitals, however, employed in each of those four different ways, will immediately put into motion very different quantities of productive labour, and augment too in very different proportions the value of the annual produce of the land and labour of the society to which they belong.

The capital of the retailer replaces, together with its profits, that of the merchant of whom he purchases goods, and thereby enables him to continue his business. The retailer himself is the only productive labourer whom it immediately employs. In his profits, consists the whole value which its employment adds to the annual produce of the land and labour of the society.

The capital of the wholesale merchant replaces, together with their profits, the capitals of the farmers and manufacturers of whom he purchases the rude and manufactured produce which he deals in, and thereby enables them to continue their respective trades. It is by this service chiefly that he contributes indirectly to support the productive labour of the society, and to increase the value of its annual produce. His capital employs too the sailors and carriers who transport his goods from one place to another, and it augments the price of those goods by the value, not only of his profits, but of their wages. This is all the productive labour which it immediately puts into motion, and all the value which it immediately adds to the annual produce. Its operation in both these respects is a good deal superior to that of the capital of the retailer.

Part of the capital of the master manufacturer is employed as a fixed capital in the instruments of his trade, and replaces, together with its profits, that of some other artificer of whom he purchases them. Part of his circulating capital is employed in purchasing materials, and replaces, with their profits, the capitals of the farmers and miners of whom he purchases them. But a great part of it is always, either annually, or in a much shorter period, distributed among the different workmen whom he employs. It augments the value of those materials by their wages, and by their masters profits upon the whole stock of wages, materials, and instruments of trade employed in the business. It puts immediately into motion, therefore, a much greater quantity of productive labour, and adds a much greater value to the annual produce of the land and labour of the society, than an equal capital in the hands of any wholesale merchant.

No equal capital puts into motion a greater quantity of productive labour than that of the farmer. Not only his labouring servants, but his labouring cattle, are productive labourers. In agriculture too nature labours along with man; and though her labour costs no expence, its produce has its value, as well as that of the most expensive workmen. The most important operations of agriculture seem intended, not so much to increase, though they do that too, as to direct the fertility of nature towards the production of the plants most profitable to man. A field overgrown with briars and brambles may frequently produce as great a quantity of vegetables as the best cultivated vineyard or cornfield. Planting and tillage frequently regulate more than they animate the active fertility of nature; and after all their labour, a great part of the work always remains to be done by her. The labourers and labouring cattle, therefore, employed in agriculture, not only occasion, like the workmen in manufactures, the reproduction of a value equal to their own consumption, or to the capital which employs them, together with its owners profits; but of a much greater value. Over and above the capital of the farmer and all its profits, they regularly occasion the reproduction of the rent of the landlord. This rent may be considered as the produce of those powers of nature, the use of which the landlord lends to the farmer. It is greater or smaller according to the supposed extent of those powers, or in other words, according to the supposed natural or improved fertility of the land. It is the work of nature which remains after deducting or compensating every thing which can be regarded as the work of man. It is seldom less than a fourth, and frequently more than a third of the whole produce. No equal quantity of productive labour employed in manufactures can ever occasion so great a reproduction. In them nature does nothing; man does all; and the reproduction must always be in proportion to the strength of the agents that occasion it. The capital employed in agriculture, therefore, not only puts into motion a greater quantity of productive labour than any equal capital employed in manufactures, but in proportion too to the quantity of productive labour which it employs, it adds a much greater value to the annual produce of the land and labour of the country, to the real wealth and revenue of its inhabitants. Of all the ways in which a capital can be employed, it is by far the most advantageous to the society.

It has been the principal cause of the rapid progress of our American colonies towards wealth and greatness, that almost their whole capitals have hitherto been employed in agriculture. They have no manufactures, those household and coarser manufactures excepted which necessarily accompany the progress of agriculture, and which are the work of the women and children in every private family. The greater part both of the exportation and coasting trade of America, is carried on by the capitals of merchants who reside in Great Britain. Even the stores and ware-houses from which goods are retailed in some provinces, particularly in Virginia and Maryland, belong many of them to merchants who reside in the mother country, and afford one of the few instances of the retail trade of a society being carried on by the capitals of those who are not resident members of it. Were the Americans, either by combination or by any other sort of violence, to stop the importation of European manu-factures, and, by thus giving a monopoly to such of their own countrymen as could manufacture the like goods, divert any considerable part of their capital into this employment, they would retard instead of accelerating the further increase in the value of their annual produce, and would ob-struct instead of promoting the progress of their country towards real wealth and greatness. This would be still more the case, were they to attempt, in the same manner, to monopolize to themselves their whole exportation trade.

The consideration of his own private profit, is the sole motive which determines the owner of any capital to employ it either in agriculture, in manufactures, or in some particular branch of the wholesale or retail trade. The different quantities of productive labour which it may put into motion, and the different values which it may add to the annual produce of the land and labour of the society, according as it is employed in one or other of those different ways, never enter into his thoughts. In coun-tries, therefore, where agriculture is the most profitable of all employ-ments, and farming and improving the most direct roads to a splendid fortune, the capitals of individuals will naturally be employed in the manner most advantageous to the whole society. The profits of agriculture, however, seem to have no superiority over those of other employments in any part of Europe. Projectors, indeed, in every corner of it, have within these few years amused the public with most magnificent accounts of the profits to be made by the cultivation and improvement of land. Without entering into any particular discussion of their calculations, a very simple observation may satisfy us that the result of them must be false. We see every day the most splendid fortunes that have been acquired in the course of a single life by trade and manufactures, frequently from a very small capital, sometimes from no capital. A single instance of such a fortune acquired by agriculture in the same time, and from such a capital, has not, perhaps, occurred in Europe during the course of the present century. In all the great countries of Europe, however, much good land still remains uncultivated, and the greater part of what is cultivated, is far from being improved to the degree of which it is capable. Agriculture, therefore, is almost everywhere capable of absorbing a much greater capital than has ever yet been employed in it. What circumstances in the policy of Europe have given the trades which are carried on in towns so great an advantage over that which is carried on in the country, that private persons frequently find it more for their advantage to employ their capitals in the most distant carrying trades of Asia and America, than in the improvement and cultivation of the most fertile fields in their own neighbourhood, I shall endeavour to explain at full length in the two following books.

Book Three: Of the different Progress of Opulence in different Nations

OF THE NATURAL PROGRESS OF OPULENCE

THE great commerce of every civilized society, is that carried on between the inhabitants of the town and those of the country. It consists in the exchange of rude for manufactured produce, either immediately, or by the intervention of money, or of some sort of paper which represents money. The country supplies the town with the means of subsistence, and the materials of manufacture. The town repays this supply by sending back a part of the manufactured produce to the inhabitants of the country. The town, in which there neither is nor can be any reproduction of substances, may very properly be said to gain its whole wealth and subsistence from the country. We must not, however, upon this account, imagine that the gain of the town is the loss of the country. The gains of both are mutual and reciprocal, and the division of labour is in this, as in all other cases, advantageous to all the different persons employed in the various occupations into which it is subdivided. The inhabitants of the country purchase of the town a greater quantity of manufactured goods, with the produce of a much smaller quantity of their own labour, than they must have employed had they attempted to prepare them themselves. The town affords a market for the surplus produce of the country, or what is over and above the maintenance of the cultivators, and it is there that the inhabitants of the country exchange it for something else which is in demand among them. The greater the number and revenue of the inhabitants of the town, the more extensive is the market which it affords to those of the country; and the more extensive that market, it is always the more advantageous to a great number. The corn which grows within a mile of the town, sells there for the same price with that which comes from twenty miles distance. But the price of the latter must generally, not only pay the expence of raising and bringing it to market, but afford too the ordinary profits of agriculture to the farmer. The proprietors and cultivators of the country, therefore, which lies in the neighbourhood of the town, over and above the ordinary profits of agriculture, gain, in the price of what they sell, the whole value of the carriage of the like produce that is brought from more distant parts, and they save, besides, the whole value of this carriage in the price of what they buy. Compare the cultivation of the lands in the neighbourhood of any considerable town, with that of those which lie at some distance from it, and you will easily satisfy yourself how much the country is benefited by the commerce of the town. Among all the absurd speculations that have been propagated concerning the balance of trade, it has never been pretended that either the country loses by its commerce with the town, or the town by that with the country which maintains it.

As subsistence is, in the nature of things, prior to conveniency and luxury, so the industry which procures the former, must necessarily be prior to that which ministers to the latter. The cultivation and improvement of the country, therefore, which affords subsistence, must, necessarily, be prior to the increase of the town, which furnishes only the means of conveniency and luxury. It is the surplus produce of the country only, or what is over and above the maintenance of the cultivators, that constitutes the subsistence of the town, which can therefore increase only with the increase of this surplus produce. The town, indeed, may not always derive its whole subsistence from the country in its neighbourhood, or even from the territory to which it belongs, but from very distant countries; and this, though it forms no exception from the general rule, has occasioned considerable variations in the progress of opulence in different ages and nations.

That order of things which necessity imposes in general, though not in every particular country, is, in every particular country, promoted by the natural inclinations of man. If human institutions had never thwarted those natural inclinations, the towns could nowhere have increased beyond what the improvement and cultivation of the territory in which they were situated could support; till such time, at least, as the whole of that territory was completely cultivated and improved. Upon equal, or nearly equal profits, most men will choose to employ their capitals rather in the improvement and cultivation of land, than either in manufactures or in foreign trade. The man who employs his capital in land, has it more under his view and command, and his fortune is much less liable to accidents, than that of the trader, who is obliged frequently to commit it, not only to the winds and the waves, but to the more uncertain elements of human folly and injustice, by giving great credits in distant countries to men, with whose character and situation he can seldom be thoroughly acquainted. The capital of the landlord, on the contrary, which is fixed in the improvement of his land, seems to be as well secured as the nature of human affairs can admit of. The beauty of the country besides, the pleasures of a country life, the tranquillity of mind which it promises, and wherever the injustice of human laws does not disturb it, the independency which it really affords, have charms that more or less attract every body; and as to cultivate the ground was the original destination of man, so in every stage of his existence he seems to retain a predilection for this primitive employment.

Without the assistance of some artificers, indeed, the cultivation of land cannot be carried on, but with great inconveniency and continual interruption. Smiths, carpenters, wheelwrights, and ploughwrights, masons, and bricklayers, tanners, shoemakers, and tailors, are people, whose service the farmer has frequent occasion for. Such artificers too stand, occasionally, in need of the assistance of one another; and as their residence is not, like that of the farmer, necessarily tied down to a precise spot, they naturally settle in the neighbourhood of one another, and thus form a small town or village. The butcher, the brewer, and the baker, soon join them, together with many other artificers and retailers, necessary or useful for supplying their occasional wants, and who contribute still further to augment the town. The inhabitants of the town and those of the country are mutually the servants of one another. The town is a continual fair or market, to which the inhabitants of the country resort, in order to exchange their rude for manufactured produce. It is this commerce which supplies the inhabitants of the town both with the materials of their work, and the means of their subsistence. The quantity of the finished work which they sell to the inhabitants of the country, necessarily regulates the quantity of the materials and provisions which they buy. Neither their employment nor subsistence, therefore, can augment, but in proportion to the augmentation of the demand from the country for finished work; and this demand can augment only in proportion to the extension of improvement and cultivation. Had human institutions, therefore, never disturbed the natural course of things, the progressive wealth and increase of the towns would, in every political society, be consequential, and in proportion to the improvement and cultivation of the territory or country.

In our North American colonies, where uncultivated land is still to be had upon easy terms, no manufactures for distant sale have ever yet been established in any of their towns. When an artificer has acquired a little more stock than is necessary for carrying on his own business in supplying the neighbouring country, he does not, in North America, attempt to establish with it a manufacture for more distant sale, but employs it in the purchase and improvement of uncultivated land. From artificer he becomes planter, and neither the large wages nor the easy subsistence which that country affords to artificers, can bribe him rather to work for other people than for himself. He feels that an artificer is the servant of his customers, from whom he derives his subsistence; but that a planter who cultivates his own land, and derives his necessary subsistence from the labour of his own family, is really a master, and independent of all the world.

In countries, on the contrary, where there is either no uncultivated land, or none that can be had upon easy terms, every artificer who has acquired more stock than he can employ in the occasional jobs of the neighbourhood, endeavours to prepare work for more distant sale. The smith erects some sort of iron, the weaver some sort of linen or woollen manufactory. Those different manufactures come, in process of time, to be gradually subdivided, and thereby improved and refined in a great variety of ways, which may easily be conceived, and which it is therefore unnecessary to explain any further.

In seeking for employment to a capital, manufactures are, upon equal or nearly equal profits, naturally preferred to foreign commerce, for the same reason that agriculture is naturally preferred to manufactures. As the capital of the landlord or farmer is more secure than that of the manufacturer, so the capital of the manufacturer, being at all times more within his view and command, is more secure than that of the foreign merchant. In every period, indeed, of every society, the surplus part both of the rude and manufactured produce, or that for which there is no demand at home, must be sent abroad in order to be exchanged for something for which there is some demand at home. But whether the capital, which carries this surplus produce abroad, be a foreign or a domestic one, is of very little importance. If the society has not acquired sufficient capital both to cultivate all its lands, and to manufacture in the completest manner the whole of its rude produce, there is even a considerable advantage that that rude produce should be exported by a foreign capital, in order that the whole stock of the society may be employed in more useful purposes. The wealth of ancient Egypt, that of China and Indostan, sufficiently demonstrate that a nation may attain a very high degree of opulence, though the greater part of its exportation trade be carried on by foreigners. The progress of our North American and West Indian colonies would have been much less rapid, had not capital but what belonged to themselves been employed in exporting their surplus produce.

According to the natural course of things, therefore, the greater part of the capital of every growing society is, first, directed to agriculture, afterwards to manufactures, and last of all to foreign commerce. This order of things is so very natural, that in every society that had any territory, it has always, I believe, been in some degree observed. Some of their lands must have been cultivated before any considerable towns could be established, and some sort of coarse industry of the manufacturing kind must have been carried on in those towns, before they could well think of employing themselves in foreign commerce.

But though this natural order of things must have taken place in some degree in every such society, it has, in all the modern states of Europe, been, in many respects, entirely inverted. The foreign commerce of some of their cities has introduced all their finer manufactures, or such as were fit for distant sale; and manufactures and foreign commerce together, have given birth to the principal improvements of agriculture. The manners and customs which the nature of their original government introduced, and which remained after that government was greatly altered, necessarily forced them into this unnatural and retrograde order.

Book Four: Of Systems of political Economy

Introduction

POLITICAL ECONOMY, considered as a branch of the science of a statesman or legislator, proposes two distinct objects: first, to provide a plentiful revenue or subsistence for the people, or more properly to enable them to provide such a revenue or subsistence for themselves; and secondly, to supply the state or commonwealth with a revenue sufficient for the public services. It proposes to enrich both the people and the sovereign.

The different progress of opulence in different ages and nations, has given occasion to two different systems of political economy, with regard to enriching the people. The one may be called the system of commerce, the other that of agriculture. I shall endeavour to explain both as fully and distinctly as I can, and shall begin with the system of commerce. It is the modern system, and is best understood in our own country and in our own times.

I. Of the Principle of the Commercial or Mercantile System

That wealth consists in money, or in gold and silver, is a popular notion which naturally arises from the double function of money, as the instrument of commerce, and as the measure of value. In consequence of its being the instrument of commerce, when we have money we can more readily obtain whatever else we have occasion for, than by means of any other commodity. The great affair, we always find, is to get money. When that is obtained, there is no difficulty in making any subsequent purchase. In consequence of its being the measure of value, we estimate that of all other commodities by the quantity of money which they will exchange for. We say of a rich man that he is worth a great deal, and of a poor man that he is worth very little money. A frugal man, or a man eager to be rich, is said to love money; and a careless, a generous, or a profuse man, is said to be indifferent about it. To grow rich is to get money; and wealth and money, in short, are, in common language, considered as in every respect synonymous.

A rich country, in the same manner as a rich man, is supposed to be a country abounding in money; and to heap up gold and silver in any country is supposed to be the readiest way to enrich it. For some time after the discovery of America, the first enquiry of the Spaniards, when they arrived upon any unknown coast, used to be, if there was any gold or silver to be found in the neighbourhood? By the information which they received, they judged whether it was worth while to make a settlement there, or if the country was worth the conquering. Plano Carpino, a monk sent ambassador from the king of France to one of the sons of the famous Genghis Khan, says that the Tartars used frequently to ask him if there was plenty of sheep and oxen in the kingdom of France. Their enquiry had the same object with that of the Spaniards. They wanted to know if the country was rich enough to be worth the conquering. Among the Tartars, as among all other nations of shepherds, who are generally ignorant of the use of money, cattle are the instruments of commerce and the measures of value. Wealth, therefore, according to them, consisted in cattle, as according to the Spaniards it consisted in gold and silver. Of the two, the Tartar notion, perhaps, was the nearest to the truth.

Mr. Locke remarks a distinction between money and other moveable goods. All other moveable goods, he says, are of so consumable a nature that the wealth which consists in them cannot be much depended on, and a nation which abounds in them one year may, without any exportation, but merely by their own waste and extravagance, be in great want of them the next. Money, on the contrary, is a steady friend, which, though it may travel about from hand to hand, yet if it can be kept from going out of the country, is not very liable to be wasted and consumed. Gold and silver, therefore, are, according to him, the most solid and substantial part of the moveable wealth of a nation, and to multiply those metals ought, he thinks, upon that account, to be the great object of its political economy.

Others admit that if a nation could be separated from all the world, it would be of no consequence how much, or how little money circulated in it. The consumable goods which were circulated by means of this money, would only be exchanged for a greater or a smaller number of pieces; but the real wealth or poverty of the country, they allow, would depend altogether upon the abundance or scarcity of those consumable goods. But it is otherwise, they think, with countries which have connections with foreign nations, and which are obliged to carry on foreign wars, and to maintain fleets and armies in distant countries. This, they say, cannot be done, but by sending abroad money to pay them with; and a nation cannot send much money abroad, unless it has a good deal at home. Every such nation, therefore, must endeavour in time of peace to accumulate gold and silver, that, when occasion requires, it may have wherewithal to carry on foreign wars.

In consequence of these popular notions, all the different nations of Europe have studied, though to little purpose, every possible means of accumulating gold and silver in their respective countries. Spain and Portugal, the proprietors of the principal mines which supply Europe with those metals, have either prohibited their exportation under the severest penalties, or subjected it to a considerable duty. The like prohibition seems anciently to have made a part of the policy of most other European nations. It is even to be found, where we should least of all expect to find it, in some old Scotch acts of parliament, which forbid under heavy penalties the carrying gold or silver *forth of the kingdom*. The like policy anciently took place both in France and England.

When those countries became commercial, the merchants found this prohibition, upon many occasions, extremely inconvenient. They could frequently buy more advantageously with gold and silver than with any other commodity, the foreign goods which they wanted, either to import into their own, or to carry to some other foreign country. They remonstrated, therefore, against this prohibition as hurtful to trade.

They represented, first, that the exportation of gold and silver in order to purchase foreign goods, did not always diminish the quantity of those metals in the kingdom. That, on the contrary, it might frequently increase that quantity; because, if the consumption of foreign goods was not thereby increased in the country, those goods might be re-exported to foreign countries, and, being there sold for a large profit, might bring back much more treasure than was originally sent out to purchase them. Mr. Mun compares this operation of foreign trade to the seedtime and harvest of agriculture. "If we only behold," says he, "the actions of the husbandman in the seedtime, when he casteth away much good corn into the ground, we shall account him rather a madman than a husbandman. But when we consider his labours in the harvest, which is the end of his endeavours, we shall find the worth and plentiful increase of his actions."

They represented, secondly, that this prohibition could not hinder the exportation of gold and silver, which, on account of the smallness of their bulk in proportion to their value, could easily be smuggled abroad. That this exportation could only be prevented by a proper attention to, what they called, the balance of trade. That when the country exported to a greater value than it imported, a balance became due to it from foreign nations, which was necessarily paid to it in gold and silver, and thereby increased the quantity of those metals in the kingdom. But that when it imported to a greater value than it exported, a contrary balance became due to foreign nations, which was necessarily paid to them in the same manner, and thereby diminished that quantity. That in this case to prohibit the exportation of those metals could not prevent it, but only by making it more dangerous, render it more expensive. That the exchange was thereby turned more against the country which owed the balance, than it otherwise might have been; the merchant who purchased a bill upon the foreign country being obliged to pay the banker who sold it, not only for the natural risk, trouble and expence of sending the money thither, but for the extraordinary risk arising from the prohibition. But that the more the exchange was against any country, the more the balance of trade became necessarily against it; the money of that country becoming necessarily of so much less value, in comparison with that of the country to which the balance was due. That if the exchange between England and Holland, for example, was five per cent. against England, it would require a hundred and five ounces of silver in England to purchase a bill for a hundred ounces of silver in Holland: that a hundred and five ounces of silver in England, therefore, would be worth only a hundred ounces of silver in Holland, and would purchase only a proportionable quantity of Dutch goods: but that a hundred ounces of silver in Holland, on the contrary, would be worth a hundred and five ounces in England, and would purchase a proportionable quantity of English goods: that the English goods which were sold to Holland would be sold so much cheaper; and the Dutch goods which were sold to England, so much dearer, by the difference of the exchange; that the one would draw so much less Dutch money to England, and the other so much more English money to Holland, as this difference amounted to: and that the balance of trade, therefore, would necessarily be so much more against England, and would require a greater balance of gold and silver to be exported to Holland.

Those arguments were partly solid and partly sophistical. They were solid so far as they asserted that the exportation of gold and silver in trade might frequently be advantageous to the country. They were solid too, in asserting that no prohibition could prevent their exportation, when private people found any advantage in exporting them. But they were sophistical in supposing, that either to preserve or to augment the quantity of those metals required more the attention of government, than to preserve or to augment the quantity of any other useful commodities, which the freedom of trade, without any such attention, never fails to supply in the proper quantity. They were sophistical too, perhaps, in asserting that the high price of exchange necessarily increased, what they called, the unfavourable balance of trade, or occasioned the exportation of a greater quantity of gold and silver. That high price, indeed, was extremely disadvantageous to the merchants who had any money to pay in foreign countries. They paid so much dearer for the bills which their bankers granted them upon those countries. But though the risk arising from the prohibition might occasion some extraordinary expence to the bankers, it would not necessarily carry any more money out of the country. This expence would generally be all laid out in the country, in smuggling the money out of it, and could seldom occasion the exportation of a single sixpence beyond the precise sum drawn for. The high price of exchange too would naturally dispose the merchants to endeavour to make their exports nearly balance their imports, in order that they might have this high exchange to pay upon as small a sum as possible. The high price of exchange, besides, must necessarily have operated as a tax, in raising the price of foreign goods, and thereby diminishing their consumption. It would tend, therefore, not to increase, but to diminish, what they called, the unfavourable balance of trade, and consequently the exportation of gold and silver.

Such as they were, however, those arguments convinced the people to whom they were addressed. They were addressed by merchants to parliaments, and to the councils of princes, to nobles, and to country gentlemen; by those who were supposed to understand trade, to those who were conscious to themselves that they knew nothing about the matter. That foreign trade enriched the country, experience demonstrated to the nobles and country gentlemen, as well as to the merchants; but how, or in what manner, none of them well knew. The merchants knew perfectly in what manner it enriched themselves. It was their business to know it. But to know in what manner it enriched the country, was no part of their business. This subject never came into their consideration, but when they had occasion to apply to their country for some change in the laws relating to foreign trade. It then became necessary to say something about the beneficial effects of foreign trade, and the manner in which those effects were obstructed by the laws as they then stood. To the judges who were to decide the business, it appeared a most satisfactory account of the matter, when they were told that foreign trade brought money into the country, but that the laws in question hindered it from bringing so much as it otherwise would do. Those arguments therefore produced the wished-for effect. The prohibition of exporting gold and silver was in France and England confined to the coin of those respective countries. The exportation of foreign coin and of bullion was made free. In Holland, and in some other places, this liberty was extended even to the coin of the country. The attention of government was turned away from guarding against the exportation of gold and silver, to watch over the balance of trade, as the only cause which could occasion any augmentation or diminution of those metals. From one fruitless care it was turned away to another care much more intricate, much more embarrassing, and just equally fruitless. The title of Mun's book, *England's Treasure in [by] Foreign Trade,* became a fundamental maxim in the political economy, not of England only, but of all other commercial countries. The inland or home trade, the most important of all, the trade in which an equal capital affords the greatest revenue, and creates the greatest employment to the people of the country, was considered as subsidiary only to foreign trade. It neither brought money into the country, it was said, nor carried any out of it. The country therefore could never become either richer or poorer by means of it, except so far as its prosperity or decay might indirectly influence the state of foreign trade.

A country that has no mines of its own must undoubtedly draw its gold and silver from foreign countries, in the same manner as one that has no vineyards of its own must draw its wines. It does not seem necessary, however, that the attention of government should be more turned towards the one than towards the other object. A country that has wherewithal to buy wine, will always get the wine which it has occasion for; and a country that has wherewithal to buy gold and silver, will never be in want of those metals. They are to be bought for a certain price like all other commodities, and as they are the price of all other commodities, so all other commodities are the price of those metals. We trust with perfect security that the freedom of trade, without any attention of government, will always supply us with the wine which we have occasion for: and we may trust with equal security that it will always supply us with all the gold and silver which we can afford to purchase or to employ, either in circulating our commodities, or in other uses.

The quantity of every commodity which human industry can either purchase or produce, naturally regulates itself in every country according to the effectual demand, or according to the demand of those who are willing to pay the whole rent, labour and profits which must be paid in order to prepare and bring it to market. But no commodities regulate themselves more easily or more exactly according to this effectual demand than gold and silver; because, on account of the small bulk and great value of those metals, no commodities can be more easily transported from one place to another, from the places where they are cheap, to those where they are dear, from the places where they exceed, to those where they fall short of this effectual demand. If there were in England, for example, an effectual demand for an additional quantity of gold, a packet boat could bring from Lisbon, or from wherever else it was to be had, fifty tons of gold, which could be coined into more than five millions of guineas. But if there were an effectual demand for grain to the same value, to import it would require, at five guineas a ton, a million of tons of shipping, or a thousand ships of a thousand tons each. The navy of England would not be sufficient.

When the quantity of gold and silver imported into any country exceeds the effectual demand, no vigilance of government can prevent their exportation. All the sanguinary laws of Spain and Portugal are not able to keep their gold and silver at home. The continual importations from Peru and Brazil exceed the effectual demand of those countries, and sink the price of those metals there below that in the neighbouring countries. If, on the contrary, in any particular country their quantity fell short of the effectual demand, so as to raise their price above that of the neighbouring countries, the government would have no occasion to take any pains to import them. If it were even to take pains to prevent their importation, it would not be able to effectuate it. Those metals, when the Spartans had got wherewithal to purchase them, broke through all the barriers which the laws of Lycurgus opposed to their entrance into Lacedemon. All the sanguinary laws of the customs are not able to prevent the importation of the teas of the Dutch and Gottenburgh East India companies; because somewhat cheaper than those of the British company. A pound of tea, however, is about a hundred times the bulk of one of the highest prices, sixteen shillings, that is commonly paid for it in silver, and more than two thousand times the bulk of the same price in gold, and consequently just so many times more difficult to smuggle.

It is partly owing to the easy transportation of gold and silver from the places where they abound to those where they are wanted, that the price of those metals does not fluctuate continually like that of the greater part of other commodities, which are hindered by their bulk from shifting their situation, when the market happens to be either over- or under-stocked with them. The price of those metals, indeed, is not altogether exempted from variation, but the changes to which it is liable are generally slow, gradual, and uniform. In Europe, for example, it is supposed, without much foundation, perhaps, that, during the course of the present and preceding century, they have been constantly, but gradually, sinking in their value, on account of the continual importations from the Spanish West Indies. But to make any sudden change in the price of gold and silver, so as to raise or lower at once, sensibly and remarkably, the money price of all other commodities, requires such a revolution in commerce as that occasioned by the discovery of America.

If, notwithstanding all this, gold and silver should at any time fall short in a country which has wherewithal to purchase them, there are more expedients for supplying their place, than that of almost any other commodity. If the materials of manufacture are wanted, industry must stop. If provisions are wanted, the people must starve. But if money is wanted, barter will supply its place, though with a good deal of incon-veniency. Buying and selling upon credit, and the different dealers com-pensating their credits with one another, once a month or once a year, will supply it with less inconveniency. A well-regulated paper money will supply it, not only without any inconveniency, but, in some cases, with some advantages. Upon every account, therefore, the attention of govern-ment never was so unnecessarily employed, as when directed to watch over the preservation or increase of the quantity of money in any country.

No complaint, however, is more common than that of a scarcity of money. Money, like wine, must always be scarce with those who have neither wherewithal to buy it, nor credit to borrow it. Those who have either, will seldom be in want either of the money, or of the wine which they have occasion for. This complaint, however, of the scarcity of money, is not always confined to improvident spendthrifts. It is sometimes general through a whole mercantile town, and the country in its neighbourhood. Overtrading is the common cause of it. Sober men, whose projects have been disproportioned to their capitals, are as likely to have neither where-withal to buy money, nor credit to borrow it, as prodigals whose expence has been disproportioned to their revenue. Before their projects can be brought to bear, their stock is gone, and their credit with it. They run about everywhere to borrow money, and every body tells them that they have none to lend. Even such general complaints of the scarcity of money do not always prove that the usual number of gold and silver pieces are not circulating in the country, but that many people want those pieces who have nothing to give for them. When the profits of trade happen to be greater than ordinary, overtrading becomes a general error both among great and small dealers. They do not always send more money abroad than usual, but they buy upon credit both at home and abroad, an unusual quantity of goods, which they send to some distant market, in hopes that the returns will come in before the demand for payment. The demand comes before the returns, and they have nothing at hand, with which they can either purchase money, or give solid security for borrowing. It is not any scarcity of gold and silver, but the difficulty which such people find in borrowing, and which their creditors find in getting payment, that occasions the general complaint of the scarcity of money.

It would be too ridiculous to go about seriously to prove, that wealth does not consist in money, or in gold and silver; but in what money purchases, and is valuable only for purchasing. Money, no doubt, makes always a part of the national capital; but it has already been shown that it generally makes but a small part, and always the most unprofitable part of it.

It is not because wealth consists more essentially in money than in goods, that the merchant finds it generally more easy to buy goods with money, than to buy money with goods; but because money is the known and established instrument of commerce, for which every thing is readily given in exchange, but which is not always with equal readiness to be got in exchange for every thing. The greater part of goods besides are more perishable than money, and he may frequently sustain a much greater loss by keeping them. When his goods are upon hand too, he is more liable to such demands for money as he may not be able to answer, than when he has got their price in his coffers. Over and above all this, his profit arises more directly from selling than from buying, and he is upon all these accounts generally much more anxious to exchange his goods for money, than his money for goods. But though a particular merchant, with abundance of goods in his warehouse, may sometimes be ruined by not being able to sell them in time, a nation or country is not liable to the same accident. The whole capital of a merchant frequently consists in perishable goods destined for purchasing money. But it is but a very small part of the annual produce of the land and labour of a country which can ever be destined for purchasing gold and silver from their neighbours. The far greater part is circulated and consumed among themselves; and even of the surplus which is sent abroad, the greater part is generally destined for the purchase of other foreign goods. Though gold and silver, therefore, could not be had in exchange for the goods destined to purchase them, the nation would not be ruined. It might, indeed, suffer some loss and inconveniency, and be forced upon some of those expedients which are necessary for supplying the place of money. The annual produce of its land and labour, however, would be the same, or very nearly the same, as usual, because the same, or very nearly the same consumable capital would be employed in maintaining it. And though goods do not always draw money so readily as money draws goods, in the long run they draw it more necessarily than even it draws them. Goods can serve many other purposes besides purchasing money, but money can serve no other purpose besides purchasing goods. Money, therefore, necessarily runs after goods, but goods do not always or necessarily run after money.

It is not by the importation of gold and silver, that the discovery of America has enriched Europe. By the abundance of the American mines, those metals have become cheaper. A service of plate can now be purchased for about a third part of the corn, or a third part of the labour, which it would have cost in the fifteenth century. With the same annual expence of labour and commodities, Europe can annually purchase about three times the quantity of plate which it could have purchased at that time. But when a commodity comes to be sold for a third part of what had been its usual price, not only those who purchased it before can purchase three times their former quantity, but it is brought down to the level of a much greater number of purchasers, perhaps to more than ten, perhaps to more than twenty times the former number. So that there may be in Europe at present not only more than three times, but more than twenty or thirty times the quantity of plate which would have been in it, even in its present state of improvement, had the discovery of the American mines never been made. So far Europe has, no doubt, gained a real conveniency, though surely a very trifling one. The cheapness of gold and silver renders those metals rather less fit for the purposes of money than they were before. In order to make the same purchases, we must load ourselves with a greater quantity of them, and carry about a shilling in our pocket where a groat would have done before. It is difficult to say which is most trifling, this inconveniency, or the opposite conveniency. Neither the one nor the other could have made any very essential change in the state of Europe. The discovery of America, however, certainly made a most essential one. By opening a new and inexhaustible market to all the commodities of Europe, it gave occasion to new divisions of labour and improvements of art, which, in the narrow circle of the ancient commerce, could never have taken place for want of a market to take off the greater part of their produce. The productive powers of labour were improved, and its produce increased in all the different countries of Europe, and together with it the real revenue and wealth of the inhabitants. The commodities of Europe were almost all new to America, and many of those of America were new to Europe. A new set of exchanges, therefore, began to take place which had never been thought of before, and which should naturally have proved as advantageous to the new, as it certainly did to the old continent. The savage injustice of the Europeans rendered an event, which ought to have been beneficial to all, ruinous and destructive to several of those unfortunate countries.

The discovery of a passage to the East Indies, by the Cape of Good Hope, which happened much about the same time, opened, perhaps, a still more extensive range to foreign commerce than even that of America, notwithstanding the greater distance. There were but two nations in America, in any respect superior to savages, and these were destroyed almost as soon as discovered. The rest were mere savages. But the empires of China, Indostan, Japan, as well as several others in the East Indies, without having richer mines of gold or silver, were in every other respect much richer, better cultivated, and more advanced in all arts and manufactures than either Mexico or Peru, even though we should credit, what plainly deserves no credit, the exaggerated accounts of the Spanish writers, concerning the ancient state of those empires. But rich and civilized nations can always exchange to a much greater value with one another, than with savages and barbarians. Europe, however, has hitherto derived much less advantage from its commerce with the East Indies, than from that with America.

Money in common language, as I have already observed, frequently signifies wealth; and this ambiguity of expression has rendered this popular notion so familiar to us, that even they, who are convinced of its absurdity, are very apt to forget their own principles, and in the course of their reasonings to take it for granted as a certain and undeniable truth. Some of the best English writers upon commerce set out with observing, that the wealth of a country consists, not in its gold and silver only, but in its lands, houses, and consumable goods of all different kinds. In the course of their reasonings, however, the lands, houses, and consumable goods seem to slip out of their memory, and the strain of their argument frequently supposes that all wealth consists in gold and silver, and that to multiply those metals is the great object of national industry and commerce.

The two principles being established, however, that wealth consisted in gold and silver, and that those metals could be brought into a country which had no mines only by the balance of trade, or by exporting to a greater value than it imported; it necessarily became the great object of political economy to diminish as much as possible the importation of foreign goods for home consumption, and to increase as much as possible the exportation of the produce of domestic industry. Its two great engines for enriching the country, therefore, were restraints upon importation, and encouragements to exportation.

The restraints upon importation were of two kinds.

First, Restraints upon the importation of such foreign goods for home consumption as could be produced at home, from whatever country they were imported.

Secondly, Restraints upon the importation of goods of almost all kinds from those particular countries with which the balance of trade was supposed to be disadvantageous.

Those different restraints consisted sometimes in high duties, and sometimes in absolute prohibitions.

Exportation was encouraged sometimes by drawbacks, sometimes by bounties, sometimes by advantageous treaties of commerce with foreign states, and sometimes by the establishment of colonies in distant countries.

Drawbacks were given upon two different occasions. When the home manufactures were subject to any duty or excise, either the whole or a part of it was frequently drawn back upon their exportation; and when foreign goods liable to a duty were imported in order to be exported again, either the whole or a part of this duty was sometimes given back upon such exportation.

Bounties were given for the encouragement either of some beginning manufactures, or of such sorts of industry of other kinds as were supposed to deserve particular favour.

By advantageous treaties of commerce, particular privileges were procured in some foreign state for the goods and merchants of the country, beyond what were granted to those of other countries.

By the establishment of colonies in distant countries, not only particular privileges, but a monopoly was frequently procured for the goods and merchants of the country which established them.

The two sorts of restraints upon importation above-mentioned, together with these four encouragements to exportation, constitute the principal means by which the commercial system proposes to increase the quantity of gold and silver in any country by turning the balance of trade in its favour.

II. Of Restraints upon the Importation from Foreign Countries of Such Goods As Can Be Produced at Home

By restraining, either by high duties, or by absolute prohibitions, the importation of such goods from foreign countries as can be produced at home, the monopoly of the home market is more or less secured to the domestic industry employed in producing them. Thus the prohibition of importing either live cattle or salt provisions from foreign countries secures to the graziers of Great Britain the monopoly of the home market for butcher's meat. The high duties upon the importation of corn, which in times of moderate plenty amount to a prohibition, give a like advantage to the growers of that commodity. The prohibition of the importation of foreign woollens is equally favourable to the woollen manufacturers. The silk manufacture, though altogether employed upon foreign materials, has lately obtained the same advantage. The linen manufacture has not yet obtained it, but is making great strides towards it. Many other sorts of manufacturers have, in the same manner, obtained in Great Britain, either altogether, or very nearly a monopoly against their countrymen. The variety of goods of which the importation into Great Britain is prohibited, either absolutely, or under certain circumstances, greatly exceeds what can easily be suspected by those who are not well acquainted with the laws of the customs.

That this monopoly of the home market frequently gives great encouragement to that particular species of industry which enjoys it, and frequently turns towards that employment a greater share of both the labour and stock of the society than would otherwise have gone to it, cannot be doubted. But whether it tends either to increase the general industry of the society, or to give it the most advantageous direction, is not, perhaps, altogether so evident.

The general industry of the society never can exceed what the capital of the society can employ. As the number of workmen that can be kept in employment by any particular person must bear a certain proportion to his capital, so the number of those that can be continually employed by all the members of a great society, must bear a certain proportion to the whole capital of that society, and never can exceed that proportion. No regulation of commerce can increase the quantity of industry in any society beyond what its capital can maintain. It can only divert a part of it into a direction into which it might not otherwise have gone; and it is by no means certain that this artificial direction is likely to be more advantageous to the society than that into which it would have gone of its own accord.

Every individual is continually exerting himself to find out the most advantageous employment for whatever capital he can command. It is his own advantage, indeed, and not that of the society, which he has in view. But the study of his own advantage naturally, or rather necessarily leads him to prefer that employment which is most advantageous to the society.

First, every individual endeavours to employ his capital as near home as he can, and consequently as much as he can in the support of domestic industry; provided always that he can thereby obtain the ordinary, or not a great deal less than the ordinary profits of stock.

Thus, upon equal or nearly equal profits, every wholesale merchant naturally prefers the home trade to the foreign trade of consumption, and the foreign trade of consumption to the carrying trade. In the home trade his capital is never so long out of his sight as it frequently is in the foreign trade of consumption. He can know better the character and situation of the persons whom he trusts, and if he should happen to be deceived, he knows better the laws of the country from which he must seek redress. In the carrying trade, the capital of the merchant is, as it were, divided between two foreign countries, and no part of it is ever necessarily brought home, or placed under his own immediate view and command.

Secondly, every individual who employs his capital in the support of domestic industry, necessarily endeavours so to direct that industry, that its produce may be of the greatest possible value.

The produce of industry is what it adds to the subject or materials upon which it is employed. In proportion as the value of this produce is great or small, so will likewise be the profits of the employer. But it is only for the sake of profit that any man employs a capital in the support of industry; and he will always, therefore, endeavour to employ it in the support of that industry of which the produce is likely to be of the greatest value, or to exchange for the greatest quantity either of money or of other goods.

But the annual revenue of every society is always precisely equal to the exchangeable value of the whole annual produce of its industry, or rather is precisely the same thing with that exchangeable value. As every individual, therefore, endeavours as much as he can both to employ his capital in the support of domestic industry, and so to direct that industry that its produce may be of the greatest value; every individual necessarily labours to render the annual revenue of the society as great as he can. He generally, indeed, neither intends to promote the public interest, nor knows how much he is promoting it. By preferring the support of domestic to that of foreign industry, he intends only his own security; and by directing that industry in such a manner as its produce may be of the greatest value, he intends only his own gain, and he is in this, as in many other cases, led by an invisible hand to promote an end which was no part of his intention. Nor is it always the worse for the society that it was no part of it. By pursuing his own interest he frequently promotes that of the society more effectually than when he really intends to promote it. I have never known much good done by those who affected to trade for the public good. It is an affectation, indeed, not very common among merchants, and very few words need be employed in dissuading them from it.

It is the maxim of every prudent master of a family, never to attempt to make at home what it will cost him more to make than to buy. The tailor does not attempt to make his own shoes, but buys them of the shoemaker. The shoemaker does not attempt to make his own clothes, but employs a tailor. The farmer attempts to make neither the one nor the other, but employs those different artificers. All of them find it for their interest to employ their whole industry in a way in which they have some advantage over their neighbours, and to purchase with a part of its produce, or what is the same thing, with the price of a part of it, whatever else they have occasion for.

What is prudence in the conduct of every private family, can scarce be folly in that of a great kingdom. If a foreign country can supply us with a commodity cheaper than we ourselves can make it, better buy it of them with some part of the produce of our own industry, employed in a way in which we have some advantage. The general industry of the country, being always in proportion to the capital which employs it, will not thereby be diminished, no more than that of the above-mentioned artificers; but only left to find out the way in which it can be employed with the greatest advantage. It is certainly not employed to the greatest advantage, when it is thus directed towards an object which it can buy cheaper than it can make. The value of its annual produce is certainly more or less diminished, when it is thus turned away from producing commodities evidently of more value than the commodity which it is directed to produce. According to the supposition, that commodity could be purchased from foreign countries cheaper than it can be made at home. It could, therefore, have been purchased with a part only of the commodities, or, what is the same thing, with a part only of the price of the commodities, which the industry employed by an equal capital would have produced at home, had it been left to follow its natural course. The industry of the country, therefore, is thus turned away from a more, to a less advantageous employment, and the exchangeable value of its annual produce, instead of being increased, according to the intention of the lawgiver, must necessarily be diminished by every such regulation.

By means of such regulations, indeed, a particular manufacture may sometimes be acquired sooner than it could have been otherwise, and after a certain time may be made at home as cheap or cheaper than in the foreign country. But though the industry of the society may be thus carried with advantage into a particular channel sooner than it could have been otherwise, it will by no means follow that the sum total, either of its industry, or of its revenue, can ever be augmented by any such regulation. The industry of the society can augment only in proportion as its capital augments, and its capital can augment only in proportion to what can be gradually saved out of its revenue. But the immediate effect of every such regulation is to diminish its revenue, and what diminishes its revenue is certainly not very likely to augment its capital faster than it would have augmented of its own accord, had both capital and industry been left to find out their natural employments.

The natural advantages which one country has over another in producing particular commodities are sometimes so great, that it is acknowledged by all the world to be in vain to struggle with them. By means of glasses, hotbeds, and hotwalls, very good grapes can be raised in Scotland, and very good wine too can be made of them at about thirty times the expence for which at least equally good can be brought from foreign countries. Would it be a reasonable law to prohibit the importation of all foreign wines, merely to encourage the making of claret and burgundy in Scotland? But if there would be a manifest absurdity in turning towards any employment, thirty times more of the capital and industry of the country, than would be necessary to purchase from foreign countries an equal quantity of the commodities wanted, there must be an absurdity, though not altogether so glaring, yet exactly of the same kind, in turning towards any such employment a thirtieth, or even a three hundredth part more of either. Whether the advantages which one country has over another, be natural or acquired, is in this respect of no consequence. As long as the one country has those advantages, and the other wants them, it will always be more advantageous for the latter, rather to buy of the former than to make. It is an acquired advantage only, which one artificer has over his neighbour, who exercises another trade; and yet they both find it more advantageous to buy of one another, than to make what does not belong to their particular trades.

Merchants and manufacturers are the people who derive the greatest advantage from this monopoly of the home market. The prohibition of the importation of foreign cattle, and of salt provisions, together with the high duties upon foreign corn, which in times of moderate plenty amount to a prohibition, are not near so advantageous to the graziers and farmers of Great Britain, as other regulations of the same kind are to its merchants and manufacturers. Manufactures, those of the finer kind especially, are more easily transported from one country to another than corn or cattle. It is in the fetching and carrying manufactures, accordingly, that foreign trade is chiefly employed. In manufactures, a very small advantage will enable foreigners to undersell our own workmen, even in the home market. It will require a very great one to enable them to do so in the rude produce of the soil. If the free importation of foreign manufactures were permitted, several of the home manufactures would probably suffer, and some of them, perhaps, go to ruin altogether, and a considerable part of the stock and industry at present employed in them, would be forced to find out some other employment. But the freest importation of the rude produce of the soil could have no such effect upon the agriculture of the country.

If the importation of foreign cattle, for example, were made ever so free, so few could be imported, that the grazing trade of Great Britain could be little affected by it. Live cattle are, perhaps, the only commodity of which the transportation is more expensive by sea than by land. By land they carry themselves to market. By sea, not only the cattle, but their food and their water too, must be carried at no small expence and inconveniency. The short sea between Ireland and Great Britain, indeed, renders the importation of Irish cattle more easy. But though the free importation of them, which was lately permitted only for a limited time, were rendered perpetual, it could have no considerable effect upon the interest of the graziers of Great Britain.

The freest importation of salt provisions, in the same manner, could have as little effect upon the interest of the graziers of Great Britain as that of live cattle. Salt provisions are not only a very bulky commodity, but when compared with fresh meat, they are a commodity both of worse quality, and as they cost more labour and expence, of higher price. They could never, therefore, come into competition with the fresh meat, though they might with the salt provisions of the country. They might be used for victualling ships for distant voyages, and such like uses, but could never make any considerable part of the food of the people. The small quantity of salt provisions imported from Ireland since their importation was rendered free, is an experimental proof that our graziers have nothing to apprehend from it. It does not appear that the price of butcher's meat has ever been sensibly affected by it.

Even the free importation of foreign corn could very little affect the interest of the farmers of Great Britain. Corn is a much more bulky commodity than butcher's meat. A pound of wheat at a penny is as dear as a pound of butcher's meat at fourpence. The small quantity of foreign corn imported even in times of the greatest scarcity, may satisfy our farmers that they can have nothing to fear from the freest importation. The average quantity imported one year with another, amounts only, according to the very well informed author of the tracts upon the corn trade, to twenty-three thousand seven hundred and twenty-eight quarters of all sorts of grain, and does not exceed the five hundredth and seventy-one part of the annual consumption. But as the bounty upon corn occasions a greater exportation in years of plenty, so it must of consequence occasion a greater importation in years of scarcity, than in the actual state of tillage would otherwise take place. By means of it, the plenty of one year does not compensate the scarcity of another, and as the average quantity exported is necessarily augmented by it, so must likewise, in the actual state of tillage, the average quantity imported. If there were no bounty, as less corn would be exported, so it is probable that, one year with another, less would be imported than at present. The corn merchants, the fetchers and carriers of corn between Great Britain and foreign countries, would have much less employment, and might suffer considerably; but the country gentlemen and farmers could suffer very little. It is in the corn merchants accordingly, rather than in the country gentlemen and farmers, that I have observed the greatest anxiety for the renewal and continuation of the bounty.

Country gentlemen and farmers are, to their great honour, of all people, the least subject to the wretched spirit of monopoly. The undertaker of a great manufactory is sometimes alarmed if another work of the same kind is established within twenty miles of him. The Dutch undertaker of the woollen manufacture at Abbeville stipulated, that no work of the same kind should be established within thirty leagues of that city. Farmers and country gentlemen, on the contrary, are generally disposed rather to promote than to obstruct the cultivation and improvement of their neighbours farms and estates. They have no secrets, such as those of the greater part of manufacturers, but are generally rather fond of communicating to their neighbours, and of extending as far as possible any new practice which they have found to be advantageous.

To prohibit by a perpetual law the importation of foreign corn and cattle, is in reality to enact, that the population and industry of the country shall at no time exceed what the rude produce of its own soil can maintain.

There seem, however, to be two cases in which it will generally be advantageous to lay some burden upon foreign, for the encouragement of domestic industry.

The first is, when some particular sort of industry is necessary for the defence of the country. The defence of Great Britain, for example, depends very much upon the number of its sailors and shipping. The act of navigation, therefore, very properly endeavours to give the sailors and shipping of Great Britain the monopoly of the trade of their own country, in some cases, by absolute prohibitions, and in others by heavy burdens upon the shipping of foreign countries. The following are the principal dispositions of this act.

First, all ships, of which the owners, masters, and three fourths of the mariners are not British subjects, are prohibited, upon pain of forfeiting ship and cargo, from trading to the British settlements and plantations, or from being employed in the coasting trade of Great Britain.

Secondly, a great variety of the most bulky articles of importation can be brought into Great Britain only, either in such ships as are above described, or in ships of the country where those goods are produced, and of which the owners, masters, and three fourths of the mariners, are of that particular country; and when imported even in ships of this latter kind, they are subject to double aliens duty.

Thirdly, a great variety of the most bulky articles of importation are prohibited from being imported, even in British ships, from any country but that in which they are produced; under pain of forfeiting ship and cargo.

Fourthly, salt fish of all kinds, whale fins, whalebone, oil, and blubber, not caught by and cured on board British vessels, when imported into Great Britain, are subjected to double aliens duty.

When the act of navigation was made, though England and Holland were not actually at war, the most violent animosity subsisted between the two nations. It had begun during the government of the long parliament, which first framed this act, and it broke out soon after in the Dutch wars during that of the Protector and of Charles the Second. It is not impossible, therefore, that some of the regulations of this famous act may have proceeded from national animosity. They are as wise, however, as if they had all been dictated by the most deliberate wisdom. National animosity at that particular time aimed at the very same object which the most deliberate wisdom would have recommended, the diminution of the naval power of Holland, the only naval power which could endanger the security of England.

The act of navigation is not favourable to foreign commerce, or to the growth of that opulence which can arise from it. The interest of a nation in its commercial relations to foreign nations is, like that of a merchant with regard to the different people with whom he deals, to buy as cheap and to sell as dear as possible. But it will be most likely to buy cheap, when by the most perfect freedom of trade it encourages all nations to bring to it the goods which it has occasion to purchase; and, for the same reason, it will be most likely to sell dear, when its markets are thus filled with the greatest number of buyers. The act of navigation, it is true, lays no burden upon foreign ships that come to export the produce of British industry. Even the ancient aliens duty, which used to be paid upon all goods exported as well as imported, has, by several subsequent acts, been taken off from the greater part of the articles of exportation. But if foreigners, either by prohibitions or high duties, are hindered from coming to sell, they cannot always afford to come to buy; because coming without a cargo, they must lose the freight from their own country to Great Britain. By diminishing the number of sellers, therefore, we necessarily diminish that of buyers, and are thus likely not only to buy foreign goods dearer, but to sell our own cheaper, than if there was a more perfect freedom of trade. As defence, however, is of much more importance than opulence, the act of navigation is, perhaps, the wisest of all the commercial regulations of England.

The second case, in which it will generally be advantageous to lay some burden upon foreign for the encouragement of domestic industry, is, when some tax is imposed at home upon the produce of the latter. In this case, it seems reasonable that an equal tax should be imposed upon the like produce of the former. This would not give the monopoly of the home market to domestic industry, nor turn towards a particular employment a greater share of the stock and labour of the country, than what would naturally go to it. It would only hinder any part of what would naturally go to it from being turned away by the tax, into a less natural direction, and would leave the competition between foreign and domestic industry, after the tax, as nearly as possible upon the same footing as before it. In Great Britain, when any such tax is laid upon the produce of domestic industry, it is usual at the same time, in order to stop the clamorous complaints of our merchants and manufacturers, that they will be undersold at home, to lay a much heavier duty upon the importation of all foreign goods of the same kind.

This second limitation of the freedom of trade according to some people should, upon some occasions, be extended much farther than to the precise foreign commodities which could come into competition with those which had been taxed at home. When the necessaries of life have been taxed in any country, it becomes proper, they pretend, to tax not only the like necessaries of life imported from other countries, but all sorts of foreign goods which can come into competition with any thing that is the produce of domestic industry. Subsistence, they say, becomes necessarily dearer in consequence of such taxes; and the price of labour must always rise with the price of the labourers' subsistence. Every commodity, therefore, which is the produce of domestic industry, though not immediately taxed itself, becomes dearer in consequence of such taxes, because the labour which produces it becomes so. Such taxes, therefore, are really equivalent, they say, to a tax upon every particular commodity produced at home. In order to put domestic upon the same footing with foreign industry, therefore, it becomes necessary, they think, to lay some duty upon every foreign commodity, equal to this enhancement of the price of the home commodities with which it can come into competition.

Whether taxes upon the necessaries of life, such as those in Great Britain upon soap, salt, leather, candles, &c. necessarily raise the price of labour, and consequently that of all other commodities, I shall consider hereafter, when I come to treat of taxes. Supposing, however, in the mean time, that they have this effect, and they have it undoubtedly, this general enhancement of the price of all commodities, in consequence of that of labour, is a case which differs in the two following respects from that of a particular commodity, of which the price was enhanced by a particular tax immediately imposed upon it.

First, it might always be known with great exactness how far the price of such a commodity could be enhanced by such a tax: but how far the general enhancement of the price of labour might affect that of every different commodity about which labour was employed, could never be known with any tolerable exactness. It would be impossible, therefore, to proportion with any tolerable exactness the tax upon every foreign, to this enhancement of the price of every home commodity.

Secondly, taxes upon the necessaries of life have nearly the same effect upon the circumstances of the people as a poor soil and a bad climate. Provisions are thereby rendered dearer in the same manner as if it required extraordinary labour and expence to raise them. As in the natural scarcity arising from soil and climate, it would be absurd to direct the people in what manner they ought to employ their capitals and industry, so is it likewise in the artificial scarcity arising from such taxes. To be left to accommodate, as well as they could, their industry to their situation, and to find out those employments in which, notwithstanding their unfavourable circumstances, they might have some advantage either in the home or in the foreign market, is what in both cases would evidently be most for their advantage. To lay a new tax upon them, because they are already overburdened with taxes, and because they already pay too dear for the necessaries of life, to make them likewise pay too dear for the greater part of other commodities, is certainly a most absurd way of making amends.

Such taxes, when they have grown up to a certain height, are a curse equal to the barrenness of the earth and the inclemency of the heavens; and yet it is in the richest and most industrious countries that they have been most generally imposed. No other countries could support so great a disorder. As the strongest bodies only can live and enjoy health, under an unwholesome regimen; so the nations only, that in every sort of industry have the greatest natural and acquired advantages, can subsist and prosper under such taxes. Holland is the country in Europe in which they abound most, and which from peculiar circumstances continues to prosper, not by means of them, as has been most absurdly supposed, but in spite of them.

As there are two cases in which it will generally be advantageous to lay some burden upon foreign, for the encouragement of domestic industry; so there are two others in which it may sometimes be a matter of deliberation; in the one, how far it is proper to continue the free importation of certain foreign goods; and in the other, how far, or in what manner, it may be proper to restore that free importation after it has been for some time interrupted.

The case in which it may sometimes be a matter of deliberation how far it is proper to continue the free importation of certain foreign goods, is, when some foreign nation restrains by high duties or prohibitions the importation of some of our manufactures into their country. Revenge in this case naturally dictates retaliation, and that we should impose the like duties and prohibitions upon the importation of some or all of their manufactures into ours. Nations accordingly seldom fail to retaliate in this manner. The French have been particularly forward to favour their own manufactures by restraining the importation of such foreign goods as could come into competition with them. In this consisted a great part of the policy of Mr. Colbert, who, notwithstanding his great abilities, seems in this case to have been imposed upon by the sophistry of merchants and manufacturers, who are always demanding a monopoly against their countrymen. It is at present the opinion of the most intelligent men in France that his operations of this kind have not been beneficial to his country. That minister, by the tariff of 1667, imposed very high duties upon a great number of foreign manufactures. Upon his refusing to moderate them in favour of the Dutch, they in 1671 prohibited the importation of the wines, brandies and manufactures of France. The war of 1672 seems to have been in part occasioned by this commercial dispute. The peace of Nimeguen put an end to it in 1678, by moderating some of those duties in favour of the Dutch, who in consequence took off their prohibition. It was about the same time that the French and English began mutually to oppress each other's industry, by the like duties and prohibitions, of which the French, however, seem to have set the first example. The spirit of hostility which has subsisted between the two nations ever since, has hitherto hindered them from being moderated on either side. In 1697 the English prohibited the importation of bone lace, the manufacture of Flanders. The government of that country, at that time under the dominion of Spain, prohibited in return the importation of English woollens. In 1700, the prohibition of importing bone lace into England, was taken off upon condition that the importation of English woollens into Flanders should be put on the same footing as before.

There may be good policy in retaliations of this kind, when there is a probability that they will procure the repeal of the high duties or prohibitions complained of. The recovery of a great foreign market will generally more than compensate the transitory inconveniency of paying dearer during a short time for some sorts of goods. To judge whether such retaliations are likely to produce such an effect, does not, perhaps, belong so much to the science of a legislator, whose deliberations ought to be governed by general principles which are always the same, as to the skill of that insidious and crafty animal, vulgarly called a statesman or politician, whose councils are directed by the momentary fluctuations of affairs. When there is no probability that any such repeal can be procured, it seems a bad method of compensating the injury done to certain classes of our people, to do another injury ourselves, not only to those classes, but to almost all the other classes of them. When our neighbours prohibit some manufacture of ours, we generally prohibit, not only the same, for that alone would seldom affect them considerably, but some other manufacture of theirs. This may no doubt give encouragement to some particular class of workmen among ourselves, and by excluding some of their rivals, may enable them to raise their price in the home market. Those workmen, however, who suffered by our neighbours' prohibition will not be benefited by ours. On the contrary, they and almost all the other classes of our citizens will thereby be obliged to pay dearer than before for certain goods. Every such law, therefore, imposes a real tax upon the whole country, not in favour of that particular class of workmen who were injured by our neighbours' prohibition, but of some other class.

The case in which it may sometimes be a matter of deliberation, how far, or in what manner, it is proper to restore the free importation of foreign goods, after it has been for some time interrupted, is, when particular manufactures, by means of high duties or prohibitions upon all foreign goods which can come into competition with them, have been so far extended as to employ a great multitude of hands. Humanity may in this case require that the freedom of trade should be restored only by slow gradations, and with a good deal of reserve and circumspection. Were those high duties and prohibitions taken away all at once, cheaper foreign goods of the same kind might be poured so fast into the home market, as to deprive all at once many thousands of our people of their ordinary employment and means of subsistence. The disorder which this would occasion might no doubt be very considerable. It would in all probability, however, be much less than is commonly imagined, for the two following reasons:

First, all those manufactures, of which any part is commonly exported to other European countries without a bounty, could be very little affected by the freest importation of foreign goods. Such manufactures must be sold as cheap abroad as any other foreign goods of the same quality and kind, and consequently must be sold cheaper at home. They would still, therefore, keep possession of the home market, and though a capricious man of fashion might sometimes prefer foreign wares, merely because they were foreign, to cheaper and better goods of the same kind that were made at home, this folly could, from the nature of things, extend to so few, that it could make no sensible impression upon the general employment of the people.

Secondly, though a great number of people should, by thus restoring the freedom of trade, be thrown all at once out of their ordinary employment and common method of subsistence, it would by no means follow that they would thereby be deprived either of employment or subsistence. By the reduction of the army and navy at the end of the late war, more than a hundred thousand soldiers and seamen, a number equal to what is employed in the greatest manufactures, were all at once thrown out of their ordinary employment; but, though they no doubt suffered some inconveniency, they were not thereby deprived of all employment and subsistence. The greater part of the seamen, it is probable, gradually betook themselves to the merchant service as they could find occasion, and in the meantime both they and the soldiers were absorbed in the great mass of the people, and employed in a great variety of occupations.

To expect, indeed, that the freedom of trade should ever be entirely restored in Great Britain, is as absurd as to expect that an Oceana or Utopia should ever be established in it. Not only the prejudices of the public, but what is much more unconquerable, the private interests of many individuals, irresistibly oppose it.

III. CONCLUSION OF THE MERCANTILE SYSTEM

CONSUMPTION is the sole end and purpose of all production; and the interest of the producer ought to be attended to, only so far as it may be necessary for promoting that of the consumer. The maxim is so perfectly self-evident, that it would be absurd to attempt to prove it. But in the mercantile system, the interest of the consumer is almost constantly sacrificed to that of the producer; and it seems to consider production, and not consumption, as the ultimate end and object of all industry and commerce.

In the restraints upon the importation of all foreign commodities which can come into competition with those of our own growth, or manufacture, the interest of the home consumer is evidently sacrificed to that of the producer. It is altogether for the benefit of the latter, that the former is obliged to pay that enhancement of price which this monopoly almost always occasions.

It is altogether for the benefit of the producer that bounties are granted upon the exportation of some of his productions. The home consumer is obliged to pay, first, the tax which is necessary for paying the bounty, and secondly, the still greater tax which necessarily arises from the enhancement of the price of the commodity in the home market.

By the famous treaty of commerce with Portugal, the consumer is prevented by high duties from purchasing of a neighbouring country, a commodity which our own climate does not produce, but is obliged to purchase it of a distant country, though it is acknowledged, that the commodity of the distant country is of a worse quality than that of the near one. The home consumer is obliged to submit to this inconveniency, in order that the producer may import into the distant country some of his productions upon more advantageous terms than he would otherwise have been allowed to do. The consumer, too, is obliged to pay, whatever enhancement in the price of those very productions, this forced exportation may occasion in the home market.

But in the system of laws which has been established for the management of our American and West Indian colonies, the interest of the home consumer has been sacrificed to that of the producer with a more extravagant profusion than in all our other commercial regulations. A great empire has been established for the sole purpose of raising up a nation of customers who should be obliged to buy from the shops of our different producers, all the goods with which these could supply them. For the sake of that little enhancement of price which this monopoly might afford our producers, the home consumers have been burdened with the whole expence of maintaining and defending that empire. For this purpose, and for this purpose only, in the two last wars, more than two hundred millions have been spent, and a new debt of more than a hundred and seventy millions has been contracted over and above all that had been expended for the same purpose in former wars. The interest of this debt alone is not only greater than the whole extraordinary profit, which, it ever could be pretended, was made by the monopoly of the colony trade, but than the whole value of that trade, or than the whole value of the goods, which at an average have been annually exported to the colonies.

It cannot be very difficult to determine who have been the contrivers of this whole mercantile system; not the consumers, we may believe, whose interest has been entirely neglected; but the producers, whose interest has been so carefully attended to; and among this latter class our merchants and manufacturers have been by far the principal architects. In the mercantile regulations, which have been taken notice of in this chapter, the interest of our manufacturers has been most peculiarly attended to; and the interest, not so much of the consumers, as that of some other sets of producers, has been sacrificed to it.

IV. Of the Agricultural Systems, or of Those Systems of Political Economy Which Represent the Produce of Land as either the Sole or the Principal Source of the Revenue and Wealth of Every Country

The agricultural systems of political economy will not require so long an explanation as that which I have thought it necessary to bestow upon the mercantile or commercial system.

That system which represents the produce of land as the sole source of the revenue and wealth of every country has, so far as I know, never been adopted by any nation, and it at present exists only in the speculations of a few men of great learning and ingenuity in France. It would not, surely, be worth while to examine at great length the errors of a system which never has done, and probably never will do any harm in any part of the world. I shall endeavour to explain, however, as distinctly as I can, the great outlines of this very ingenious system.

Mr. Colbert, the famous minister of Lewis XIV, was a man of probity, of great industry and knowledge of detail; of great experience and acuteness in the examination of public accounts, and of abilities, in short, every way fitted for introducing method and good order into the collection and expenditure of the public revenue. That minister had unfortunately embraced all the prejudices of the mercantile system, in its nature and essence a system of restraint and regulation, and such as could scarce fail to be agreeable to a laborious and plodding man of business, who had been accustomed to regulate the different departments of public offices, and to establish the necessary checks and controls for confining each to its proper sphere. The industry and commerce of a great country he endeavoured to regulate upon the same model as the departments of a public office; and instead of allowing every man to pursue his own interest his own way, upon the liberal plan of equality, liberty and justice, he bestowed upon certain branches of industry extraordinary privileges, while he laid others under as extraordinary restraints. He was not only disposed, like other European ministers, to encourage more the industry of the towns than that of the country; but, in order to support the industry of the towns, he was willing even to depress and keep down that of the country. In order to render provisions cheap to the inhabitants of the towns, and thereby to encourage manufactures and foreign commerce, he prohibited altogether the exportation of corn, and thus excluded the inhabitants of the country from every foreign market for by far the most important part of the produce of their industry. This prohibition, joined to the restraints imposed by the ancient provincial laws of France upon the transportation of corn from one province to another, and to the arbitrary and degrading taxes which are levied upon the cultivators in almost all the provinces, discouraged and kept down the agriculture of that country very much below the state to which it would naturally have risen in so very fertile a soil and so very happy a climate. This state of discouragement and depression was felt more or less in every different part of the country, and many different inquiries were set on foot concerning the causes of it. One of those causes appeared to be the preference given, by the institutions of Mr. Colbert, to the industry of the towns above that of the country.

If the rod be bent too much one way, says the proverb, in order to make it straight you must bend it as much the other. The French philosophers, who have proposed the system which represents agriculture as the sole source of the revenue and wealth of every country, seem to have adopted this proverbial maxim; and as in the plan of Mr. Colbert the industry of the towns was certainly overvalued in comparison with that of the country; so in their system it seems to be as certainly undervalued.

The different orders of people who have ever been supposed to contribute in any respect towards the annual produce of the land and labour of the country, they divide into three classes. The first is the class of the proprietors of land. The second is the class of the cultivators, of farmers and country labourers, whom they honour with the peculiar appellation of the productive class. The third is the class of artificers, manufacturers, and merchants, whom they endeavour to degrade by the humiliating appellation of the barren or unproductive class.

According to this liberal and generous system, the most advantageous method in which a landed nation can raise up artificers, manufacturers, and merchants of its own, is to grant the most perfect freedom of trade to the artificers, manufacturers and merchants of all other nations. It thereby raises the value of the surplus produce of its own land, of which the continual increase gradually establishes a fund, which in due time necessarily raises up all the artificers, manufacturers and merchants whom it has occasion for.

When a landed nation, on the contrary, oppresses either by high duties or by prohibitions the trade of foreign nations, it necessarily hurts its own interest in two different ways. First, by raising the price of all foreign goods and of all sorts of manufactures, it necessarily sinks the real value of the surplus produce of its own land, with which, or, what comes to the same thing, with the price of which, it purchases those foreign goods and manufactures. Secondly, by giving a sort of monopoly of the home market to its own merchants, artificers, and manufacturers, it raises the rate of mercantile and manufacturing profit in proportion to that of agricultural profit, and consequently either draws from agriculture a part of the capital which had before been employed in it, or hinders from going to it a part of what would otherwise have gone to it. This policy, therefore, discourages agriculture in two different ways; first, by sinking the real value of its produce, and thereby lowering the rate of its profit; and, secondly, by raising the rate of profit in all other employments. Agriculture is rendered less advantageous, and trade and manufactures more advantageous than they otherwise would be; and every man is tempted by his own interest to turn, as much as he can, both his capital and his industry from the former to the latter employments.

Though, by this oppressive policy, a landed nation should be able to raise up artificers, manufacturers, and merchants of its own, somewhat sooner than it could do by the freedom of trade; a matter, however, which is not a little doubtful; yet it would raise them up, if one may say so, prematurely, and before it was perfectly ripe for them. By raising up too hastily one species of industry, it would depress another more valuable species of industry. By raising up too hastily a species of industry which only replaces the stock which employs it, together with the ordinary profit, it would depress a species of industry which, over and above replacing that stock with its profit, affords likewise a neat produce, a free rent to the landlord. It would depress productive labour, by encouraging too hastily that labour which is altogether barren and unproductive.

In what manner, according to this system, the sum total of the annual produce of the land is distributed among the three classes above mentioned, and in what manner the labour of the unproductive class does no more than replace the value of its own consumption, without increasing in any respect the value of that sum total, is represented by Mr. Quesnai, the very ingenious and profound author of this system, in some arithmetical formularies. The first of these formularies, which by way of eminence he peculiarly distinguishes by the name of the Economical Table, represents the manner in which he supposes this distribution takes place, in a state of the most perfect liberty, and therefore of the highest prosperity; in a state where the annual produce is such as to afford the greatest possible neat produce, and where each class enjoys its proper share of the whole annual produce. Some subsequent formularies represent the manner, in which, he supposes, this distribution is made in different states of restraint and regulation; in which, either the class of proprietors, or the barren and unproductive class, is more favoured than the class of cultivators, and in which, either the one or the other encroaches more or less upon the share which ought properly to belong to this productive class. Every such encroachment, every violation of that natural distribution, which the most perfect liberty would establish, must, according to this system, necessarily degrade more or less, from one year to another, the value and sum total of the annual produce, and must necessarily occasion a gradual declension in the real wealth and revenue of the society; a declension of which the progress must be quicker or slower, according to the degree of this encroachment, according as that natural distribution, which the most perfect liberty would establish, is more or less violated. Those subsequent formularies represent the different degrees of declension, which, according to this system, correspond to the different degrees in which this natural distribution of things is violated.

Some speculative physicians seem to have imagined that the health of the human body could be preserved only by a certain precise regimen of diet and exercise, of which every, the smallest, violation necessarily occasioned some degree of disease or disorder proportioned to the degree of the violation. Experience, however, would seem to show, that the human body frequently preserves, to all appearance at least, the most perfect state of health under a vast variety of different regimens; even under some which are generally believed to be very far from being perfectly wholesome. But the healthful state of the human body, it would seem, contains in itself some unknown principle of preservation, capable either of preventing or of correcting, in many respects, the bad effects even of a very faulty regimen. Mr. Quesnai, who was himself a physician, and a very speculative physician, seems to have entertained a notion of the same kind concerning the political body, and to have imagined that it would thrive and prosper only under a certain precise regimen, the exact regimen of perfect liberty and perfect justice. He seems not to have considered that in the political body, the natural effort which every man is continually making to better his own condition, is a principle of preservation capable of preventing and correcting, in many respects, the bad effects of a political economy, in some degree both partial and oppressive. Such a political economy, though it no doubt retards more or less, is not always capable of stopping altogether the natural progress of a nation towards wealth and prosperity, and still less of making it go backwards. If a nation could not prosper without the enjoyment of perfect liberty and perfect justice, there is not in the world a nation which could ever have prospered. In the political body, however, the wisdom of nature has fortunately made ample provision for remedying many of the bad effects of the folly and injustice of man; in the same manner as it has done in the natural body, for remedying those of his sloth and intemperance.

The capital error of this system, however, seems to lie in its representing the class of artificers, manufacturers, and merchants, as altogether barren and unproductive. The following observations may serve to show the impropriety of this representation.

First, this class, it is acknowledged, reproduces annually the value of its own annual consumption, and continues, at least, the existence of the stock or capital which maintains and employs it. But upon this account alone the denomination of barren or unproductive should seem to be very improperly applied to it. We should not call a marriage barren or unproductive, though it produced only a son and a daughter, to replace the father and mother, and though it did not increase the number of the human species, but only continued it as it was before. Farmers and country labourers, indeed, over and above the stock which maintains and employs them, reproduce annually a neat produce, a free rent to the landlord. As a marriage which affords three children is certainly more productive than one which affords only two; so the labour of farmers and country labourers is certainly more productive than that of merchants, artificers, and manufacturers. The superior produce of the one class, however, does not render the other barren or unproductive.

Secondly, it seems, upon this account, altogether improper to consider artificers, manufacturers, and merchants in the same light as menial servants. The labour of menial servants does not continue the existence of the fund which maintains and employs them. Their maintenance and employment is altogether at the expence of their masters, and the work which they perform is not of a nature to repay that expence. That work consists in services which perish generally in the very instant of their performance, and does not fix or realize itself in any vendible commodity which can replace the value of their wages and maintenance. The labour, on the contrary, of artificers, manufacturers and merchants, naturally does fix and realize itself in some such vendible commodity. It is upon this account that, in the chapter in which I treat of productive and unproductive labour, I have classed artificers, manufacturers, and merchants, among the productive labourers, and menial servants among the barren or unproductive.

Thirdly, it seems, upon every supposition, improper to say, that the labour of artificers, manufacturers, and merchants, does not increase the real revenue of the society. Though we should suppose, for example, as it seems to be supposed in this system, that the value of the daily, monthly, and yearly consumption of this class was exactly equal to that of its daily, monthly, and yearly production; yet it would not from thence follow that its labour added nothing to the real revenue, to the real value of the annual produce of the land and labour of the society. An artificer, for example, who, in the first six months after harvest, executes ten pounds' worth of work, though he should in the same time consume ten pounds' worth of corn and other necessaries, yet really adds the value of ten pounds to the annual produce of the land and labour of the society. While he has been consuming a half yearly revenue of ten pounds' worth of corn and other necessaries, he has produced an equal value of work capable of purchasing, either to himself or to some other person, an equal half yearly revenue. The value, therefore, of what has been consumed and produced during these six months is equal, not to ten, but to twenty pounds.

Fourthly, farmers and country labourers can no more augment, without parsimony, the real revenue, the annual produce of the land and labour of their society, than artificers, manufacturers, and merchants. The annual produce of the land and labour of any society can be augmented only in two ways; either, first, by some improvement in the productive powers of the useful labour actually maintained within it; or, secondly, by some increase in the quantity of that labour.

The improvement in the productive powers of useful labour depends, first, upon the improvement in the ability of the workman; and, secondly, upon that of the machinery with which he works. But the labour of artificers and manufacturers, as it is capable of being more subdivided, and the labour of each workman reduced to a greater simplicity of operation, than that of farmers and country labourers, so it is likewise capable of both these sorts of improvement in a much higher degree. In this respect, therefore, the class of cultivators can have no sort of advantage over that of artificers and manufacturers.

Fifthly and lastly, though the revenue of the inhabitants of every country was supposed to consist altogether, as this system seems to suppose, in the quantity of subsistence which their industry could procure to them; yet even upon this supposition, the revenue of a trading and manufacturing country must, other things being equal, always be much greater than that of one without trade or manufactures. By means of trade and manufactures, a greater quantity of subsistence can be annually imported into a particular country than what its own lands, in the actual state of their cultivation, could afford. The inhabitants of a town, though they frequently possess no lands of their own, yet draw to themselves by their industry such a quantity of the rude produce of the lands of other people as supplies them, not only with the materials of their work, but with the fund of their subsistence. What a town always is with regard to the country in its neighbourhood, one independent state or country may frequently be with regard to other independent states or countries. It is thus that Holland draws a great part of its subsistence from other countries: live cattle from Holstein and Jutland, and corn from almost all the different countries of Europe. A small quantity of manufactured produce purchases a great quantity of rude produce. A trading and manufacturing country, therefore, naturally purchases with a small part of its manufactured produce a great part of the rude produce of other countries; while, on the contrary, a country without trade and manufactures is generally obliged to purchase, at the expence of a great part of its rude produce, a very small part of the manufactured produce of other countries. The one exports what can subsist and accommodate but a very few, and imports the subsistence and accommodation of a great number. The other exports the accommodation and subsistence of a great number, and imports that of a very few only. The inhabitants of the one must always enjoy a much greater quantity of subsistence than what their own lands, in the actual state of their cultivation, could afford. The inhabitants of the other must always enjoy a much smaller quantity.

This system, however, with all its imperfections, is, perhaps, the nearest approximation to the truth that has yet been published upon the subject of political economy, and is upon that account well worth the consideration of every man who wishes to examine with attention the principles of that very important science. Though in representing the labour which is employed upon land as the only productive labour, the notions which it inculcates are perhaps too narrow and confined; yet in representing the wealth of nations as consisting, not in the unconsumable riches of money, but in the consumable goods annually reproduced by the labour of the society; and in representing perfect liberty as the only effectual expedient for rendering this annual reproduction the greatest possible, its doctrine seems to be in every respect as just as it is generous and liberal. Its followers are very numerous; and as men are fond of paradoxes, and of appearing to understand what surpasses the comprehension of ordinary people, the paradox which it maintains, concerning the unproductive nature of manufacturing labour, has not perhaps contributed a little to increase the number of its admirers. They have for some years past made a pretty considerable sect, distinguished in the French republic of letters by the name of, The Economists. Their works have certainly been of some service to their country; not only by bringing into general discussion, many subjects which had never been well examined before, but by influencing in some measure the public administration in favour of agriculture. It has been in consequence of their representations, accordingly, that the agriculture of France has been delivered from several of the oppressions which it before laboured under. The term during which such a lease can be granted, as will be valid against every future purchaser or proprietor of the land, has been prolonged from nine to twenty-seven years. The ancient provincial restraints upon the transportation of corn from one province of the kingdom to another, have been entirely taken away, and the liberty of exporting it to all foreign countries, has been established as the common law of the kingdom in all ordinary cases. This sect, in their works, which are very numerous, and which treat not only of what is properly called Political Economy, or of the nature and causes of the wealth of nations, but of every other branch of the system of civil government, all follow implicitly, and without any sensible variation, the doctrine of Mr. Quesnai. There is upon this account little variety in the greater part of their works. The most distinct and best connected account of this doctrine is to be found in a little book written by Mr. Mercier de la Riviere, sometime Intendant of Martinico, entitled, *The natural and essential Order of Political Societies*. The admiration of this whole sect for their master, who was himself a man of the greatest modesty and simplicity, is not inferior to that of any of the ancient philosophers for the founders of their respective systems. "There have been, since the world began," says a very diligent and respectable author, the Marquis de Mirabeau, "three great inventions which have principally given stability to political societies, independent of many other inventions which have enriched and adorned them. The first, is the invention of writing, which alone gives human nature the power of transmitting, without alteration, its laws, its contracts, its annals, and its discoveries. The second, is the invention of money, which binds together all the relations between civilized societies. The third, is the Economical Table, the result of the other two, which completes them both by perfecting their object; the great discovery of our age, but of which our posterity will reap the benefit."

As the political economy of the nations of modern Europe, has been more favourable to manufactures and foreign trade, the industry of the towns, than to agriculture, the industry of the country; so that of other nations has followed a different plan, and has been more favourable to agriculture than to manufactures and foreign trade.

The policy of China favours agriculture more than all other employments.

The policy of ancient Egypt too, and that of the Gentoo government of Indostan, seem to have favoured agriculture more than all other employments.

The sovereigns of China, of ancient Egypt, and of the different kingdoms into which Indostan has at different times been divided, have always derived the whole, or by far the most considerable part, of their revenue from some sort of land-tax or land-rent. This land-tax or land-rent, like the tithe in Europe, consisted in a certain proportion, a fifth, it is said, of the produce of the land, which was either delivered in kind, or paid in money, according to a certain valuation, and which therefore varied from year to year according to all the variations of the produce. It was natural therefore, that the sovereigns of those countries should be particularly attentive to the interests of agriculture, upon the prosperity or declension of which immediately depended the yearly increase or diminution of their own revenue.

The greatest and most important branch of the commerce of every nation, it has already been observed, is that which is carried on between the inhabitants of the town and those of the country. The inhabitants of the town draw from the country the rude produce which constitutes both the materials of their work and the fund of their subsistence; and they pay for this rude produce by sending back to the country a certain portion of it manufactured and prepared for immediate use. The trade which is carried on between those two different sets of people, consists ultimately in a certain quantity of rude produce exchanged for a certain quantity of manufactured produce. The dearer the latter, therefore, the cheaper the former; and whatever tends in any country to raise the price of manufactured produce, tends to lower that of the rude produce of the land, and thereby to discourage agriculture. The smaller the quantity of manufactured produce which any given quantity of rude produce, or, which comes to the same thing, which the price of any given quantity of rude produce is capable of purchasing, the smaller the exchangeable value of that given quantity of rude produce; the smaller the encouragement which either the landlord has to increase its quantity by improving, or the farmer by cultivating the land. Whatever, besides, tends to diminish in any country the number of artificers and manufacturers, tends to diminish the home market, the most important of all markets for the rude produce of the land, and thereby still further to discourage agriculture.

Those systems, therefore, which preferring agriculture to all other employments, in order to promote it, impose restraints upon manufactures and foreign trade, act contrary to the very end which they propose, and indirectly discourage that very species of industry which they mean to promote. They are so far, perhaps, more inconsistent than even the mercantile system. That system, by encouraging manufactures and foreign trade more than agriculture, turns a certain portion of the capital of the society from supporting a more advantageous, to support a less advantageous species of industry. But still it really and in the end encourages that species of industry which it means to promote. Those agricultural systems, on the contrary, really and in the end discourage their own favourite species of industry.

It is thus that every system which endeavours, either by extraordinary encouragements to draw towards a particular species of industry a greater share of the capital of the society than what would naturally go to it, or by extraordinary restraints to force from a particular species of industry some share of the capital which would otherwise be employed in it, is in reality subversive of the great purpose which it means to promote. It retards, instead of accelerating, the progress of the society towards real wealth and greatness, and diminishes, instead of increasing, the real value of the annual produce of its land and labour.

All systems either of preference or of restraint, therefore, being thus completely taken away, the obvious and simple system of natural liberty establishes itself of its own accord. Every man, as long as he does not violate the laws of justice, is left perfectly free to pursue his own interest his own way, and to bring both his industry and capital into competition with those of any other man or order of men. The sovereign is completely discharged from a duty in the attempting to perform which he must always be exposed to innumerable delusions, and for the proper performance of which no human wisdom or knowledge could ever be sufficient: the duty of superintending the industry of private people, and of directing it towards the employments most suitable to the interest of the society. According to the system of natural liberty, the sovereign has only three duties to attend to, three duties of great importance, indeed, but plain and intelligible to common understandings: first, the duty of protecting the society from the violence and invasion of other independent societies; secondly, the duty of protecting, as far as possible, every member of the society from the injustice or oppression of every other member of it, or the duty of establishing an exact administration of justice; and, thirdly, the duty of erecting and maintaining certain public works and certain public institutions, which it can never be for the interest of any individual or small number of individuals to erect and maintain, because the profit could never repay the expence to any individual or small number of individuals, though it may frequently do much more than repay it to a great society.

Book Five: Of the Revenue of the Sovereign or Commonwealth

I. Of the Expences of the Sovereign or Commonwealth

PART ONE: Of the Expence of Defence

THE first duty of the sovereign, that of protecting the society from the violence and invasion of other independent societies, can be performed only by means of a military force. But the expence both of preparing this military force in time of peace, and of employing it in time of war, is very different in the different states of society, in the different periods of improvement.

The number of those who can go to war, in proportion to the whole number of the people, is necessarily much smaller in a civilized, than in a rude state of society. In a civilized society, as the soldiers are maintained altogether by the labour of those who are not soldiers, the number of the former can never exceed what the latter can maintain, over and above maintaining, in a manner suitable to their respective stations, both themselves and the other officers of government, and law, whom they are obliged to maintain. In the little agrarian states of ancient Greece, a fourth or a fifth part of the whole body of the people considered themselves as soldiers, and would sometimes, it is said, take the field. Among the civilized nations of modern Europe, it is commonly computed, that not more than one hundredth part of the inhabitants of any country can be employed as soldiers, without ruin to the country which pays the expence of their service.

The art of war, as it is certainly the noblest of all arts, so in the progress of improvement it necessarily becomes one of the most complicated among them. The state of the mechanical, as well as of some other arts, with which it is necessarily connected, determines the degree of perfection to which it is capable of being carried at any particular time. But in order to carry it to this degree of perfection, it is necessary that it should become the sole or principal occupation of a particular class of citizens, and the division of labour is as necessary for the improvement of this, as of every other art.

In these circumstances, there seem to be but two methods, by which the state can make any tolerable provision for the public defence.

It may either, first, by means of a very rigorous police, and in spite of the whole bent of the interest, genius and inclinations of the people, enforce the practice of military exercises, and oblige either all the citizens of the military age, or a certain number of them, to join in some measure the trade of a soldier to whatever other trade or profession they may happen to carry on.

Or secondly, by maintaining and employing a certain number of citizens in the constant practice of military exercises, it may render the trade of a soldier a particular trade, separate and distinct from all others.

If the state has recourse to the first of those two expedients, its military force is said to consist in a militia; if to the second, it is said to consist in a standing army. The practice of military exercises is the sole or principal occupation of the soldiers of a standing army, and the maintenance or pay which the state affords them is the principal and ordinary fund of their subsistence. The practice of military exercises is only the occasional occupation of the soldiers of a militia, and they derive the principal and ordinary fund of their subsistence from some other occupation. In a militia, the character of the labourer, artificer, or tradesman, predominates over that of the soldier: in a standing army, that of the soldier predominates over every other character; and in this distinction seems to consist the essential difference between those two different species of military force.

The first duty of the sovereign, that of defending the society from the violence and injustice of other independent societies, grows gradually more and more expensive, as the society advances in civilization. The military force of the society, which originally cost the sovereign no expence either in time of peace or in time of war, must, in the progress of improvement, first be maintained by him in time of war, and afterwards even in time of peace.

In modern war the great expence of firearms gives an evident advantage to the nation which can best afford that expence; and consequently, to an opulent and civilized, over a poor and barbarous nation. In ancient times the opulent and civilized found it difficult to defend themselves against the poor and barbarous nations. In modern times the poor and barbarous find it difficult to defend themselves against the opulent and civilized. The invention of firearms, an invention which at first sight appears to be so pernicious, is certainly favourable both to the permanency and to the extension of civilization.

PART TWO: Of the Expence of Justice

The second duty of the sovereign, that of protecting, as far as possible, every member of the society from the injustice or oppression of every other member of it, or the duty of establishing an exact administration of justice requires two very different degrees of expence in the different periods of society.

Among nations of hunters, as there is scarce any property, or at least none that exceeds the value of two or three days' labour; so there is seldom any established magistrate or any regular administration of justice. Men who have no property can injure one another only in their persons or reputations. But when one man kills, wounds, beats, or defames another, though he to whom the injury is done suffers, he who does it receives no benefit. It is otherwise with the injuries to property. The benefit of the person who does the injury is often equal to the loss of him who suffers it. Envy, malice, or resentment, are the only passions which can prompt one man to injure another in his person or reputation. But the greater part of men are not very frequently under the influence of those passions; and the very worst men are so only occasionally. As their gratification too, how agreeable soever it may be to certain characters, is not attended with any real or permanent advantage, it is in the greater part of men commonly restrained by prudential considerations. Men may live together in society with some tolerable degree of security, though there is no civil magistrate to protect them from the injustice of those passions. But avarice and ambition in the rich, in the poor the hatred of labour and the love of present ease and enjoyment, are the passions which prompt to invade property, passions much more steady in their operation, and much more universal in their influence. Wherever there is great property, there is great inequality. For one very rich man, there must be at least five hundred poor, and the affluence of the few supposes the indigence of the many. The affluence of the rich excites the indignation of the poor, who are often both driven by want, and prompted by envy, to invade his possessions. It is only under the shelter of the civil magistrate that the owner of that valuable property, which is acquired by the labour of many years, or perhaps of many successive generations, can sleep a single night in security. The acquisition of valuable and extensive property, therefore, necessarily requires the establishment of civil government.

It is in the age of shepherds, in the second period of society, that the inequality of fortune first begins to take place, and introduces among men a degree of authority and subordination which could not possibly exist before. The inferior shepherds and herdsmen feel that the security of their own herds and flocks depends upon the security of those of the great shepherd or herdsman; that the maintenance of their lesser authority depends upon that of his greater authority, and that upon their subordination to him depends his power of keeping their inferiors in subordination to them. They constitute a sort of little nobility, who feel themselves interested to defend the property and to support the authority of their own little sovereign, in order that he may be able to defend their property and to support their authority. Civil government, so far as it is instituted for the security of property, is in reality instituted for the defence of the rich against the poor, or of those who have some property against those who have none at all.

The judicial authority of such a sovereign, however, far from being a cause of expence, was for a long time a source of revenue to him. The persons who applied to him for justice were always willing to pay for it, and a present never failed to accompany a petition.

The office of judge is in itself so very honourable, that men are willing to accept of it, though accompanied with very small emoluments. The inferior office of justice of peace, though attended with a good deal of trouble, and in most cases with no emoluments at all, is an object of ambition to the greater part of our country gentlemen. The salaries of all the different judges, high and low, together with the whole expence of the administration and execution of justice, even where it is not managed with very good economy, makes, in any civilized country, but a very inconsiderable part of the whole expence of government.

The whole expence of justice too might easily be defrayed by the fees of court; and, without exposing the administration of justice to any real hazard of corruption, the public revenue might thus be entirely discharged from a certain, though, perhaps, but a small incumbrance.

The separation of the judicial from the executive power seems originally to have arisen from the increasing business of the society, in consequence of its increasing improvement. The administration of justice became so laborious and so complicated a duty as to require the undivided attention of the persons to whom it was entrusted. The person entrusted with the executive power, not having leisure to attend to the decision of private causes himself, a deputy was appointed to decide them in his stead. In the progress of the Roman greatness, the consul was too much occupied with the political affairs of the state, to attend to the administration of justice. A prætor, therefore, was appointed to administer it in his stead. In the progress of the European monarchies which were founded upon the ruins of the Roman empire, the sovereigns and the great lords came universally to consider the administration of justice as an office, both too laborious and too ignoble for them to execute in their own persons. They universally, therefore, discharged themselves of it by appointing a deputy, bailiff, or judge.

When the judicial is united to th executive power, it is scarce possible that justice should not frequently be sacrificed to, what is vulgarly called, politics. The persons entrusted with the great interests of the state may, even without any corrupt views, sometimes imagine it necessary to sacrifice to those interests the rights of a private man. But upon the impartial administration of justice depends the liberty of every individual, the sense which he has of his own security. In order to make every individual feel himself perfectly secure in the possession of every right which belongs to him, it is not only necessary that the judicial should be separated from the executive power, but that it should be rendered as much as possible independent of that power. The judge should not be liable to be removed from his office according to the caprice of that power. The regular payment of his salary should not depend upon the good will, or even upon the good economy of that power.

PART THREE: Of the Expence of public Works and public Institutions

The third and last duty of the sovereign or commonwealth is that of erecting and maintaining those public institutions and those public works, which, though they may be in the highest degree advantageous to a great society, are, however, of such a nature, that the profit could never repay the expence to any individual or small number of individuals, and which it therefore cannot be expected that any individual or small number of individuals should erect or maintain. The performance of this duty requires too very different degrees of expence in the different periods of society.

After the public institutions and public works necessary for the defence of the society, and for the administration of justice, both of which have already been mentioned, the other works and institutions of this kind are chiefly those for facilitating the commerce of the society, and those for promoting the instruction of the people. The institutions for instruction are of two kinds; those for the education of the youth, and those for the instruction of people of all ages. The consideration of the manner in which the expence of those different sorts of public works and institutions may be most properly defrayed, will divide this third part of the present chapter into three different articles.

Article I

OF THE PUBLIC WORKS AND INSTITUTIONS FOR FACILITATING THE COMMERCE OF THE SOCIETY

AND, FIRST, OF THOSE WHICH ARE NECESSARY FOR FACILITATING COMMERCE IN GENERAL

That the erection and maintenance of the public works which facilitate the commerce of any country, such as good roads, bridges, navigable canals, harbours, &c. must require very different degrees of expence in the different periods of society, is evident without any proof. The expence of making and maintaining the public roads of any country must evidently increase with the annual produce of the land and labour of that country, or with the quantity and weight of the goods which it becomes necessary to fetch and carry upon those roads. The strength of a bridge must be suited to the number and weight of the carriages, which are likely to pass over it. The depth and the supply of water for a navigable canal must be proportioned to the number and tonnage of the lighters, which are likely to carry goods upon it; the extent of a harbour to the number of the shipping which are likely to take shelter in it.

It does not seem necessary that the expence of those public works should be defrayed from that public revenue, as it is commonly called, of which the collection and application are in most countries assigned to the executive power. The greater part of such public works may easily be so managed, as to afford a particular revenue sufficient for defraying their own expence, without bringing any burden upon the general revenue of the society.

A highway, a bridge, a navigable canal, for example, may in most cases be both made and maintained by a small toll upon the carriages which make use of them: a harbour, by a moderate port duty upon the tonnage of the shipping which load or unload in it. The coinage, another institution for facilitating commerce, in many countries, not only defrays its own expence, but affords a small revenue or seignorage to the sovereign. The post office, another institution for the same purpose, over and above defraying its own expence, affords in almost all countries a very considerable revenue to the sovereign.

OF THE PUBLIC WORKS AND INSTITUTIONS WHICH ARE NECESSARY FOR FACILI-
TATING PARTICULAR BRANCHES OF COMMERCE

The object of the public works and institutions above mentioned is to facilitate commerce in general. But in order to facilitate some particular branches of it, particular institutions are necessary, which again require a particular and extraordinary expence.

Some particular branches of commerce, which are carried on with barbarous and uncivilized nations, require extraordinary protection. An ordinary store or countinghouse could give little security to the goods of the merchants who trade to the western coast of Africa. To defend them from the barbarous natives, it is necessary that the place where they are deposited, should be, in some measure, fortified. The disorders in the government of Indostan have been supposed to render a like precaution necessary even among that mild and gentle people; and it was under pretence of securing their persons and property from violence, that both the English and French East India Companies were allowed to erect the first forts which they possessed in that country. Among other nations, whose vigorous government will suffer no strangers to possess any fortified place within their territory, it may be necessary to maintain some ambassador, minister, or consul, who may both decide, according to their own customs, the differences arising among his own countrymen; and, in their disputes with the natives, may, by means of his public character, interfere with more authority, and afford them a more powerful protection, than they could expect from any private man. The interests of commerce have frequently made it necessary to maintain ministers in foreign countries, where the purposes, either of war or alliance, would not have required any. The commerce of the Turkey Company first occasioned the establishment of an ordinary ambassador at Constantinople. The first English embassies to Russia arose altogether from commercial interests. The constant interference which those interests necessarily occasioned between the subjects of the different states of Europe, has probably introduced the custom of keeping, in all neighbouring countries, ambassadors or ministers constantly resident even in the time of peace. This custom, unknown to ancient times, seems not to be older than the end of the fifteenth or beginning of the sixteenth century; that is, than the time when commerce first began to extend itself to the greater part of the nations of Europe, and when they first began to attend to its interests.

The protection of trade in general has always been considered as essential to the defence of the commonwealth, and, upon that account, a necessary part of the duty of the executive power. The collection and application of the general duties of customs, therefore, have always been left to that power. But the protection of any particular branch of trade is a part of the general protection of trade; a part, therefore, of the duty of that power; and if nations always acted consistently, the particular duties levied for the purposes of such particular protection, should always have been left equally to its disposal. But in this respect, as well as in many others, nations have not always acted consistently; and in the greater part of the commercial states of Europe, particular companies of merchants have had the address to persuade the legislature to entrust to them the performance of this part of the duty of the sovereign, together with all the powers which are necessarily connected with it.

These companies, though they may, perhaps, have been useful for the first introduction of some branches of commerce, by making, at their own expence, an experiment which the state might not think it prudent to make, have in the long run proved, universally, either burdensome or useless, and have either mismanaged or confined the trade.

Article II

OF THE EXPENCE OF THE INSTITUTIONS FOR THE EDUCATION OF YOUTH

The institutions for the education of the youth may furnish a revenue sufficient for defraying their own expence. The fee or honorary which the scholar pays to the master naturally constitutes a revenue of this kind.

Even where the reward of the master does not arise altogether from this natural revenue, it still is not necessary that it should be derived from that general revenue of the society, of which the collection and application are, in most countries, assigned to the executive power. Through the greater part of Europe, accordingly, the endowment of schools and colleges makes either no charge upon that general revenue, or but a very small one. It every where arises chiefly from some local or provincial revenue, from the rent of some landed estate, or from the interest of some sum of money allotted and put under the management of trustees for this particular purpose, sometimes by the sovereign himself, and sometimes by some private donor.

The education of the common people requires, perhaps, in a civilized and commercial society, the attention of the public more than that of people of some rank and fortune. People of some rank and fortune are generally eighteen or nineteen years of age before they enter upon that particular business, profession, or trade, by which they propose to distinguish themselves in the world. They have before that full time to acquire, or at least to fit themselves for afterwards acquiring, every accomplishment which can recommend them to the public esteem, or render them worthy of it. Their parents or guardians are generally sufficiently anxious that they should be so accomplished, and are, in most cases, willing enough to lay out the expence which is necessary for that purpose. If they are not always properly educated, it is seldom from the want of expence laid out upon their education; but from the improper application of that expence.

It is otherwise with the common people. They have little time to spare for education. Their parents can scarce afford to maintain them even in infancy. As soon as they are able to work, they must apply to some trade by which they can earn their subsistence. That trade too is generally so simple and uniform as to give little exercise to the understanding; while, at the same time, their labour is both so constant and so severe, that it leaves them little leisure and less inclination to apply to, or even to think of anything else.

But though the common people cannot, in any civilized society, be so well instructed as people of some rank and fortune, the most essential parts of education, however, to read, write, and account, can be acquired at so early a period of life, that the greater part even of those who are to be bred to the lowest occupations, have time to acquire them before they can be employed in those occupations. For a very small expence the public can facilitate, can encourage, and can even impose upon almost the whole body of the people, the necessity of acquiring those most essential parts of education.

The public can facilitate this acquisition by establishing in every parish or district a little school, where children may be taught for a reward so moderate, that even a common labourer may afford it; the master being partly, but not wholly paid by the public; because, if he was wholly, or even principally paid by it, he would soon learn to neglect his business. In Scotland the establishment of such parish schools has taught almost the whole common people to read, and a very great proportion of them to write and account. In England the establishment of charity schools has had an effect of the same kind, though not so universally, because the establishment is not so universal. If in those little schools the books, by which the children are taught to read, were a little more instructive than they commonly are; and if, instead of a little smattering of Latin, which the children of the common people are sometimes taught there, and which can scarce ever be of any use to them; they were instructed in the elementary parts of geometry and mechanics, the literary education of this rank of people would perhaps be as complete as it can be. There is scarce a common trade which does not afford some opportunities of applying to it the principles of geometry and mechanics, and which would not therefore gradually exercise and improve the common people in those principles, the necessary introduction to the most sublime as well as to the most useful sciences.

The public can encourage the acquisition of those most essential parts of education by giving small premiums, and little badges of distinction, to the children of the common people who excel in them.

The public can impose upon almost the whole body of the people the necessity of acquiring those most essential parts of education, by obliging every man to undergo an examination or probation in them before he can obtain the freedom in any corporation, or be allowed to set up any trade either in a village or town corporate.

Article III

OF THE EXPENCE OF THE INSTITUTIONS FOR THE INSTRUCTION OF PEOPLE OF ALL AGES

The institutions for the instruction of people of all ages are chiefly those for religious instruction. This is a species of instruction of which the object is not so much to render the people good citizens in this world, as to prepare them for another and a better world in a life to come. The teachers of the doctrine which contains this instruction, in the same manner as other teachers, may either depend altogether for their subsistence upon the voluntary contributions of their hearers; or they may derive it from some other fund to which the law of their country may entitle them; such as a landed estate, a tythe or land tax, an established salary or stipend.

PART FOUR: *Of the Expence of supporting the Dignity of the Sovereign*

Over and above the expence necessary for enabling the sovereign to perform his several duties, a certain expence is requisite for the support of his dignity. This expence varies both with the different periods of improvement, and with the different forms of government.

In an opulent and improved society, where all the different orders of people are growing every day more expensive in their houses, in their furniture, in their tables, in their dress, and in their equipage; it cannot well be expected that the sovereign should alone hold out against the fashion. He naturally, therefore, or rather necessarily becomes more expensive in all those different articles too. His dignity even seems to require that he should become so.

As in point of dignity, a monarch is more raised above his subjects than the chief magistrate of any republic is ever supposed to be above his fellow citizens; so a greater expence is necessary for supporting that higher dignity. We naturally expect more splendor in the court of a king, than in the mansion house of a doge or burgomaster.

II. OF THE SOURCES OF THE GENERAL OR PUBLIC REVENUE OF THE SOCIETY

THE REVENUE which must defray, not only the expence of defending the society and of supporting the dignity of the chief magistrate, but all the other necessary expences of government, for which the constitution of the state has not provided any particular revenue, may be drawn, either, first, from some fund which peculiarly belongs to the sovereign or commonwealth, and which is independent of the revenue of the people; or, secondly, from the revenue of the people.

I. The subjects of every state ought to contribute towards the support of the government, as nearly as possible, in proportion to their respective abilities; that is, in proportion to the revenue which they respectively enjoy under the protection of the state. The expence of government to the individuals of a great nation, is like the expence of management to the joint tenants of a great estate, who are all obliged to contribute in proportion to their respective interests in the estate. In the observation or neglect of this maxim consists, what is called the equality or inequality of taxation.

II. The tax which each individual is bound to pay ought to be certain, and not arbitrary. The time of payment, the manner of payment, the quantity to be paid, ought all to be clear and plain to the contributor, and to every other person. Where it is otherwise, every person subject to the tax is put more or less in the power of the taxgatherer, who can either aggravate the tax upon any obnoxious contributor, or extort, by the terror of such aggravation, some present or perquisite to himself.

III. Every tax ought to be levied at the time, or in the manner, in which it is most likely to be convenient for the contributor to pay it. A tax upon the rent of land or of houses, payable at the same term at which such rents are usually paid, is levied at the time when it is most likely to be convenient for the contributor to pay; or, when he is most likely to have wherewithal to pay. Taxes upon such consumable goods as are articles of luxury, are all finally paid by the consumer, and generally in a manner that is very convenient for him. He pays them by little and little, as he has occasion to buy the goods. As he is at liberty too, either to buy, or not to buy, as he pleases, it must be his own fault if he ever suffers any considerable inconveniency from such taxes.

IV. Every tax ought to be so contrived as both to take out and to keep out of the pockets of the people as little as possible, over and above what it brings into the public treasury of the state. A tax may either take out or keep out of the pockets of the people a great deal more than it brings into the public treasury, in the four following ways. First, the levying of it may require a great number of officers, whose salaries may eat up the greater part of the produce of the tax, and whose perquisites may impose another additional tax upon the people. Secondly, it may obstruct the industry of the people, and discourage them from applying to certain branches of business which might give maintenance and employment to great multitudes. While it obliges the people to pay, it may thus diminish, or perhaps destroy, some of the funds which might enable them more easily to do so. Thirdly, by the forfeitures and other penalties which those unfortunate individuals incur who attempt unsuccessfully to evade the tax, it may frequently ruin them, and thereby put an end to the benefit which the community might have received from the employment of their capitals. An injudicious tax offers a great temptation to smuggling. But the penalties of smuggling must rise in proportion to the temptation. The law, contrary to all the ordinary principles of justice, first creates the temptation, and then punishes those who yield to it; and it commonly enhances the punishment too in proportion to the very circumstance which ought certainly to alleviate it, the temptation to commit the crime. Fourthly, by subjecting the people to the frequent visits and the odious examination of the taxgatherers, it may expose them to much unnecessary trouble, vexation, and oppression; and though vexation is not, strictly speaking, expence, it is certainly equivalent to the expence at which every man would be willing to redeem himself from it. It is in some one or other of these four different ways that taxes are frequently so much more burdensome to the people than they are beneficial to the sovereign.

AN ESSAY ON THE
PRINCIPLE OF POPULATION

by

THOMAS ROBERT MALTHUS

CONTENTS

An Essay on the Principle of Population

Part One: Of the Checks to Population in the Less Civilized Parts of the World and in Past Times

    I. Statement of the Subject

    II. Of the General Checks to Population, and the Mode of Their Operation

    III. General Deductions from the Preceding View of Society

Part Two: Of Our Future Prospects Respecting the Removal or Mitigation of the Evils Arising from the Principle of Population

    I. Of Moral Restraint, and Our Obligation to Practise This Virtue

    II. Of the Effects Which Would Result to Society from the Prevalence of Moral Restraint

    III. Of the Only Effectual Mode of Improving the Condition of the Poor

    IV. Objections to This Mode Considered

    V. Of the Consequences of Pursuing the Opposite Mode

    VI. Effects of the Knowledge of the Principal Cause of Poverty on Civil Liberty

    VII. Continuation of the Same Subject

    VIII. Plan of the Gradual Abolition of the Poor-Laws Proposed

    IX. Of the Modes of Correcting the Prevailing Opinions on Population

    X. Of the Direction of Our Charity

    XI. Of Our Rational Expectations Respecting the Future Improvement of Society

THOMAS ROBERT MALTHUS

1766–1834

THOMAS ROBERT MALTHUS, author of *An Essay on the Principle of Population,* was the son of Daniel Malthus, a country gentleman living near Guildford, Surrey, England. He was born in 1766 and was instructed by his father as well as in private schools. At the age of nineteen he went to Cambridge University, where he distinguished himself as a scholar and took holy orders. For several months he held a curacy at Albury, Surrey. His chief interest, however, was not in the ministry but in social problems.

Daniel Malthus was a friend of David Hume, Scottish historian and philosopher, and of Jean-Jacques Rousseau, world-famous French writer and theorist. The times were stormy, and the spirit of revolution was in the air. The Marquis de Condorcet was propounding in France extravagantly optimistic theories regarding human perfectibility, and William Godwin in England was writing a book, *An Enquiry Concerning Political Justice,* which was soon not only to startle the world by reason of its anarchistic implications but was also to stimulate the younger Malthus to express his own views.

At first in his family circle and in conversation with his father and friends, young Malthus discussed the arguments used by Godwin and Condorcet. He could not doubt their talent as writers. What gave him pause, he said, was their seeming unwillingness to face the difficulties that made the realization of their ideals impossible. These difficulties, according to Malthus, were based on an inexorable law of nature—namely, that population tends to outstrip the means of subsistence.

Daniel Malthus was so impressed by his son's reasoning powers that he prevailed upon him to publish his views. The first *Essay on the Principle of Population* appeared anonymously in 1798.

The root idea underlying the *Essay* is clearly stated at its outset. "I think," says Malthus, "I may fairly make two postulata. First, that food is necessary to the existence of man. Secondly, that the passion between the sexes is necessary, and will remain nearly in its present state."

Implicit in Malthus's view are belief in the beneficent rule of God, a new conception of "vice" and "misery" as agents which tend to reduce population, and a plea for the abolition of Poor Laws, which, in his opinion, undermine a sense of responsibility in the needy and encourage overpopulation. An unforgettable turn is given to his arguments by his statement that "population, when unchecked, increases in a geometrical ratio," while "subsistence only increases in an arithmetical ratio."

Publication of the *Essay* led to an animated controversy. Prime Minister William Pitt and Archdeacon William Paley, England's famous theologian, both admitted that they were favorably impressed by Malthus's arguments, but other publicists attacked his position. He now found himself the target of indignant critics who not only questioned the accuracy of his mathematics, but who also accused him of "defending" wars, famines, and plagues as agents in depopulation and of denying to the poor even the solace of charity.

Stung by these criticisms, Malthus proceeded to strengthen his case. He gathered material bearing on "general checks to population." He read Greek and Roman history and added to his store of information regarding birth rates in Asiatic races. In 1799 he traveled on the continent of Europe, collecting facts and figures in relation to what was becoming his mental obsession—the problem of population.

In 1803 Malthus published a second edition of his *Essay,* embodying in it about four times as much matter as that contained in the original version. He spoke now of "moral restraint" as a major factor in bringing about a reduction of population, and by moral restraint he meant "a restraint from marriage from prudential motives, with a conduct strictly moral during the period of this restraint." The new edition was really an entirely new work, and Malthus acknowledged its authorship. Four more editions, substantially the same as the second edition, were to appear before he died in 1834. The present digest is based on the eighth edition.

At the age of thirty-eight Malthus married his cousin, Harriet Eckersall. This late marriage resulted in three children. In 1805, the year following his marriage, he became professor of history and political economy at Haileybury College, an institution established by the East India Company for the purpose of training young men who were to enter its service. With Grote, Ricardo, James Mill, and Tooke he helped to found the Political Economy Club in London in 1821.

Apart from the *Essay on the Principle of Population*, Malthus wrote voluminously on economic topics. Among his works are *Observations on the Effects of the Corn Laws* (1814), *An Inquiry into the Nature and Progress of Rent* (1815), *Principles of Political Economy* (1820), and *The Measure of Value Stated and Illustrated* (1823).

Charles Darwin made public acknowledgment of his intellectual debt to Malthus. "In October 1838," he writes in his autobiography, "that is, fifteen months after I had begun my systematic inquiry, I happened to read for amusement Malthus on *Population*, and being well prepared to appreciate the struggle for existence which everywhere goes on, from long-continued observation of the habits of animals and plants, it at once struck me that under these circumstances favourable variations would tend to be preserved and unfavourable ones to be destroyed." Alfred Russel Wallace, co-discoverer of the theory of evolution, also acknowledged his indebtedness to Malthus.

AN ESSAY ON THE PRINCIPLE
OF POPULATION

Part One: Of the Checks to Population in the Less Civilised Parts of the World and in Past Times

I. STATEMENT OF THE SUBJECT. RATIOS OF THE INCREASE OF POPULATION AND FOOD

IN AN INQUIRY concerning the improvement of society, the mode of conducting the subject which naturally presents itself, is—

1. To investigate the causes that have hitherto impeded the progress of mankind towards happiness; and,

2. To examine the probability of the total or partial removal of these causes in future.

To enter fully into this question, and to enumerate all the causes that have hitherto influenced human improvement, would be much beyond the power of an individual. The principal object of the present essay is to examine the effects of one great cause intimately united with the very nature of man; which, though it has been constantly and powerfully operating since the commencement of society, has been little noticed by the writers who have treated this subject. The facts which establish the existence of this cause have, indeed, been repeatedly stated and acknowledged; but its natural and necessary effects have been almost totally overlooked; though probably among these effects may be reckoned a very considerable portion of that vice and misery, and of that unequal distribution of the bounties of nature, which it has been the unceasing object of the enlightened philanthropist in all ages to correct.

The cause to which I allude, is the constant tendency in all animated life to increase beyond the nourishment prepared for it.

It is observed by Dr. [Benjamin] Franklin, that there is no bound to the prolific nature of plants or animals but what is made by their crowding and interfering with each other's means of subsistence. Were the face of the earth, he says, vacant of other plants, it might be gradually sowed and overspread with one kind only, as, for instance, with fennel: and were it empty of other inhabitants, it might in a few ages be replenished from one nation only, as, for instance, with Englishmen.

This is incontrovertibly true. Throughout the animal and vegetable kingdoms Nature has scattered the seeds of life abroad with the most profuse and liberal hand; but has been comparatively sparing in the room and the nourishment necessary to rear them. The germs of existence contained in this earth, if they could freely develop themselves, would fill millions of worlds in the course of a few thousand years. Necessity, that imperious, all-pervading law of nature, restrains them within the prescribed bounds. The race of plants and the race of animals shrink under this great restrictive law; and man cannot by any efforts of reason escape from it.

In plants and irrational animals, the view of the subject is simple. They are all impelled by a powerful instinct to the increase of their species, and this instinct is interrupted by no doubts about providing for their offspring. Wherever, therefore, there is liberty, the power of increase is exerted, and the superabundant effects are repressed afterwards by want of room and nourishment.

The effects of this check on man are more complicated. Impelled to the increase of his species by an equally powerful instinct, reason interrupts his career, and asks him whether he may not bring beings into the world for whom he cannot provide the means of support. If he attend to this natural suggestion, the restriction too frequently produces vice. If he hear it not, the human race will be constantly endeavouring to increase beyond the means of subsistence. But as, by that law of our nature which makes food necessary to the life of man, population can never actually increase beyond the lowest nourishment capable of supporting it, a strong check on population, from the difficulty of acquiring food, must be constantly in operation. This difficulty must fall somewhere, and must necessarily be severely felt in some or other of the various forms of misery, or the fear of misery, by a large portion of mankind.

That population has this constant tendency to increase beyond the means of subsistence, and that it is kept to its necessary level by these causes, will sufficiently appear from a review of the different states of society in which man has existed. But, before we proceed to this review, the subject will perhaps be seen in a clearer light, if we endeavour to ascertain what would be the natural increase of population, if left to exert itself with perfect freedom; and what might be expected to be the rate of increase in the productions of the earth, under the most favourable circumstances of human industry.

It will be allowed that no country has hitherto been known, where the manners were so pure and simple, and the means of subsistence so abundant, that no check whatever has existed to early marriages from the difficulty of providing for a family, and that no waste of the human species has been occasioned by vicious customs, by towns, by unhealthy occupations, or too severe labour. Consequently in no state that we have yet known, has the power of population been left to exert itself with perfect freedom.

Whether the law of marriage be instituted or not, the dictate of nature and virtue seems to be an early attachment to one woman; and where there were no impediments of any kind in the way of a union to which such an attachment would lead, and no causes of depopulation afterwards, the increase of the human species would be evidently much greater than any increase which has been hitherto known.

In the northern states of America, where the means of subsistence have been more ample, the manners of the people more pure, and the checks to early marriages fewer, than in any of the modern states of Europe, the population has been found to double itself, for above a century and a half successively, in less than twenty-five years. Yet, even during these periods, in some of the towns, the deaths exceeded the births, a circumstance which clearly proves that in those parts of the country which supplied this deficiency, the increase must have been much more rapid than the general average.

In the back settlements, where the sole employment is agriculture, and vicious customs and unwholesome occupations are little known, the population has been found to double itself in fifteen years. Even this extraordinary rate of increase is probably short of the utmost power of population. Very severe labour is requisite to clear a fresh country; such situations are not in general considered as particularly healthy; and the inhabitants, probably, are occasionally subject to the incursions of the Indians, which may destroy some lives, or at any rate diminish the fruits of industry.

According to a table of Euler, calculated on a mortality of 1 in 36, if the births be to the deaths in the proportion of 3 to 1, the period of doubling will be only twelve years and four-fifths. And this proportion is not only a possible supposition, but has actually occurred for short periods in more countries than one.

Sir William Petty supposes a doubling possible in so short a time as ten years.

But, to be perfectly sure that we are far within the truth, we will take the slowest of these rates of increase, a rate in which all concurring testimonies agree, and which has been repeatedly ascertained to be from procreation only.

It may safely be pronounced, therefore, that population, when unchecked, goes on doubling itself every twenty-five years, or increases in a geometrical ratio.

The rate according to which the productions of the earth may be supposed to increase, will not be so easy to determine. Of this, however, we may be perfectly certain, that the ratio of their increase in a limited territory must be of a totally different nature from the ratio of the increase of population. A thousand millions are just as easily doubled every twenty-five years by the power of population as a thousand. But the food to support the increase from the greater number will by no means be obtained with the same facility. Man is necessarily confined in room. When acre has been added to acre till all the fertile land is occupied, the yearly increase of food must depend upon the melioration of the land already in possession. This is a fund, which, from the nature of all soils, instead of increasing, must be gradually diminishing. But population, could it be supplied with food, would go on with unexhausted vigour; and the increase of one period would furnish the power of a greater increase the next, and this without any limit.

From the accounts we have of China and Japan, it may be fairly doubted, whether the best directed efforts of human industry could double the produce of these countries even once in any number of years. There are many parts of the globe, indeed, hitherto uncultivated and almost unoccupied; but the right of exterminating, or driving into a corner where they must starve, even the inhabitants of these thinly peopled regions, will be questioned in a moral view. The process of improving their minds and directing their industry would necessarily be slow; and during this time, as population would regularly keep pace with the increasing produce, it would rarely happen that a great degree of knowledge and industry would have to operate at once upon rich unappropriated soil. Even where this might take place, as it does sometimes in new colonies, a geometrical ratio increases with such extraordinary rapidity, that the advantage could not last long. If the United States of America continue increasing, which they certainly will do, though not with the same rapidity as formerly, the Indians will be driven farther and farther back into the country, till the whole race is ultimately exterminated, and the territory is incapable of further extension.

These observations are, in a degree, applicable to all the parts of the earth where the soil is imperfectly cultivated. To exterminate the inhabitants of the greatest part of Asia and Africa, is a thought that could not be admitted for a moment. To civilise and direct the industry of the various tribes of Tartars and Negroes, would certainly be a work of considerable time, and of variable and uncertain success.

Europe is by no means so fully peopled as it might be. In Europe there is the fairest chance that human industry may receive its best direction. The science of agriculture has been much studied in England and Scotland; and there is still a great portion of uncultivated land in these countries. Let us consider at what rate the produce of this island (Great Britain) might be supposed to increase under circumstances the most favourable to improvement.

If it be allowed that by the best possible policy, and great encouragements to agriculture, the average produce of the island could be doubled in the first twenty-five years, it will be allowing, probably, a greater increase than could with reason be expected.

In the next twenty-five years, it is impossible to suppose that the produce could be quadrupled. It would be contrary to all our knowledge of the properties of land. The improvement of the barren parts would be a work of time and labour; and it must be evident to those who have the slightest acquaintance with agricultural subjects, that in proportion as cultivation extended, the additions that could yearly be made to the former average produce must be gradually and regularly diminishing. That we may be the better able to compare the increase of population and food, let us make a supposition, which, without pretending to accuracy, is clearly more favourable to the power of production in the earth than any experience we have had of its qualities will warrant.

Let us suppose that the yearly additions which might be made to the former average produce, instead of decreasing, which they certainly would do, were to remain the same; and that the produce of this island might be increased every twenty-five years, by a quantity equal to what it at present produces. The most enthusiastic speculator cannot suppose a greater increase than this. In a few centuries it would make every acre of land in the island like a garden.

If this supposition be applied to the whole earth, and if it be allowed that the subsistence for man which the earth affords might be increased every twenty-five years by a quantity equal to what it at present produces, this will be supposing a rate of increase much greater than we can imagine that any possible exertions of mankind could make it.

It may be fairly pronounced, therefore, that, considering the present average state of the earth, the means of subsistence, under circumstances the most favourable to human industry, could not possibly be made to increase faster than in an arithmetical ratio.

The necessary effects of these two different rates of increase, when brought together, will be very striking. Let us call the population of this island eleven millions; and suppose the present produce equal to the easy support of such a number. In the first twenty-five years the population would be twenty-two millions, and the food being also doubled, the means of subsistence would be equal to this increase. In the next twenty-five years, the population would be forty-four millions, and the means of subsistence only equal to the support of thirty-three millions. In the next period the population would be eighty-eight millions, and the means of subsistence just equal to the support of half that number. And, at the conclusion of the first century, the population would be a hundred and seventy-six millions, and the means of subsistence only equal to the support of fifty-five millions, leaving a population of a hundred and twenty-one millions totally unprovided for.

Taking the whole earth, instead of this island, emigration would of course be excluded; and, supposing the present population equal to a thousand millions, the human species would increase as the numbers, 1, 2, 4, 8, 16, 32, 64, 128, 256; and subsistence as 1, 2, 3, 4, 5, 6, 7, 8, 9. In two centuries the population would be to the means of subsistence as 256 to 9; in three centuries as 4096 to 13, and in two thousand years the difference would be almost incalculable.

In this supposition no limits whatever are placed to the produce of the earth. It may increase for ever, and be greater than any assignable quantity; yet still the power of population being in every period so much superior, the increase of the human species can only be kept down to the level of the means of subsistence by the constant operation of the strong law of necessity, acting as a check upon the greater power.

II. Of the General Checks to Population, and the Mode of Their Operation

The ultimate check to population appears then to be a want of food, arising necessarily from the different ratios according to which population and food increase. But this ultimate check is never the immediate check, except in cases of actual famine.

The immediate check may be stated to consist in all those customs, and all those diseases, which seem to be generated by a scarcity of the means of subsistence; and all those causes, independent of this scarcity, whether of a moral or physical nature, which tend prematurely to weaken and destroy the human frame.

These checks to population, which are constantly operating with more or less force in every society, and keep down the number to the level of the means of subsistence, may be classed under two general heads—the preventive and the positive checks.

The preventive check, as far as it is voluntary, is peculiar to man, and arises from that distinctive superiority in his reasoning faculties which enables him to calculate distant consequences. The checks to the indefinite increase of plants and irrational animals are all either positive or, if preventive, involuntary. But man cannot look around him, and see the distress which frequently presses upon those who have large families; he cannot contemplate his present possessions or earnings, which he now nearly consumes himself, and calculate the amount of each share, when with very little addition they must be divided, perhaps, among seven or eight, without feeling a doubt whether, if he follow the bent of his inclinations, he may be able to support the offspring which he will probably bring into the world. In a state of equality, if such can exist, this would be the simple question. In the present state of society other considerations occur. Will he not lower his rank in life, and be obliged to give up in great measure his former habits? Does any mode of employment present itself by which he may reasonably hope to maintain a family? Will he not at any rate subject himself to greater difficulties, and more severe labour, than in his single state? Will he not be unable to transmit to his children the same advantages of education and improvement that he had himself possessed? Does he even feel secure that, should he have a large family, his utmost exertions can save them from rags and squalid poverty, and their consequent degradation in the community? And may he not be reduced to the grating necessity of forfeiting his independence, and of being obliged to the sparing hand of charity for support?

These considerations are calculated to prevent, and certainly do prevent, a great number of persons in all civilised nations from pursuing the dictate of nature in an early attachment to one woman.

If this restraint do not produce vice, it is undoubtedly the least evil that can arise from the principle of population. Considered as a restraint on a strong natural inclination, it must be allowed to produce a certain degree of temporary unhappiness; but evidently slight, compared with the evils which result from any of the other checks to population; and merely of the same nature as many other sacrifices of temporary to permanent gratification, which it is the business of a moral agent continually to make.

When this restraint produces vice, the evils which follow are but too conspicuous. A promiscuous intercourse to such a degree as to prevent the birth of children, seems to lower, in the most marked manner, the dignity of human nature. It cannot be without its effect on men, and nothing can be more obvious than its tendency to degrade the female character, and to destroy all its most amiable and distinguishing characteristics. Add to which, that among those unfortunate females with which all great towns abound, more real distress and aggravated misery are, perhaps, to be found, than in any other department of human life.

When a general corruption of morals, with regard to the sex, pervades all the classes of society, its effects must necessarily be to poison the springs of domestic happiness, to weaken conjugal and parental affection, and to lessen the united exertions and ardour of parents in the care and education of their children;—effects which cannot take place without a decided diminution of the general happiness and virtue of society; particularly as the necessity of art in the accomplishment and conduct of intrigues, and in the concealment of their consequences, necessarily leads to many other vices.

The positive checks to population are extremely various, and include every cause, whether arising from vice or misery, which in any degree contribute to shorten the natural duration of human life. Under this head, therefore, may be enumerated all unwholesome occupations, severe labour and exposure to the seasons, extreme poverty, bad nursing of children, large towns, excesses of all kinds, the whole train of common diseases and epidemics, wars, plague, and famine.

On examining these obstacles to the increase of population which are classed under the heads of preventive and positive checks, it will appear that they are all resolvable into moral restraint, vice, and misery.

Of the preventive checks, the restraint from marriage which is not followed by irregular gratifications may properly be termed moral restraint.

Promiscuous intercourse, unnatural passions, violations of the marriage bed, and improper arts to conceal the consequences of irregular connections, are preventive checks that clearly come under the head of vice.

Of the positive checks, those which appear to arise unavoidably from the laws of nature, may be called exclusively misery; and those which we obviously bring upon ourselves, such as wars, excesses, and many others which it would be in our power to avoid, are of a mixed nature. They are brought upon us by vice, and their consequences are misery.

The sum of all these preventive and positive checks, taken together, forms the immediate check to population; and it is evident that, in every country where the whole of the procreative power cannot be called into action, the preventive and the positive checks must vary inversely as each other; that is, in countries either naturally unhealthy, or subject to a great mortality, from whatever cause it may arise, the preventive check will prevail very little. In those countries, on the contrary, which are naturally healthy, and where the preventive check is found to prevail with considerable force, the positive check will prevail very little, or the mortality be very small.

In every country some of these checks are, with more or less force, in constant operation; yet, notwithstanding their general prevalence, there are few states in which there is not a constant effort in the population to increase beyond the means of subsistence. This constant effort as constantly tends to subject the lower classes of society to distress, and to prevent any great permanent melioration of their condition.

These effects, in the present state of society, seem to be produced in the following manner. We will suppose the means of subsistence in any country just equal to the easy support of its inhabitants. The constant effort towards population, which is found to act even in the most vicious societies, increases the number of people before the means of subsistence are increased. The food, therefore, which before supported eleven millions, must now be divided among eleven millions and a half. The poor consequently must live much worse, and many of them be reduced to severe distress. The number of labourers also being above the proportion of work in the market, the price of labour must tend to fall, while the price of provisions would at the same time tend to rise. The labourer therefore must do more work to earn the same as he did before. During this season of distress, the discouragements to marriage and the difficulty of rearing a family are so great, that the progress of population is retarded. In the meantime, the cheapness of labour, the plenty of labourers, and the necessity of an increased industry among them, encourage cultivators to employ more labour upon their land, to turn up fresh soil, and to manure and improve more completely what is already in tillage, till ultimately the means of subsistence may become in the same proportion to the population as at the period from which we set out. The situation of the labourer being then again tolerably comfortable, the restraints to population are in some degree loosened; and, after a short period, the same retrograde and progressive movements with respect to happiness are repeated.

This sort of oscillation will not probably be obvious to common view; and it may be difficult even for the most attentive observer to calculate its periods. Yet that, in the generality of old states, some alternation of this kind does exist, though in a much less marked, and in a much more irregular manner, than I have described it, no reflecting man, who considers the subject deeply, can well doubt.

One principal reason why this oscillation has been less remarked, and less decidedly confirmed by experience than might naturally be expected, is, that the histories of mankind which we possess are, in general, histories only of the higher classes. We have not many accounts that can be depended upon, of the manners and customs of that part of mankind where these retrograde and progressive movements chiefly take place. A satisfactory history of this kind, of one people and of one period, would require the constant and minute attention of many observing minds in local and general remarks on the state of the lower classes of society, and the causes that influenced it; and, to draw accurate inferences upon this subject, a succession of such historians for some centuries would be necessary. This branch of statistical knowledge has, of late years, been attended to in some countries, and we may promise ourselves a clearer insight into the internal structure of human society from the progress of these inquiries. But the science may be said yet to be in its infancy, and many of the objects on which it would be desirable to have information, have been either omitted or not stated with sufficient accuracy. Among these, perhaps, may be reckoned the proportion of the number of adults to the number of marriages; the extent to which vicious customs have prevailed in consequence of the restraints upon matrimony; the comparative mortality among the children of the most distressed part of the community, and of those who live rather more at their ease; the variations in the real price of labour; the observable differences in the state of the lower classes of society, with respect to ease and happiness, at different times during a certain period; and very accurate registers of births, deaths, and marriages, which are of the utmost importance in this subject.

A faithful history, including such particulars, would tend greatly to elucidate the manner in which the constant check upon population acts; and would probably prove the existence of the retrograde and progressive movements that have been mentioned; though the times of their vibration must necessarily be rendered irregular from the operation of many interrupting causes; such as, the introduction or failure of certain manufactures; a greater or less prevalent spirit of agricultural enterprise; years of plenty, or years of scarcity; wars, sickly seasons, poor-laws, emigrations and other causes of a similar nature.

A circumstance which has, perhaps, more than any other, contributed to conceal this oscillation from common view, is the difference between the nominal and real price of labour. It very rarely happens that the nominal price of labour universally falls; but we well know that it frequently remains the same, while the nominal price of provisions has been gradually rising. This, indeed, will generally be the case, if the increase of manufactures and commerce be sufficient to employ the new labourers that are thrown into the market, and to prevent the increased supply from lowering the money price. But an increased number of labourers receiving the same money wages will necessarily, by their competition, increase the money price of corn. This is, in fact, a real fall in the price of labour; and, during this period, the condition of the lower classes of the community must be gradually growing worse. But the farmers and capitalists are growing rich from the real cheapness of labour. Their increasing capitals enable them to employ a greater number of men; and, as the population had probably suffered some check from the greater difficulty of supporting a family, the demand for labour, after a certain period, would be great in proportion to the supply, and its price would of course rise, if left to find its natural level; and thus the wages of labour, and consequently the condition of the lower classes of society, might have progressive and retrograde movements, though the price of labour might never nominally fall.

In savage life, where there is no regular price of labour, it is little to be doubted that similar oscillations take place. When population has increased nearly to the utmost limits of the food, all the preventive and the positive checks will naturally operate with increased force. Vicious habits with respect to the sex will be more general, the exposing of children more frequent, and both the probability and fatality of wars and epidemics will be considerably greater; and these causes will probably continue their operation till the population is sunk below the level of the food; and then the return to comparative plenty will again produce an increase, and, after a certain period, its further progress will again be checked by the same causes.

But without attempting to establish these progressive and retrograde movements in different countries, which would evidently require more minute histories than we possess, and which the progress of civilisation naturally tends to counteract, the following propositions are intended to be proved:—

1. Population is necessarily limited by the means of subsistence.

2. Population invariably increases where the means of subsistence increase, unless prevented by some very powerful and obvious checks.

3. These checks, and the checks which repress the superior power of population, and keep its effects on a level with the means of subsistence, are all resolvable into moral restraint, vice, and misery.

III. General Deductions from the Preceding View of Society

That the checks which have been mentioned are the immediate causes of the slow increase of population, and that these checks result principally from an insufficiency of subsistence, will be evident from the comparatively rapid increase which has invariably taken place, whenever, by some sudden enlargement in the means of subsistence, these checks have in any considerable degree been removed.

It has been universally remarked that all new colonies settled in healthy countries, where room and food were abundant, have constantly made a rapid progress in population. Many of the colonies from ancient Greece, in the course of one or two centuries, appear to have rivalled, and even surpassed, their mother cities. Syracuse and Agrigentum in Sicily, Tarentum and Locri in Italy, Ephesus and Miletus in Lesser Asia, were by all accounts at least equal to any of the cities of ancient Greece. All these colonies had established themselves in countries inhabited by savage and barbarous nations, which easily gave place to the new settlers, who had of course plenty of good land. It is calculated that the Israelites, though they increased very slowly while they were wandering in the land of Canaan, on settling in a fertile district of Egypt, doubled their numbers every fifteen years during the whole period of their stay. But not to dwell on remote instances, the European settlements in America bear ample testimony to the truth of a remark, that has never I believe been doubted. Plenty of rich land to be had for little or nothing is so powerful a cause of population, as generally to overcome all obstacles.

No settlements could easily have been worse managed than those of Spain, in Mexico, Peru, and Quito. The tyranny, superstition, and vices of the mother country were introduced in ample quantities among her children. Exorbitant taxes were exacted by the crown, the most arbitrary restrictions were imposed on their trade, and the governors were not behind hand in rapacity and extortion for themselves as well as their masters. Yet under all these difficulties the colonies made a quick progress in population. The city of Quito, which was but a hamlet of Indians, is represented by Ulloa as containing fifty or sixty thousand inhabitants above fifty years ago. Lima, which was founded since the conquest, is mentioned by the same author as equally or more populous before the fatal earthquake in 1746. Mexico is said to contain a hundred thousand inhabitants, which, notwithstanding the exaggerations of the Spanish writers, is supposed to be five times greater than what it contained in the time of Montezuma.

In the Portuguese colony of Brazil, governed with almost equal tyranny, there were supposed to be above thirty years ago six hundred thousand inhabitants of European extraction.

The Dutch and French colonies, though under the government of exclusive companies of merchants, still persisted in thriving under every disadvantage.

But the English North American colonies, now the powerful people of the United States of America, far outstripped all the others in the progress of their population. To the quantity of rich land which they possessed in common with the Spanish and Portuguese colonies, they added a greater degree of liberty and equality. Though not without some restrictions on their foreign commerce, they were allowed the liberty of managing their own internal affairs. The political institutions which prevailed were favourable to the alienation and division of property. Lands which were not cultivated by the proprietor within a limited time were declared grantable to any other person. In Pennsylvania there was no right of primogeniture, and in the provinces of New England the eldest son had only a double share. There were no tithes in any of the states, and scarcely any taxes. And on account of the extreme cheapness of good land, and a situation favourable to the exportation of grain, a capital could not be more advantageously employed than in agriculture, which, at the same time that it affords the greatest quantity of healthy work, supplies the most valuable produce to the society.

The consequence of these favourable circumstances united was a rapidity of increase almost without parallel in history. Throughout all the northern provinces the population was found to double itself in 25 years. The original number of persons which had settled in the four provinces of New England in 1643 was 21,200. Afterwards it was calculated that more left them than went to them. In the year 1760 they were increased to half a million. They had therefore all along doubled their number in 25 years. In New Jersey the period of doubling appeared to be 22 years, and in Rhode Island still less. In the back settlements, where the inhabitants applied themselves solely to agriculture, and luxury was not known, they were supposed to double their number in 15 years. Along the seacoast, which would naturally be first inhabited, the period of doubling was about 35 years, and in some of the maritime towns the population was absolutely at a stand. From the late census made in America it appears that, taking all the states together, they have still continued to double their numbers within 25 years; and as the whole population is now so great as not to be materially affected by the emigrations from Europe, and as it is known that in some of the towns and districts near the seacoast the progress of population has been comparatively slow, it is evident that in the interior of the country in general the period of doubling from procreation only must have been considerably less than 25 years.

The population of the United States of America, according to the fourth census in 1820, was 7,861,710. We have no reason to believe that Great Britain is less populous at present for the emigration of the small parent stock which produced these numbers. On the contrary, a certain degree of emigration is known to be favourable to the population of the mother country. It has been particularly remarked that the two Spanish provinces from which the greatest number of people emigrated to America became in consequence more populous.

Whatever was the original number of British emigrants which increased so fast in North America, let us ask, Why does not an equal number produce an equal increase in the same time in Great Britain? The obvious reason to be assigned is the want of food; and that this want is the most efficient cause of the three immediate checks to population, which have been observed to prevail in all societies, is evident from the rapidity with which even old states recover the desolations of war, pestilence, famine, and the convulsions of nature. They are then for a short time placed a little in the situation of new colonies, and the effect is always answerable to what might be expected. If the industry of the inhabitants be not destroyed, subsistence will soon increase beyond the wants of the reduced numbers; and the invariable consequence will be that population, which before perhaps was nearly stationary, will begin immediately to increase, and will continue its progress till the former population is recovered.

The fertile province of Flanders, which has been so often the seat of the most destructive wars, after a respite of a few years has always appeared as rich and populous as ever. The undiminished population of France, is an instance very strongly in point. The effects of the dreadful plague in London in 1666 were not perceptible 15 or 20 years afterwards. It may even be doubted whether Turkey and Egypt are upon an average much less populous for the plagues which periodically lay them waste. If the number of people which they contain be considerably less now than formerly, it is rather to be attributed to the tyranny and oppression of the governments under which they groan, and the consequent discouragements to agriculture, than to the losses which they sustain by the plague. The traces of the most destructive famines in China, Indostan, Egypt, and other countries, are by all accounts very soon obliterated; and the most tremendous convulsions of nature, such as volcanic eruptions and earthquakes, if they do not happen so frequently as to drive away the inhabitants or destroy their spirit of industry, have been found to produce but a trifling effect on the average population of any state.

It has appeared from the registers of different countries that the progress of their population is checked by the periodical though irregular returns of plagues and sickly seasons. Dr. Short, in his curious researches into bills of mortality, often uses the expression "terrible correctives of the redundance of mankind;" and in a table of all the plagues, pestilences, and famines of which he could collect accounts, shows the constancy and universality of their operation.

The epidemical years in his table, or the years in which the plague or some great and wasting epidemic prevailed (for smaller sickly seasons seem not to be included) are 431, of which 32 were before the Christian era. If we divide therefore the years of the present era by 399, it will appear that the periodical returns of such epidemics, to some countries that we are acquainted with, have been on an average only at the interval of about $4\frac{1}{2}$ years.

Of the 254 great famines and dearths enumerated in the table, 15 were before the Christian era, beginning with that which occurred in Palestine in the time of Abraham. If, subtracting these 15, we divide the years of the present era by the remainder, it will appear that the average interval between the visits of this dreadful scourge has been only about $7\frac{1}{2}$ years.

How far these "terrible correctives to the redundance of mankind" have been occasioned by the too rapid increase of population, is a point which it would be very difficult to determine with any degree of precision. The causes of most of our diseases appear to us to be so mysterious, and probably are really so various, that it would be rashness to lay too much stress on any single one; but it will not perhaps be too much to say that *among* these causes we ought certainly to rank crowded houses and insufficient or unwholesome food, which are the natural consequences of an increase of population faster than the accommodations of a country with respect to habitations and food will allow.

Almost all the histories of epidemics which we possess tend to confirm this supposition, by describing them in general as making their principal ravages among the lower classes of people. In Dr. Short's tables this circumstance is frequently mentioned; and it further appears that a very considerable proportion of the epidemic years either followed or were accompanied by seasons of dearth and bad food. In other places he also mentions great plagues as diminishing particularly the numbers of the lower or servile sort of people; and in speaking of different diseases he observes that those which are occasioned by bad and unwholesome food generally last the longest.

We know from constant experience that fevers are generated in our jails, our manufactories, our crowded workhouses, and in the narrow and close streets of our large towns—all which situations appear to be similar in their effects to squalid poverty; and we cannot doubt that causes of this kind aggravated in degree contributed to the production and prevalence of those great and wasting plagues formerly so common in Europe, but which now from the mitigation of these causes are everywhere considerably abated, and in many places appear to be completely extirpated.

Of the other great scourge of mankind, famine, it may be observed that it is not in the nature of things that the increase of population should absolutely produce one. This increase though rapid is necessarily gradual; and as the human frame cannot be supported even for a very short time without food, it is evident that no more human beings can grow up than there is provision to maintain. But though the principle of population cannot absolutely produce a famine, it prepares the way for one, and by frequently obliging the lower classes of people to subsist nearly on the smallest quantity of food that will support life, turns even a slight deficiency from the failure of the seasons into a severe dearth, and may be fairly said therefore to be one of the principal causes of famine.

It also appears that when the increasing produce of a country and the increasing demand for labour so far meliorate the condition of the labourer as greatly to encourage marriage, the custom of early marriages is generally continued till the population has gone beyond the increased produce, and sickly seasons appear to be the natural and necessary consequence. The continental registers exhibit many instances of rapid increase interrupted in this manner by mortal diseases; and the inference seems to be that those countries where subsistence is increasing sufficiently to encourage population, but not to answer all its demands, will be more subject to periodical epidemics than those where the increase of population is more nearly accommodated to the average produce.

The converse of this will of course be true. In those countries which are subject to periodical sicknesses, the increase of population, or the excess of births above the deaths, will be greater in the intervals of these periods than is usual in countries not so much subject to these diseases. If Turkey and Egypt have been nearly stationary in their average population for the last century in the intervals of their periodical plagues, the births must have exceeded the deaths in a much greater proportion than in such countries as France and England.

Europe was without doubt formerly more subject to plagues and wasting epidemics than at present, and this will account in a great measure for the greater proportion of births to deaths in former times mentioned by many authors, as it has always been a common practice to estimate these proportions from too short periods, and generally to reject the years of plague as accidental.

The average proportion of births to deaths in England during the last century may be considered as about 12 to 10, or 120 to 100. The proportion in France for ten years, ending in 1780, was about 115 to 100. Though these proportions undoubtedly varied at different periods during the century, yet we have reason to think that they did not vary in any very considerable degree; and it will appear therefore that the population of France and England had accommodated itself more nearly to the average produce of each country than many other states. The operation of the preventive check—wars—the silent though certain destruction of life in large towns and manufactories, and the close habitations and insufficient food of many of the poor, prevent population from outrunning the means of subsistence, and, if I may use an expression which certainly at first appears strange, supersede the necessity of great and ravaging epidemics to destroy what is redundant. If a wasting plague were to sweep off two millions in England, and six millions in France, it cannot be doubted that after the inhabitants had recovered from the dreadful shock, the proportion of births to deaths would rise much above the usual average in either country during the last century.

In New Jersey the proportion of births to deaths, on an average of 7 years ending with 1743, was 300 to 100. In France and England the average proportion cannot be reckoned at more than 120 to 100. Great and astonishing as this difference is, we ought not to be so wonder-struck at it as to attribute it to the miraculous interposition of Heaven. The causes of it are not remote, latent, and mysterious, but near us, round about us, and open to the investigation of every inquiring mind. It accords with the most liberal spirit of philosophy to believe that no stone can fall, or plant rise, without the immediate agency of divine power. But we know from experience that these operations of what we call Nature have been conducted almost invariably according to fixed laws. And since the world began, the causes of population and depopulation have been probably as constant as any of the laws of nature with which we are acquainted.

The passion between the sexes has appeared in every age to be so nearly the same that it may always be considered in algebraic language as a given quantity. The great law of necessity which prevents population from increasing in any country beyond the food which it can either produce or acquire is a law so open to our view, so obvious and evident to our understandings, that we cannot for a moment doubt it. The different modes which nature takes to repress a redundant population do not indeed appear to us so certain and regular; but though we cannot always predict the mode, we may with certainty predict the fact. If the proportion of the births to the deaths for a few years indicates an increase of numbers much beyond the proportional increased or acquired food of the country, we may be perfectly certain that unless an emigration take place, the deaths will shortly exceed the births, and that the increase which had been observed for a few years cannot be the real average increase of the population of the country. If there were no other depopulating causes, and if the preventive check did not operate very strongly, every country would without doubt be subject to periodical plagues and famines.

The only true criterion of a real and permanent increase in the population of any country is the increase of the means of subsistence. But even this criterion is subject to some slight variations, which however are completely open to our observation. In some countries population seems to have been forced; that is, the people have been habituated by degrees to live almost upon the smallest possible quantity of food. There must have been periods in such countries when population increased permanently without an increase in the means of subsistence. China, India, and the countries possessed by the Bedoween Arabs appear to answer to this description. The average produce of these countries seems to be but barely sufficient to support the lives of the inhabitants, and of course any deficiency from the badness of the seasons must be fatal. Nations in this state must necessarily be subject to famines.

In America, where the reward of labour is at present so liberal, the lower classes might retrench very considerably in a year of scarcity without materially distressing themselves. A famine therefore seems to be almost impossible. It may be expected that in the progress of the population of America the labourers will in time be much less liberally rewarded. The numbers will in this case permanently increase without a proportional increase in the means of subsistence.

In the different countries of Europe there must be some variations in the proportion of the number of inhabitants, and the quantity of food consumed arising from the different habits of living which prevail in each state. The labourers in the south of England are so accustomed to eat fine wheaten bread, that they will suffer themselves to be half starved before they will submit to live like the Scotch peasants.

They might perhaps in time, by the constant operation of the hard law of necessity, be reduced to live even like the lower classes of the Chinese, and the country would then with the same quantity of food support a greater population. But to effect this must always be a difficult, and every friend to humanity will hope an abortive, attempt.

I have mentioned some cases where population may permanently increase without a proportional increase in the means of subsistence. But it is evident that the variation in different states between the food and the numbers supported by it is restricted to a limit beyond which it cannot pass. In every country the population of which is not absolutely decreasing the food must be necessarily sufficient to support and continue the race of labourers.

Other circumstances being the same, it may be affirmed that countries are populous according to the quantity of human food which they produce or can acquire; and happy according to the liberality with which this food is divided, or the quantity which a day's labour will purchase. Corn countries are more populous than pasture countries, and rice countries more populous than corn countries. But their happiness does not depend either upon their being thinly or fully inhabited, upon their poverty or their riches, their youth or their age, but on the proportion which the population and the food bear to each other.

This proportion is generally the most favourable in new colonies, where the knowledge and industry of an old state operate on the fertile unappropriated land of a new one. In other cases the youth or the age of a state is not in this respect of great importance. It is probable that the food of Great Britain is divided in more liberal shares to her inhabitants at the present period than it was two thousand, three thousand, or four thousand years ago. And it has appeared that the poor and thinly inhabited tracts of the Scotch Highlands are more distressed by a redundant population than the most populous parts of Europe.

If a country were never to be overrun by a people more advanced in arts, but left to its own natural progress in civilisation, from the time that its produce might be considered as an unit to the time that it might be considered as a million, during the lapse of many thousand years, there might not be a single period when the mass of the people could be said to be free from distress, either directly or indirectly, for want of food. In every state in Europe since we have first had accounts of it, millions and millions of human existences have been repressed from this simple cause, though perhaps in some of these states an absolute famine may never have been known.

Must it not then be acknowledged by an attentive examiner of the histories of mankind that in every age and in every state in which man has existed or does now exist,

The increase to population is necessarily limited by the means of subsistence:

Population invariably increases when the means of subsistence increase, unless prevented by powerful and obvious checks:

These checks, and the checks which keep the population down to the level of the means of subsistence, are moral restraint, vice, and misery?

Part Two: Of Our Future Prospects Respecting the Removal or Mitigation of the Evils Arising from the Principle of Population

I. Of Moral Restraint, and Our Obligation to Practise This Virtue

As it ppears that in the actual state of every society which has come within our review the natural progress of population has been constantly and powerfully checked, and as it seems evident that no improved form of government, no plans of emigration, no benevolent institutions, and no degree or direction of national industry can prevent the continued action of a great check to population in some form or other, it follows that we must submit to it as an inevitable law of nature; and the only inquiry that remains is how it may take place with the least possible prejudice to the virtue and happiness of human society.

All the immediate checks to population which have been observed to prevail in the same and different countries seem to be resolvable into moral restraint, vice, and misery; and if our choice be confined to these three, we cannot long hesitate in our decision respecting which it would be most eligible to encourage.

In the first edition of this essay I observed that as from the laws of nature it appeared that some check to population must exist, it was better that this check should arise from a foresight of the difficulties attending a family and the fear of dependent poverty than from the actual presence of want and sickness. This idea will admit of being pursued farther; and I am inclined to think that from the prevailing opinions respecting population, which undoubtedly originated in barbarous ages, and have been continued and circulated by that part of every community which may be supposed to be interested in their support, we have been prevented from attending to the clear dictates of reason and nature on this subject.

Natural and moral evil seem to be the instruments employed by the Deity in admonishing us to avoid any mode of conduct which is not suited to our being, and will consequently injure our happiness. If we are intemperate in eating and drinking, our health is disordered; if we indulge the transports of anger, we seldom fail to commit acts of which we afterwards repent; if we multiply too fast, we die miserably of poverty and contagious diseases. The laws of nature in all these cases are similar and uniform. They indicate to us that we have followed these impulses too far, so as to trench upon some other law, which equally demands attention. The uneasiness we feel from repletion, the injuries that we inflict on ourselves or others in anger, and the inconveniences we suffer on the approach of poverty, are all admonitions to us to regulate these impulses better; and if we heed not this admonition, we justly incur the penalty of our disobedience, and our sufferings operate as a warning to others.

From the inattention of mankind hitherto to the consequences of increasing too fast, it must be presumed that these consequences are not so immediately and powerfully connected with the conduct which leads to them as in the other instances; but the delayed knowledge of particular effects does not alter their nature, or our obligation to regulate our conduct accordingly, as soon as we are satisfied of what this conduct ought to be. In many other instances it has not been till after long and painful experience that the conduct most favourable to the happiness of man has been forced upon his attention. The kind of food and the mode of preparing it best suited to the purposes of nutrition and the gratification of the palate, the treatment and remedies of different disorders, the bad effects on the human frame of low and marshy situations, the invention of the most convenient and comfortable clothing, the construction of good houses, and all the advantages and extended enjoyments which distinguish civilised life, were not pointed out to the attention of man at once, but were the slow and late result of experience and of the admonitions received by repeated failures.

Diseases have been generally considered as the inevitable inflictions of Providence, but perhaps a great part of them may more justly be considered as indications that we have offended against some of the laws of nature. The plague at Constantinople and in other towns of the East is a constant admonition of this kind to the inhabitants. The human constitution cannot support such a state of filth and torpor; and as dirt, squalid poverty, and indolence are in the highest degree unfavourable to happiness and virtue, it seems a benevolent dispensation that such a state should by the laws of nature produce disease and death as a beacon to others to avoid splitting on the same rock.

The prevalence of the plague in London till the year 1666 operated in a proper manner on the conduct of our ancestors; and the removal of nuisances, the construction of drains, the widening of the streets, and the giving more room and air to the houses, had the effect of eradicating completely this dreadful disorder, and of adding greatly to the health and happiness of the inhabitants.

In the history of every epidemic it has almost invariably been observed that the lower classes of people, whose food was poor and insufficient, and who lived crowded together in small and dirty houses, were the principal victims. In what other manner can Nature point out to us that, if we increase too fast for the means of subsistence so as to render it necessary for a considerable part of the society to live in this miserable manner, we have offended against one of her laws? This law she has declared exactly in the same manner as she declares that intemperance in eating and drinking will be followed by ill health, and that, however grateful it may be to us at the moment to indulge this propensity to excess, such indulgence will ultimately produce unhappiness. It is as much a law of nature that repletion is bad for the human frame, as that eating and drinking, unattended with this consequence, are good for it.

An implicit obedience to the impulses of our natural passions would lead us into the wildest and most fatal extravagances, and yet we have the strongest reasons for believing that all these passions are so necessary to our being that they could not be generally weakened or diminished without injuring our happiness. The most powerful and universal of all our desires is the desire of food, and of those things—such as clothing, houses, &c.—which are immediately necessary to relieve us from the pains of hunger and cold. It is acknowledged by all that these desires put in motion the greatest part of that activity from which the multiplied improvements and advantages of civilised life are derived, and that the pursuit of these objects and the gratification of these desires form the principal happiness of the larger half of mankind, civilised or uncivilised, and are indispensably necessary to the more refined enjoyments of the other half. We are all conscious of the inestimable benefits that we derive from these desires when directed in a certain manner, but we are equally conscious of the evils resulting from them when not directed in this manner—so much so that society has taken upon itself to punish most severely what it considers as an irregular gratification of them. And yet the desires in both cases are equally natural, and, abstractedly considered, equally virtuous. The act of the hungry man who satisfies his appetite by taking a loaf from the shelf of another is in no respect to be distinguished from the act of him who does the same thing with a loaf of his own, but by its consequences. From the consideration of these consequences we feel the most perfect conviction that if people were not prevented from gratifying their natural desires with the loaves in the possession of others, the number of loaves would universally diminish. This experience is the foundation of the laws relating to property and of the distinctions of virtue and vice in the gratification of desires otherwise perfectly the same.

If the pleasure arising from the gratification of these propensities were universally diminished in vividness, violations of property would become less frequent; but this advantage would be greatly overbalanced by the narrowing of the sources of enjoyment. The diminution in the quantity of all those productions which contribute to human gratification would be much greater in proportion than the diminution of thefts, and the loss of general happiness on the one side would be beyond comparison greater than the gain of happiness on the other. When we contemplate the constant and severe toils of the greatest part of mankind, it is impossible not to be forcibly impressed with the reflection that the sources of human happiness would be most cruelly diminished if the prospect of a good meal, a warm house, and a comfortable fireside in the evening were not incitements sufficiently vivid to give interest and cheerfulness to the labours and privations of the day.

After the desire of food, the most powerful and general of our desires is the passion between the sexes, taken in an enlarged sense. Of the happiness spread over human life by this passion very few are unconscious. Virtuous love, exalted by friendship, seems to be that sort of mixture of sensual and intellectual enjoyment particularly suited to the nature of man, and most powerfully calculated to awaken the sympathies of the soul, and produce the most exquisite gratifications. Perhaps there is scarcely a man who has once experienced the genuine delight of virtuous love, however great his intellectual pleasures may have been, who does not look back to that period as the sunny spot in his whole life, where his imagination loves most to bask, which he recollects and contemplates with the fondest regret, and which he would wish to live over again.

It has been said by Mr. [William] Godwin, in order to show the evident inferiority of the pleasures of sense, "Strip the commerce of the sexes of all its attendant circumstances, and it would be generally despised." He might as well say to a man who admires trees, Strip them of their spreading branches and lovely foliage, and what beauty can you see in a bare pole? But it was the tree with the branches and foliage, and not without them, that excited admiration. It is "the symmetry of person, the vivacity, the voluptuous softness of temper, the affectionate kindness of feeling, the imagination, and the wit" of a woman, as Mr. Godwin says, which excites the passion of love and not the mere distinction of her being a female.

It is a very great mistake to suppose that the passion between the sexes only operates and influences human conduct when the immediate gratification of it is in contemplation. The formation and steady pursuit of some particular plan of life has been justly considered as one of the most permanent sources of happiness; but I am inclined to believe that there are not many of these plans formed which are not connected in a considerable degree with the prospect of the gratification of this passion, and with the support of children arising from it. The evening meal, the warm house, and the comfortable fireside would lose half their interest if we were to exclude the idea of some object of affection with whom they were to be shared.

We have also great reason to believe that the passion between the sexes has the most powerful tendency to soften and meliorate the human character, and keep it more alive to all the kindlier emotions of benevolence and pity. Observations on savage life have generally tended to prove that nations in which this passion appeared to be less vivid, were distinguished by a ferocious and malignant spirit, and particularly by tyranny and cruelty to the sex. If indeed this bond of conjugal affection were considerably weakened, it seems probable either that the man would make use of his superior physical strength, and turn his wife into a slave, as among the generality of savages, or at best that every little inequality of temper, which must necessarily occur between two persons, would produce a total alienation of affection; and this could hardly take place without a diminution of parental fondness and care, which would have the most fatal effect on the happiness of society.

It may be further remarked, and observations on the human character in different countries warrant us in the conclusion, that the passion is stronger, and its general effects in producing gentleness, kindness, and suavity of manners, much more powerful, where obstacles are thrown in the way of very early and universal gratification. In some of the southern countries, where every impulse may be almost immediately indulged, the passion sinks into mere animal desire, is soon weakened and almost extinguished by excess, and its influence on the character is extremely confined. But in European countries, where, though the women are not secluded, yet manners have imposed considerable restraints on this gratification, the passion not only rises in force, but in the universality and beneficial tendency of its effects; and has often the greatest influence in the formation and improvement of the character, where it is the least gratified.

Considering then the passion between the sexes in all its bearings and relations, and including the endearing engagement of parent and child resulting from it, few will be disposed to deny that it is one of the principal ingredients of human happiness. Yet experience teaches us that much evil flows from the irregular gratification of it; and though the evil be of little weight in the scale when compared with the good, yet its absolute quantity cannot be inconsiderable, on account of the strength and universality of the passion. It is evident however from the general conduct of all governments in their distribution of punishments, that the evil resulting from this cause is not so great and so immediately dangerous to society, as the irregular gratification of the desire of property; but placing this evil in the most formidable point of view, we should evidently purchase a diminution of it at a very high price by the extinction or diminution of the passion which causes it; a change which would probably convert human life either into a cold and cheerless blank or a scene of savage and merciless ferocity.

A careful attention to the remote as well as immediate effect of all the human passions and all the general laws of nature, leads us strongly to the conclusion that under the present constitution of things few or none of them will admit of being greatly diminished, without narrowing the sources of good more powerfully than the sources of evil. And the reason seems to be obvious. They are in fact the materials of all our pleasures as well as of all our pains; of all our happiness as well as of all our misery; of all our virtues as well as of all our vices. It must therefore be regulation and direction that are wanted, not diminution or extinction.

It is justly observed by Paley [in his *Natural Theology*] that "Human passions are either necessary to human welfare, or capable of being made, and in a great majority of instances are in fact made, conducive to its happiness. These passions are strong and general; and perhaps would not answer their purpose unless they were so. But strength and generality, when it is expedient that particular circumstances should be respected, become if left to themselves excess and misdirection. From which excess and misdirection the vices of mankind (the causes no doubt of much misery) appear to spring. This account, while it shows us the principle of vice, shows us at the same time the province of reason and self-government."

Our virtue therefore as reasonable beings evidently consists in educing from the general materials which the Creator has placed under our guidance the greatest sum of human happiness; and as natural impulses are abstractedly considered good, and only to be distinguished by their consequences, a strict attention to these consequences and the regulation of our conduct conformably to them must be considered as our principal duty.

The fecundity of the human species is in some respects a distinct consideration from the passion between the sexes, as it evidently depends more upon the power of women in bearing children than upon the strength and weakness of this passion. It is a law however exactly similar in its great features to all the other laws of nature. It is strong and general, and apparently would not admit of any very considerable diminution without being inadequate to its object; the evils arising from it are incidental to those necessary qualities of strength and generality; and these evils are capable of being very greatly mitigated and rendered comparatively light by human energy and virtue. We cannot but conceive that it is an object of the Creator that the earth should be replenished; and it appears to me clear that this could not be effected without a tendency in population to increase faster than food; and as, with the present law of increase, the peopling of the earth does not proceed very rapidly, we have undoubtedly some reason to believe that this law is not too powerful for its apparent object. The desire of the means of subsistence would be comparatively confined in its effects, and would fail of producing that general activity so necessary to the improvement of the human faculties, were it not for the strong and universal effort of population to increase with greater rapidity than its supplies. If these two tendencies were exactly balanced, I do not see what motive there would be sufficiently strong to overcome the acknowledged indolence of man, and make him proceed in the cultivation of the soil. The population of any large territory, however fertile, would be as likely to stop at five hundred or five thousand, as at five millions or fifty millions. Such a balance therefore would clearly defeat one great purpose of creation; and if the question be merely a question of degree, a question of a little more or a little less strength, we may fairly distrust our competence to judge of the precise quantity necessary to answer the object with the smallest sum of incidental evil. In the present state of things we appear to have under our guidance a great power, capable of peopling a desert region in a small number of years; and yet under other circumstances capable of being confined by human energy and virtue to any limits, however narrow, at the expense of a small comparative quantity of evil. The analogy of all the other laws of nature would be completely violated, if in this instance alone there were no provision for accidental failures, no resources against the vices of mankind, or the partial mischiefs resulting from other general laws. To effect the apparent object without any attendant evil, it is evident that a perpetual change in the law of increase would be necessary, varying with the varying circumstances of each country. But instead of this it is not only more consonant to the analogy of the other parts of nature, but we have reason to think that it is more conducive to the formation and improvement of the human mind, that the laws should be uniform and the evils incidental to it, under certain circumstances, left to be mitigated or removed by man himself. His duties in this case vary with his situation; he is thus kept more alive to the consequences of his actions; and his faculties have evidently greater play and opportunity of improvement, than if the evil were removed by a perpetual change of the law according to circumstances.

Even if from passions too easily subdued, or the facility of illicit intercourse, a state of celibacy were a matter of indifference, and not a state of some privation, the end of nature in the peopling of the earth would be apparently liable to be defeated. It is of the very utmost importance to the happiness of mankind that population should not increase too fast; but it does not appear that the object to be accomplished would admit of any considerable diminution in the desire of marriage. It is clearly the duty of each individual not to marry till he has a prospect of supporting his children; but it is at the same time to be wished that he should retain undiminished his desire of marriage, in order that he may exert himself to realise this prospect, and be stimulated to make provision for the support of greater numbers.

It is evidently therefore regulation and direction which are required with regard to the principle of population, not diminution or alteration. And if moral restraint be the only virtuous mode of avoiding the incidental evils arising from this principle, our obligation to practise it will evidently rest exactly upon the same foundation as our obligation to practise any of the other virtues.

Whatever indulgence we may be disposed to allow to occasional failures in the discharge of a duty of acknowledged difficulty, yet of the strict line of duty we cannot doubt. Our obligation not to marry till we have a fair prospect of being able to support our children will appear to deserve the attention of the moralist, if it can be proved that an attention to this obligation is of most powerful effect in the prevention of misery; and that if it were the general custom to follow the first impulse of nature and marry at the age of puberty, the universal prevalence of every known virtue in the greatest conceivable degree, would fail of rescuing society from the most wretched and desperate state of want, and all the diseases and famines which usually accompany it.

II. Of the Effects Which Would Result to Society from the Prevalence of Moral Restraint

One of the principal reasons which have prevented an assent to the doctrine of the constant tendency of population to increase beyond the means of subsistence, is a great unwillingness to believe that the Deity would by the laws of nature bring beings into existence, which by the laws of nature could not be supported in that existence. But if, in addition to that general activity and direction of our industry put in motion by these laws, we further consider that the incidental evils arising from them are constantly directing our attention to the proper check to population, moral restraint; and if it appear that by a strict obedience to the duties pointed out to us by the light of nature and reason, and confirmed and sanctioned by revelation, these evils may be avoided, the objection will, I trust, be removed, and all apparent imputation on the goodness of the Deity be done away.

The heathen moralists never represented happiness as attainable on earth but through the medium of virtue; and among their virtues prudence ranked in the first class, and by some was even considered as including every other. The Christian religion places our present as well as future happiness in the exercise of those virtues which tend to fit us for a state of superior enjoyment; and the subjection of the passions to the guidance of reason, which, if not the whole, is a principal branch of prudence, is in consequence most particularly inculcated.

If, for the sake of illustration, we might be permitted to draw a picture of society in which each individual endeavoured to attain happiness by the strict fulfillment of those duties which the most enlightened of the ancient philosophers deduced from the laws of nature, and which have been directly taught and received such powerful sanctions in the moral code of Christianity, it would present a very different scene from that which we now contemplate. Every act which was prompted by the desire of immediate gratification, but which threatened an ultimate overbalance of pain, would be considered as a breach of duty, and consequently no man whose earnings were only sufficient to maintain two children would put himself in a situation in which he might have to maintain four or five, however he might be prompted to it by the passion of love. This prudential restraint, if it were generally adopted, by narrowing the supply of labour in the market, would in the natural course of things soon raise its price. The period of delayed gratification would be passed in saving the earnings which were above the wants of a single man, and in acquiring habits of sobriety, industry, and economy, which would enable him in a few years to enter into the matrimonial contract without fear of its consequences. The operation of the preventive check in this way, by constantly keeping the population within the limits of the food though constantly following its increase, would give a real value to the rise of wages and the sums saved by labourers before marriage, very different from those forced advances in the price of labour or arbitrary parochial donations which, in proportion to their magnitude and extensiveness, must of necessity be followed by a proportional advance in the price of provisions. As the wages of labour would thus be sufficient to maintain with decency a large family, and as every married couple would set out with a sum for contingencies, all abject poverty would be removed from society, or would at least be confined to a very few who had fallen into misfortunes against which no prudence or foresight could provide.

The interval between the age of puberty and the period at which each individual might venture on marriage must, according to the supposition, be passed in strict chastity, because the law of chastity cannot be violated without producing evil. The effect of anything like a promiscuous intercourse, which prevents the birth of children, is evidently to weaken the best affections of the heart, and in a very marked manner to degrade the female character; and any other intercourse would, without improper arts, bring as many children into the society as marriage, with a much greater probability of their becoming a burden to it.

These considerations show that the virtue of chastity is not, as some have supposed, a forced produce of artificial society, but that it has the most real and solid foundation in nature and reason, being apparently the only virtuous means of avoiding the vice and misery which result so often from the principle of population.

In such a society as we have been supposing it might be necessary for some of both sexes to pass many of the early years of life in the single state, and if this were general there would certainly be room for a much greater number to marry afterwards, so that fewer, upon the whole, would be condemned to pass their lives in celibacy. If the custom of not marrying early prevailed generally, and if violations of chastity were equally dishonourable in both sexes, a more familiar and friendly intercourse between them might take place without danger. Two young people might converse together intimately without its being immediately supposed that they either intended marriage or intrigue, and a much better opportunity would thus be given to both sexes of finding out kindred dispositions, and of forming those strong and lasting attachments without which the married state is generally more productive of misery than of happiness. The earlier years of life would not be spent without love, though without the full gratification of it. The passion, instead of being extinguished as it now too frequently is by early sensuality, would only be repressed for a time that it might afterwards burn with a brighter, purer, and steadier flame, and the happiness of the married state, instead of only affording the means of immediate indulgence, would be looked forward to as the prize of industry and virtue, and the reward of a genuine and constant attachment.

The passion of love is a powerful stimulus in the formation of character and often prompts to the most noble and generous exertions, but this is only when the affections are centred in one object, and generally when full gratification is delayed by difficulties. The heart is perhaps never so much disposed to virtuous conduct, and certainly at no time is the virtue of chastity so little difficult to men as when under the influence of such a passion. Late marriages taking place in this way would be very different from those of the same name at present, where the union is too frequently prompted solely by interested views, and the parties meet not unfrequently with exhausted constitutions and generally with exhausted affections. The late marriages at present are indeed principally confined to the men, of whom there are few, however advanced in life, who if they determine to marry do not fix their choice on a young wife. A young woman without fortune, when she has passed her twenty-fifth year, begins to fear, and with reason, that she may lead a life of celibacy, and with a heart capable of forming a strong attachment feels as each year creeps on her hopes of finding an object on which to rest her affections gradually diminishing, and the uneasiness of her situation aggravated by the silly and unjust prejudices of the world. If the general age of marriage among women were later the period of youth and hope would be prolonged, and fewer would be ultimately disappointed.

That a change of this kind would be a most decided advantage to the more virtuous half of society we cannot for a moment doubt. However impatiently the privation might be borne by the men, it would be supported by the women readily and cheerfully, and if they could look forward with just confidence to marriage at twenty-seven or twenty-eight, I fully believe that if the matter were left to their free choice, they would clearly prefer waiting till this period to the being involved in all the cares of a large family at twenty-five. The most eligible age of marriage however could not be fixed, but must depend entirely on circumstances and situation. There is no period of human life at which nature most strongly prompts to an union of the sexes than from seventeen or eighteen to twenty. In every society above that state of depression, which almost excludes reason and foresight, these early tendencies must necessarily be restrained; and if in the actual state of things such a restraint on the impulses of nature be found unavoidable, at what time can we be consistently released from it but at that period, whatever it may be, when in the existing circumstances of the society a fair prospect presents itself of maintaining a family?

The difficulty of moral restraint will perhaps be objected to this doctrine. To him who does not acknowledge the authority of the Christian religion I have only to say that after the most careful investigation this virtue appears to be absolutely necessary in order to avoid certain evils which would otherwise result from the general laws of nature. According to his own principles it is his duty to pursue the greatest good consistent with these laws, and not to fail in this important end, and produce an overbalance of misery by a partial obedience to some of the dictates of nature while he neglects others. The path of virtue, though it be the only path which leads to permanent happiness, has always been represented by the heathen moralists as of difficult ascent.

To the Christian I would say that the Scriptures most clearly and precisely point it out to us as our duty to restrain our passions within the bounds of reason, and it is a palpable disobedience of this law to indulge our desires in such a manner as reason tells us will unavoidably end in misery. The Christian cannot consider the difficulty of moral restraint as any argument against its being his duty, since in almost every page of the sacred writings man is described as encompassed on all sides by temptations which it is extremely difficult to resist; and though no duties are enjoined which do not contribute to his happiness on earth as well as in a future state, yet an undeviating obedience is never represented as an easy task.

There is in general so strong a tendency to love in early youth that it is extremely difficult at this period to distinguish a genuine from a transient passion. If the earlier years of life were passed by both sexes in moral restraint, from the greater facility that this would give to the meeting of kindred dispositions, it might even admit of a doubt whether more happy marriages would not take place, and consequently more pleasure from the passion of love, than in a state such as that of America the circumstances of which allow of a very early union of the sexes. But if we compare the intercourse of the sexes in such a society as I have been supposing with that which now exists in Europe, taken under all its circumstances, it may safely be asserted that, independently of the load of misery which would be removed, the sum of pleasurable sensations from the passion of love would be increased in a very great degree.

If we could suppose such a system general, the accession of happiness to society in its internal economy would scarcely be greater than in its external relations. It might fairly be expected that war, that great pest of the human race, would under such circumstances soon cease to extend its ravages so widely and so frequently as it does at present.

One of its first causes and most powerful impulses was undoubtedly an insufficiency of room and food; and greatly as the circumstances of mankind have changed since it first began, the same cause still continues to operate and to produce, though in a smaller degree, the same effects. The ambition of princes would want instruments of destruction if the distresses of the lower classes of people did not drive them under their standards. A recruiting sergeant always prays for a bad harvest and a want of employment, or in other words a redundant population.

In the earlier ages of the world when war was the great business of mankind, and the drains of population from this cause were beyond

comparison greater than in modern times, the legislators and statesmen
of each country, adverting principally to the means of offence and
defence, encouraged an increase of people in every possible way, fixed
a stigma on barrenness and celibacy, and honoured marriage. The popular religions followed these prevailing opinions. In many countries the
prolific power of nature was the object of solemn worship. In the
religion of Mahomet, which was established by the sword, and the
promulgation of which in consequence could not be unaccompanied
by an extraordinary destruction of its followers, the procreation of children
to glorify the Creator was laid down as one of the principal duties of
man, and he who had the most numerous offspring was considered as
having best answered the end of his creation. The prevalence of such
moral sentiments had naturally a great effect in encouraging marriage,
and the rapid procreation which followed was partly the effect and partly
the cause of incessant war. The vacancies occasioned by former desolations made room for the rearing of fresh supplies, and the overflowing
rapidity with which these supplies followed constantly furnished fresh
incitements and fresh instruments for renewed hostilities. Under the
influence of such moral sentiments, it is difficult to conceive how the fury
of incessant war should ever abate.

It is a pleasing confirmation of the truth and divinity of the Christian
religion, and of its being adapted to a more improved state of human
society, that it places our duties respecting marriage and the procreation
of children in a different light from that in which they were before beheld.

Without entering minutely into the subject, which would evidently
lead too far, I think it will be admitted that if we apply the spirit of
St. Paul's declarations respecting marriage to the present state of society
and the known constitution of our nature, the natural inference seems
to be that, when marriage does not interfere with higher duties, it is
right; when it does, it is wrong. According to the general principles of
moral science, says Paley [in his *Moral Philosophy*], "the method of
coming at the will of God from the light of nature is to inquire into the
tendency of the action to promote or diminish the general happiness."
There are perhaps few actions that tend so directly to diminish the
general happiness as to marry without the means of supporting children.
He who commits this act therefore clearly offends against the will of
God; and having become a burden on the society in which he lives, and
plunged himself and family into a situation in which virtuous habits are
preserved with more difficulty than in any other, he appears to have
violated his duty to his neighbours and to himself, and thus to have
listened to the voice of passion in opposition to his higher obligations.

In a society such as I have supposed, all the members of which
endeavour to obtain happiness by obedience to the moral code derived

from the light of nature, and enforced by strong sanctions in revealed religion, it is evident that no such marriages could take place; and the prevention of a redundant population in this way would remove one of the principal encouragements to offensive war, and at the same time tend powerfully to eradicate those two fatal political disorders, internal tyranny and internal tumult, which mutually produce each other.

Indisposed to a war of offence, in a war of defence such a society would be strong as a rock of adamant. Where every family possessed the necessaries of life in plenty, and a decent portion of its comforts and conveniences, there could not exist that hope of change, or at best that melancholy and disheartening indifference to it, which sometimes prompts the lower classes of people to say, "Let what will come, we cannot be worse off than we are now." Every heart and hand will be united to repel an invader when each individual felt the value of the solid advantages which he enjoyed, and a prospect of change presented only a prospect of being deprived of them.

As it appears therefore that it is in the power of each individual to avoid all the evil consequences to himself and society resulting from the principle of population by the practice of a virtue clearly dictated to him by the light of nature and expressly enjoined in revealed religion, and as we have reason to think that the exercise of this virtue to a certain degree would tend rather to increase than diminish individual happiness, we can have no reason to impeach the justice of the Deity because his general laws make this virtue necessary, and punish our offences against it by the evils attendant upon vice and the pains that accompany the various forms of premature death. A really virtuous society such as I have supposed would avoid these evils. It is the apparent object of the Creator to deter us from vice by the pains which accompany it, and to lead us to virtue by the happiness that it produces. This object appears to our conceptions to be worthy of a benevolent Creator. The laws of nature respecting population tend to promote this object. No imputation therefore on the benevolence of the Deity can be founded on these laws which is not equally applicable to any of the evils necessarily incidental to an imperfect state of existence.

III. OF THE ONLY EFFECTUAL MODE OF IMPROVING THE CONDITION OF THE POOR

HE WHO PUBLISHES a moral code or system of duties, however firmly he may be convinced of the strong obligation on each individual strictly to conform to it, has never the folly to imagine that it will be universally or even generally practised. But this is no valid objection against the publication of the code. If it were, the same objection would always have applied, we should be totally without general rules, and to the vices of mankind arising from temptation would be added a much longer list than we have at present of vices from ignorance.

Judging merely from the light of nature, if we feel convinced of the misery arising from a redundant population on the one hand, and of the evils and unhappiness, particularly to the female sex, arising from promiscuous intercourse, on the other, I do not see how it is possible for any person who acknowledges the principle of utility as the great criterion of moral rules, to escape the conclusion that moral restraint, or the abstaining from marriage till we are in a condition to support a family, with a perfectly moral conduct during that period, is the strict line of duty; and when revelation is taken into the question, this duty undoubtedly receives very powerful confirmation. At the same time I believe that few of my readers can be less sanguine than I am in their expectations of any sudden and great change in the general conduct of men on this subject; and the chief reason why in the last chapter I allowed myself to suppose the universal prevalence of this virtue was that I might endeavour to remove any imputation on the goodness of the Deity, by showing that the evils arising from the principle of population were exactly of the same nature as the generality of other evils which excite fewer complaints, that they were increased by human ignorance and indolence, and diminished by human knowledge and virtue; and on the supposition that each individual strictly fulfilled his duty would be almost totally removed, and this without any general diminution of those sources of pleasure arising from the regulated indulgence of the passions, which have been justly considered as the principal ingredients of human happiness.

If it will answer any purpose of illustration, I see no harm in drawing the picture of a society, in which each individual is supposed strictly to fulfil his duties; nor does a writer appear to be justly liable to the imputation of being visionary, unless he make such universal or general obedience necessary to the practical utility of his system, and to that degree of moderate and partial improvement which is all that can rationally be expected from the most complete knowledge of our duties.

But in this respect there is an essential difference between that improved state of society which I have supposed in the last chapter and most of the other speculations on this subject. The improvement there supposed, if we ever should make approaches towards it, is to be effected in the way in which we have been in the habit of seeing all the greatest improvements effected by a direct application to the interest and happiness of each individual. It is not required of us to act from motives to which we are unaccustomed; to pursue a general good which we may not distinctly comprehend, or the effect of which may be weakened by distance and diffusion. The happiness of the whole is to be the result of the happiness of individuals, and to begin first with them. No co-operation is required. Every step tells. He who performs his duty faithfully will reap the full fruits of it, whatever may be the number of others who fail. This duty is intelligible to the humblest capacity. It is merely that he is not to bring beings into the world for whom he cannot find the means of support. When once this subject is cleared from the obscurity thrown over it by parochial laws and private benevolence, every man must feel the strongest conviction of such an obligation. If he cannot support his children, they must starve; and if he marry in the face of a fair probability that he shall not be able to support his children, he is guilty of all the evils which he thus brings upon himself, his wife, and his offspring. It is clearly his interest, and will tend greatly to promote his happiness, to defer marrying, till by industry and economy he is in a capacity to support the children that he may reasonably expect from his marriage; and as he cannot in the meantime gratify his passions without violating an express command of God, and running a great risk of injuring himself or some of his fellow creatures, considerations of his own interest and happiness will dictate to him the strong obligation to a moral conduct while he remains unmarried.

However powerful may be the impulses of passion, they are generally in some degree modified by reason. And it does not seem entirely visionary to suppose that, if the true and permanent cause of poverty were clearly explained and forcibly brought home to each man's bosom, it would have some and perhaps not an inconsiderable influence on his conduct; at least the experiment has never yet been fairly tried. Almost everything that has been hitherto done for the poor has tended, as if with solicitous care, to throw a veil of obscurity over this subject and to hide from them the true cause of their poverty. When the wages of labour are hardly sufficient to maintain two children, a man marries and has five or six; he of course finds himself miserably distressed. He accuses the insufficiency of the price of labour to maintain a family. He accuses his parish for their tardy and sparing fulfilment of their obligation to assist him. He accuses the avarice of the rich who suffer him to want what they can so well spare. He accuses the partial and unjust institutions of society which have awarded him an inadequate share of the produce of the earth. He accuses perhaps the dispensations of Providence which have assigned to him a place in society so beset with unavoidable distress and dependence. In searching for objects of accusation, he never adverts to the quarter from which his misfortunes originate. The last person that he would think of accusing is himself, on whom in fact the principal blame lies except so far as he has been deceived by the higher classes of society. He may perhaps wish that he had not married, because he now feels the inconveniences of it; but it never enters into his head that he can have done anything wrong. He has always been told that to raise up subjects for his king and country is a very meritorious act. He has done this and yet is suffering for it; and it cannot but strike him as most extremely unjust and cruel in his king and country to allow him thus to suffer in return for giving them what they are continually declaring that they particularly want.

Till these erroneous ideas have been corrected, and the language of nature and reason has been generally heard on the subject of population, instead of the language of error and prejudice, it cannot be said that any fair experiment has been made with the understandings of the common people; and we cannot justly accuse them of improvidence and want of industry, till they act as they do now, after it has been brought home to their comprehensions, that they are themselves the cause of their own poverty; that the means of redress are in their own hands, and in the hands of no other persons whatever; that the society in which they live, and the government which presides over it, are without any *direct* power in this respect; and that however ardently they may desire to relieve them, and whatever attempts they may make to do so, they are really and truly unable to execute what they benevolently wish, but unjustly promise; that when the wages of labour will not maintain a family it is an incontrovertible sign that their king and country do not want more subjects, or at least that they cannot support them; that, if they marry in this case, so far from fulfilling a duty to society, they are throwing a useless burden on it, at the same time that they are plunging themselves into distress, and that they are acting directly contrary to the will of God, and bringing down upon themselves various diseases, which might all, or the greater part, have been avoided if they had attended to the repeated admonitions which he gives by the general laws of nature to every being capable of reason.

Paley, in his *Moral Philosophy,* observes that "in countries in which subsistence is become scarce, it behoves the state to watch over the public morals with increased solicitude; for nothing but the instinct of nature, under the restraint of chastity, will induce men to undertake the labour, or consent to the sacrifice of personal liberty and indulgence, which the support of a family in such circumstances requires." That it is always the duty of a state to use every exertion likely to be effectual in discouraging vice and promoting virtue, and that no temporary circumstances ought to cause any relaxation in these exertions, is certainly true. The means therefore proposed are always good; but the particular end in view in this case appears to be absolutely criminal. We wish to force people into marriage, when from the acknowledged scarcity of subsistence they will have little chance of being able to support their children. We might as well force people into the water who are unable to swim. In both cases we rashly tempt Providence. Nor have we more reason to believe that a miracle will be worked to save us from the misery and mortality resulting from our conduct in the one case than in the other.

The object of those who really wish to better the condition of the lower classes of society must be to raise the relative proportion between the price of labour and the price of provisions, so as to enable the labourer to command a larger share of the necessaries and comforts of life. We have hitherto principally attempted to attain this end by encouraging the married poor, and consequently increasing the number of labourers, and overstocking the market with a commodity which we still say that we wish to be dear. It would seem to have required no great spirit of divination to foretell the certain failure of such a plan of proceeding. There is nothing, however, like experience. It has been tried in many different countries and for many hundred years, and the success has always been answerable to the nature of the scheme. It is really time now to try something else.

When it was found that oxygen or pure vital air would not cure consumption as was expected, but rather aggravated their symptoms, trial was made of an air of the most opposite kind. I wish we had acted with the same philosophical spirit in our attempts to cure the disease of poverty; and having found that the pouring in of fresh supplies of labour only tended to aggravate the symptoms, had tried what would be the effect of withholding a little these supplies.

In all old and fully peopled states it is from this method and this alone that we can rationally expect any essential and permanent melioration in the condition of the labouring classes of the people.

In an endeavour to raise the proportion of the quantity of provisions to the number of consumers in any country, our attention would naturally be first directed to the increasing of the absolute quantity of provisions; but finding that as fast as we did this the number of consumers more than kept pace with it, and that with all our exertions we were still as far as ever behind, we should be convinced that our efforts directed only in this way would never succeed. It would appear to be setting the tortoise to catch the hare. Finding therefore that from the laws of nature we could not proportion the food to the population, our next attempt should naturally be to proportion the population to the food. If we can persuade the hare to go to sleep, the tortoise may have some chance of overtaking her.

We are not however to relax our efforts in increasing the quantity of provisions, but to combine another effort with it, that of keeping the population, when once it has been overtaken, at such a distance behind as to effect the relative proportion which we desire, and thus unite the two grand *desiderata,* a great actual population and a state of society in which abject poverty and dependence are comparatively but little known, two objects which are far from being incompatible.

If we be really serious in what appears to be the object of such general research, the mode of essentially and permanently bettering the condition of the poor, we must explain to them the true nature of their situation, and show them that the withholding of the supplies of labour is the only possible way of really raising its price, and that they themselves being the possessors of this commodity have alone the power to do this.

I cannot but consider this mode of diminishing poverty as so perfectly clear in theory, and so invariably confirmed by the analogy of every other commodity which is brought to market, that nothing but its being shown to be calculated to produce greater evils than it proposes to remedy can justify us in not making the attempt to put it into execution.

IV. Objections to This Mode Considered

One objection which perhaps will be made to this plan is that from which alone it derives its value—a market rather understocked with labour. This must undoubtedly take place in a certain degree; but by no means in such a degree as to affect the wealth and prosperity of the country. But putting this subject of a market understocked with labour in the most unfavourable point of view, if the rich will not submit to a slight inconvenience necessarily attendant on the attainment of what they profess to desire, they cannot really be in earnest in their professions. Their benevolence to the poor must be either childish play or hypocrisy; it must be either to amuse themselves or to pacify the minds of the common people with a mere show of attention to their wants. To wish to better the condition of the poor by enabling them to command a greater quantity of the necessaries and comforts of life, and then to complain of higher wages, is the act of a silly boy who gives away his cake and then cries for it. A market overstocked with labour, and an ample remuneration to each labourer, are objects perfectly incompatible with each other. In the annals of the world they never existed together: and to couple them even in imagination betrays a gross ignorance of the simplest principles of political economy.

A second objection that may be made to this plan is the diminution of population that it would cause. It is to be considered however that this diminution is merely relative; and when once this relative diminution has been effected by keeping the population stationary while the supply of food has increased, it might then start afresh and continue increasing for ages with the increase of food, maintaining always nearly the same relative proportion to it. I can easily conceive that this country, with a proper direction of the national industry, might in the course of some centuries contain two or three times its present population, and yet every man in the kingdom be much better fed and clothed than he is at present. While the springs of industry continue in vigour, and a sufficient part of that industry is directed to agriculture, we need be under no apprehensions of a deficient population; and nothing perhaps would tend so strongly to excite a spirit of industry and economy among the poor as a thorough knowledge that their happiness must always depend principally upon themselves; and that, if they obey their passions in opposition to their reason, or be not industrious and frugal while they are single to save a sum for the common contingencies of the married state, they must expect to suffer the natural evils which Providence has prepared for those who disobey its repeated admonitions.

A third objection which may be started to this plan, and the only one which appears to me to have any kind of plausibility, is that, by endeavouring to urge the duty of moral restraint on the poor, we may increase the quantity of vice relating to the sex.

I should be extremely sorry to say anything which could either directly or remotely be construed unfavourably to the cause of virtue; but I certainly cannot think that the vices which relate to the sex are the only vices which are to be considered in a moral question; or that they are even the greatest and most degrading to the human character. They can rarely or never be committed without producing unhappiness somewhere or other, and therefore ought always to be strongly reprobated; but there are other vices the effects of which are still more pernicious; and there are other situations which lead more certainly to moral offences than the refraining from marriage. Powerful as may be the temptations to a breach of chastity, I am inclined to think that they are impotent in comparison of the temptations arising from continued distress. A large class of women and many men, I have no doubt, pass a considerable part of their lives consistently with the laws of chastity; but I believe there will be found very few who pass through the ordeal of squalid and hopeless poverty, or even of long-continued embarrassed circumstances, without a great moral degradation of character.

In the higher and middle classes of society it is a melancholy and distressing sight to observe not unfrequently a man of a noble and ingenuous disposition, once feelingly alive to a sense of honour and integrity, gradually sinking under the pressure of circumstances, making his excuses at first with a blush of conscious shame, afraid of seeing the faces of his friends from whom he may have borrowed money, reduced to the meanest tricks and subterfuges to delay or avoid the payment of his just debts, till ultimately grown familiar with falsehood and at enmity with the world he loses all the grace and dignity of man.

To the general prevalence of indigence, and the extraordinary encouragements which we afford in this country to a total want of foresight and prudence among the common people, is to be attributed a considerable part of those continual depredations on property, and other more atrocious crimes, which drive us to the painful resource of such a number of executions. According to Mr. [Patrick] Colquhoun, above twenty thousand miserable individuals of various classes rise up every morning without knowing how or by what means they are to be supported during the passing day, or where in many instances they are to lodge on the succeeding night. It is by these unhappy persons that the principal depredations on the public are committed; and supposing but few of them to be married, and driven to these acts from the necessity of supporting their children, yet still it is probably true that the too great frequency of marriage amongst the poorest classes of society is one of the principal causes of the temptations to these crimes. A considerable part of these unhappy wretches will probably be found to be the offspring of such marriages, educated in workhouses where every vice is propagated, or bred up at home in filth and rags, with an utter ignorance of every moral obligation. A still greater part perhaps consists of persons who, being unable for some time to get employment owing to the full supply of labour, have been urged to these extremities by their temporary wants; and having thus lost their characters, are rejected even when their labour may be wanted by the well-founded caution of civil society.

When indigence does not produce overt acts of vice, it palsies every virtue. Under the continued temptations to a breach of chastity, occasional failures may take place, and the moral sensibility in other respects not be very strikingly impaired; but the continued temptations which beset hopeless poverty, and the strong sense of injustice that generally accompanies it from an ignorance of its true cause, tend so powerfully to sour the disposition, to harden the heart, and deaden the moral sense, that generally speaking virtue takes her flight clear away from the tainted spot, and does not often return.

Even with respect to the vices which relate to the sex, marriage has been found to be by no means a complete remedy. Among the higher classes, our Doctors' Commons, and the lives that many married men are known to lead, sufficiently prove this; and the same kind of vice, though not so much heard of among the lower classes of people, is probably in all our great towns not much less frequent.

Add to this that abject poverty, particularly when joined with idleness, is a state the most unfavourable to chastity that can well be conceived. The passion is as strong, or nearly so, as in other situations; and every restraint on it from personal respect, or a sense of morality, is generally removed. There is a degree of squalid poverty in which, if a girl was brought up, I should say that her being really modest at twenty was an absolute miracle. Those persons must have extraordinary minds indeed, and such as are not usually formed under similar circumstances, who can continue to respect themselves when no other person whatever respects them. If the children thus brought up were even to marry at twenty, it is probable that they would have passed some years in vicious habits before that period.

If after all, however, these arguments should appear insufficient, if we reprobate the idea of endeavouring to encourage the virtue of moral restraint among the poor from a fear of producing vice; and if we think that to facilitate marriage by all possible means is a point of the first consequence to the morality and happiness of the people, let us act consistently, and before we proceed endeavour to make ourselves acquainted with the mode by which alone we can effect our object.

V. Of the Consequences of Pursuing the Opposite Mode

It is an evident truth that, whatever may be the rate of increase in the means of subsistence, the increase of population must be limited by it, at least after the food has once been divided into the smallest shares that will support life. All the children born beyond what would be required to keep up the population to this level must necessarily perish, unless room be made for them by the deaths of grown persons. It has appeared indeed clearly in the course of this work, that in all old states the marriages and births depend principally upon the deaths, and that there is no encouragement to early unions so powerful as a great mortality. To act consistently therefore we should facilitate, instead of foolishly and vainly endeavouring to impede, the operations of nature in producing this mortality; and if we dread the too frequent visitation of the horrid form of famine, we should sedulously encourage the other forms of destruction which we compel nature to use. Instead of recommending cleanliness to the poor, we should encourage contrary habits. In our towns we should make the streets narrower, crowd more people into the houses, and court the return of the plague. In the country we should build our villages near stagnant pools, and particularly encourage settlements in all marshy and unwholesome situations. But above all we should reprobate specific remedies for ravaging diseases; and those benevolent, but much mistaken men, who have thought they were doing a service to mankind by projecting schemes for the total extirpation of particular disorders. If by these and similar means the annual mortality were increased from 1 in 36 or 40, to one in 18 or 20, we might probably every one of us marry at the age of puberty, and yet few be absolutely starved.

If however we all marry at this age and yet still continue our exertions to impede the operations of nature, we may rest assured that all our efforts will be vain. Nature will not, nor cannot, be defeated in her purposes. The necessary mortality must come in some form or other; and the extirpation of one disease will only be the signal for the birth of another perhaps more fatal. We cannot lower the waters of misery by pressing them down in different places, which must necessarily make them rise somewhere else; the only way in which we can hope to effect our purpose, is by drawing them off. To this course nature is constantly directing our attention by the chastisements which await a contrary conduct. These chastisements are more or less severe, in proportion to the degree in which her admonitions produce their intended effect. In this country at present these admonitions are by no means entirely neglected. The preventive check to population prevails to a considerable degree, and her chastisements are in consequence moderate: but if we were all to marry at the age of puberty they would be severe indeed. Political evils would probably be added to physical. A people goaded by constant distress, and visited by frequent returns of famine, could not be kept down but by a cruel despotism. We should approach to the state of the people in Egypt or Abyssinia; and I would ask whether in that case it is probable that we should be more virtuous?

Physicians have long remarked the great changes which take place in diseases; and that while some appear to yield to the efforts of human care and skill, others seem to become in proportion more malignant and fatal. Dr. William Heberden published not long since some valuable observations on this subject deduced from the London bills of mortality. In his preface, speaking of these bills, he says, "The gradual changes they exhibit in particular diseases correspond to the alterations, which in time are known to take place in the channels through which the great stream of mortality is constantly flowing." In the body of his work afterwards, speaking of some particular diseases, he observes with that candour which always distinguishes true science: "It is not easy to give a satisfactory reason for all the changes which may be observed to take place in the history of diseases. Nor is it any disgrace to physicians if their causes are often so gradual in their operation, or so subtle as to elude investigation."

I hope I shall not be accused of presumption in venturing to suggest that under certain circumstances such changes must take place; and perhaps without any alteration in those proximate causes which are usually looked to on these occasions. If this should appear to be true, it will not seem extraordinary that the most skilful and scientific physicians, whose business it is principally to investigate proximate causes, should sometimes search for these causes in vain.

In the country which keeps its population at a certain standard, if the average number of marriages and births be given, it is evident that the average number of deaths will also be given; and, to use Dr. Heberden's metaphor, the channels through which the great stream of mortality is constantly flowing, will always convey off a given quantity. Now if we stop up any of these channels it is perfectly clear that the stream of mortality must run with greater force through some of the other channels; that is, if we eradicate some diseases others will become proportionally more fatal. In this case the only distinguishable cause is the damming up a necessary outlet of mortality. Nature, in the attainment of her great purposes, seems always to seize upon the weakest part. If this part be made strong by human skill, she seizes upon the next weakest part, and so on in succession; not like a capricious deity, with an intention to sport with our sufferings and constantly to defeat our labours; but like a kind though sometimes severe instructor, with the intention of teaching us to make all parts strong, and to chase vice and misery from the earth. In avoiding one fault we are too apt to run into some other; but we always find Nature faithful to her great object at every false step we commit, ready to admonish us of our errors by the infliction of some physical or moral evil. If the prevalence of the preventive check to population in a sufficient degree were to remove many of those diseases which now afflict us, yet be accompanied by a considerable increase of the vice of promiscuous intercourse, it is probable that the disorders and unhappiness, the physical and moral evils arising from this vice would increase in strength and degree; and admonishing us severely of our error would point to the only line of conduct approved by nature, reason, and religion, abstinence from marriage till we can support our children, and chastity till that period arrives.

In the case just stated, in which the population and the number of marriages are supposed to be fixed, the necessity of a change in the mortality of some diseases from the diminution or extinction of others is capable of mathematical demonstration. The only obscurity which can possibly involve this subject, arises from taking into consideration the effect that might be produced by a diminution of mortality in increasing the population or in decreasing the number of marriages. That the removal of any of the particular causes of mortality can have no further effect upon population than the means of subsistence will allow, and that it has no certain and necessary influence on these means of subsistence, are facts of which the reader must be already convinced. Of its operation in tending to prevent marriage by diminishing the demand for fresh supplies of children I have no doubt; and there is reason to think that it had this effect in no inconsiderable degree on the extinction of the plague, which had so long and so dreadfully ravaged this country.

If on contemplating the increase of vice which might contingently follow an attempt to inculcate the duty of moral restraint, and the increase of misery that must necessarily follow the attempts to encourage marriage and population, we come to the conclusion not to interfere in any respect, but to leave every man to his own free choice and responsible only to God for the evil which he does in either way; this is all I contend for; I would on no account do more; but I contend that at present we are very far from doing this.

Among the lower classes of society, where the point is of the greatest importance, the poor-laws afford a direct, constant, and systematical encouragement to marriage by removing from each individual that heavy responsibility which he would incur by the laws of nature for bringing beings into the world which he could not support. Our private benevolence has the same direction as the poor-laws, and almost invariably tends to encourage marriage and to equalise as much as possible the circumstances of married and single men.

Among the higher classes of people the superior distinctions which married women receive, and the marked inattentions to which single women of advanced age are exposed, enable many men who are agreeable neither in mind nor person and are besides in the wane of life to choose a partner among the young and fair, instead of being confined as nature seems to dictate to persons of nearly their own age and accomplishments. It is scarcely to be doubted that the fear of being an old maid, and of that silly and unjust ridicule which folly sometimes attaches to this name, drives many women into the marriage union with men whom they dislike, or at best to whom they are perfectly indifferent. Such marriages must to every delicate mind appear little better than legal prostitutions, and they often burden the earth with unnecessary children, without compensating for it by an accession of happiness and virtue to the parties themselves.

Throughout all the ranks of society the prevailing opinions respecting the duty and obligation of marriage cannot but have a very powerful influence. The man who thinks that in going out of the world without leaving representatives behind him he shall have failed in an important duty to society, will be disposed to force rather than to repress his inclinations on this subject; and when his reason represents to him the difficulties attending a family he will endeavour not to attend to these suggestions, will still determine to venture, and will hope that in the discharge of what he conceives to be his duty he shall not be deserted by Providence.

In a civilised country such as England, where a taste for the decencies and comforts of life prevails among a very large class of people, it is not possible that the encouragements to marriage from positive institutions and prevailing opinions should entirely obscure the light of nature and reason on this subject; but still they contribute to make it comparatively weak and indistinct. And till this obscurity is removed, and the poor are undeceived with respect to the principal cause of their poverty, and taught to know that their happiness or misery must depend chiefly upon themselves, it cannot be said that with regard to the great question of marriage we leave every man to his own free and fair choice.

VI. Effects of the Knowledge of the Principal Cause of Poverty on Civil Liberty

It may appear, perhaps, that a doctrine which attributes the greatest part of the sufferings of the lower classes of society exclusively to themselves is unfavourable to the cause of liberty, as affording a tempting opportunity to governments of oppressing their subjects at pleasure and laying the whole blame on the laws of nature and the imprudence of the poor. We are not, however, to trust to first appearances; and I am strongly disposed to believe that those who will be at the pains to consider this subject deeply will be convinced that nothing would so powerfully contribute to the advancement of rational freedom as a thorough knowledge generally circulated of the principal cause of poverty, and that the ignorance of this cause, and the natural consequences of this ignorance, form at present one of the chief obstacles to its progress.

The pressure of distress on the lower classes of people, together with the habit of attributing this distress to their rulers, appears to me to be the rock of defence, the castle, the guardian spirit of despotism. It affords to the tyrant the fatal and unanswerable plea of necessity. It is the reason why every free government tends constantly to destruction, and that its appointed guardians become daily less jealous of the encroachments of power. It is the reason why so many noble efforts in the cause of freedom have failed, and why almost every revolution after long and painful sacrifices has terminated in a military despotism. While any dissatisfied man of talents has power to persuade the lower classes of people that all their poverty and distress arise solely from the iniquity of the government, though, perhaps, the greatest part of what they suffer is unconnected with this cause, it is evident that the seeds of fresh discontents and fresh revolutions are continually sowing. When an established government has been destroyed, finding that their poverty is not removed, their resentment naturally falls upon the successors to power; and when these have been immolated without producing the desired effect, other sacrifices are called for, and so on without end. Are we to be surprised that under such circumstances the majority of well-disposed people, finding that a government with proper restrictions is unable to support itself against the revolutionary spirit, and weary and exhausted with perpetual change to which they can see no end, should give up the struggle in despair, and throw themselves into the arms of the first power which can afford them protection against the horrors of anarchy?

A mob, which is generally the growth of a redundant population goaded by resentment for real sufferings, but totally ignorant of the quarter from which they originate, is of all monsters the most fatal to freedom. It fosters a prevailing tyranny, and engenders one where it was not; and though in its dreadful fits of resentment it appears occasionally to devour its unsightly offspring, yet no sooner is the horrid deed committed than, however unwilling it may be to propagate such a breed, it immediately groans with a new birth.

Of the tendency of mobs to produce tyranny we may not, perhaps, be long without an example in this country. As a friend to freedom, and naturally an enemy to large standing armies, it is with extreme reluctance that I am compelled to acknowledge that, had it not been for the great organised force in the country, the distresses of the people during the late scarcities [of 1800 and 1801], encouraged by the extreme ignorance and folly of many among the higher classes, might have driven them to commit the most dreadful outrages, and ultimately to involve the country in all the horrors of famine. Should such periods often recur (a recurrence which we have too much reason to apprehend from the present state of the country), the prospect which opens to our view is melancholy in the extreme. The English constitution will be seen hastening with rapid strides to the *Euthanasia* foretold by [David] Hume, unless its progress be interrupted by some popular commotion; and this alternative presents a picture still more appalling to the imagination. If political discontents were blended with the cries of hunger, and a revolution were to take place by the instrumentality of a mob clamouring for want of food, the consequences would be unceasing change and unceasing carnage, the bloody career of which nothing but the establishment of some complete despotism could arrest.

We can scarcely believe that the appointed guardians of British liberty should quietly have acquiesced in those gradual encroachments of power which have taken place of late years, but from the apprehension of these still more dreadful evils. Great as has been the influence of corruption, I cannot yet think so meanly of the country gentlemen of England, as to believe that they would thus have given up a part of their birthright of liberty, if they had not been actuated by a real and genuine fear that it was then in greater danger from the people than from the crown. They appeared to surrender themselves to government, on condition of being protected from the mob; but they never would have made this melancholy and disheartening surrender, if such a mob had not existed either in reality or in imagination. That the fears on this subject were artfully exaggerated and increased beyond the limits of just apprehension is undeniable; but I think it is also undeniable that the frequent declamations which were heard against the unjust institutions of society, and the delusive arguments on equality which were circulated among the lower classes, gave us just reason to suppose that if the *vox populi* had been allowed to speak, it would have appeared to be the voice of error and absurdity instead of the *vox Dei*.

To say that our conduct is not to be regulated by circumstances is to betray an ignorance of the most solid and incontrovertible principles of morality. Though the admission of this principle may sometimes afford a cloak to changes of opinion that do not result from the purest motives, yet the admission of a contrary principle would be productive of infinitely worse consequences. The phrase of "existing circumstances" has, I believe, not unfrequently created a smile in the English House of Commons, but the smile should have been reserved for the application of the phrase, and not have been excited by the phrase itself. A very frequent repetition of it has indeed of itself rather a suspicious air; and its application should always be watched with the most jealous and anxious attention; but no man ought to be judged *in limine* for saying that existing circumstances had obliged him to alter his opinions and conduct. The country gentlemen were perhaps too easily convinced that existing circumstances called upon them to give up some of the most valuable privileges of Englishmen; but as far as they were really convinced of this obligation, they acted consistently with the clearest rule of morality.

The degree of power to be given to the civil government and the measure of our submission to it, must be determined by general expediency; and, in judging of this expediency, every circumstance is to be taken into consideration, particularly the state of public opinion and the degree of ignorance and delusion prevailing among the common people. The patriot who might be called upon by the love of his country to join with heart and hand in a rising of the people for some specific attainable object of reform, if he knew that they were enlightened respecting their own situation and would stop short when they had attained their demand, would be called upon by the same motive to submit to very great oppression rather than give the slightest countenance to a popular tumult, the members of which, at least the greater number of them, were persuaded that the destruction of the Parliament, the Lord Mayor, and the monopolisers, would make bread cheap, and that a revolution would enable them all to support their families. In this case it is more the ignorance and delusion of the lower classes of the people that occasion the oppression, than the actual disposition of the government to tyranny. That there is, however, in all power a constant tendency to encroach is an incontrovertible truth, and cannot be too strongly inculcated. The checks which are necessary to secure the liberty of the subject will always in some degree embarrass and delay the operations of the executive government. The members of this government feeling these inconveniences while they are exerting themselves, as they conceive, in the service of their country, and conscious perhaps of no ill intention towards the people, will naturally be disposed on every occasion to demand the suspension or abolition of these checks; but if once the convenience of ministers be put in competition with the liberties of the people and we get into a habit of relying on fair assurances and personal character, instead of examining with the most scrupulous and jealous care the merits of each particular case, there is an end of British freedom. If we once admit the principle that the government must know better with regard to the quantity of power which it wants than we can possibly do with our limited means of information, and that therefore it is our duty to surrender up our private judgments, we may just as well at the same time surrender up the whole of our constitution. Government is a quarter in which liberty is not nor cannot be very faithfully preserved. If we are wanting to ourselves, and inattentive to our great interest in this respect, it is the height of folly and unreasonableness to expect that government will attend to them for us. Should the British constitution ultimately lapse into a despotism as has been prophesied, I shall think that the country gentlemen of England will have much more to answer for than the ministers.

To do the country gentlemen justice, however, I should readily acknowledge that in the partial desertion of their posts as guardians of British freedom, which has already taken place, they have been actuated more by fear than corruption. And the principal reason of this fear was, I conceive, the ignorance and delusions of the common people, and the prospective horrors which were contemplated if in such a state of mind they should by any revolutionary movement obtain an ascendant.

The circulation of [Thomas] Paine's *Rights of Man* it is supposed has done great mischief among the lower and middling classes of people in this country. This is probably true; but not because man is without rights or that these rights ought not to be known; but because Mr. Paine has fallen into some fundamental errors respecting the principles of government, and in many important points has shown himself totally unacquainted with the structure of society, and the different moral effects to be expected from the physical difference between this country and America. Mobs of the same description as those collections of people known by this name in Europe could not exist in America. The number of people without property is there, from the physical state of the country, comparatively small: and therefore the civil power, which is to protect property, cannot require the same degree of strength. Mr. Paine very justly observes that whatever the apparent cause of any riots may be, the real one is always want of happiness; but when he goes on to say it shows that something is wrong in the system of government that injures the felicity by which society is to be preserved, he falls into the common error of attributing all want of happiness to government. It is evident that this want of happiness might have existed, and from ignorance might have been the principal cause of the riots, and yet be almost wholly unconnected with any of the proceedings of government. The redundant population of an old state furnishes materials of unhappiness unknown to such a state as that of America; and if an attempt were to be made to remedy this unhappiness by distributing the produce of the taxes to the poorer classes of society, according to the plan proposed by Mr. Paine, the evil would be aggravated a hundredfold, and in a very short time no sum that the society could possibly raise would be adequate to the proposed object.

Nothing would so effectually counteract the mischiefs occasioned by Mr. Paine's *Rights of Man* as a general knowledge of the real rights of man. What these rights are it is not my business at present to explain; but there is one right which man has generally been thought to possess, which I am confident he neither does nor can possess—a right to subsistence when his labour will not fairly purchase it. Our laws indeed say that he has this right, and bind the society to furnish employment and food to those who cannot get them in the regular market; but in so doing they attempt to reverse the laws of nature, and it is in consequence to be expected not only that they should fail in their object, but that the poor, who were intended to be benefited, should suffer most cruelly from the inhuman deceit thus practised upon them.

The Abbé Raynal has said that *"Avant toutes les loix sociales l'homme avoit le droit de subsister."* He might with just as much propriety have said that before the institution of social laws every man had a right to live a hundred years. Undoubtedly he had then and has still a good right to live a hundred years, nay a thousand *if he can,* without interfering with the right of others to live; but the affair in both cases is principally an affair of power not of right. Social laws very greatly increase this power, by enabling a much greater number to subsist than could subsist without them, and so far very greatly enlarge *le droit de subsister;* but neither before nor after the institution of social laws could an unlimited number subsist; and before as well as since, he who ceased to have the power ceased to have the right.

If the great truths on these subjects were more generally circulated and the lower classes of people could be convinced that by the laws of nature, independently of any particular institutions except the great one of property, which is absolutely necessary in order to attain any considerable produce, no person has any claim of *right* on society for subsistence if his labour will not purchase it, the greatest part of the mischievous declamation on the unjust institutions of society would fall powerless to the ground. The poor are by no means inclined to be visionary. Their distresses are always real, though they are not attributed to the real causes. If these causes were properly explained to them, and they were taught to know what part of their present distress was attributable to government, and what part to causes totally unconnected with it, discontent and irritation among the lower classes of people would show themselves much less frequently than at present; and when they did show themselves would be much less to be dreaded. The efforts of turbulent and discontented men in the middle classes of society might safely be disregarded if the poor were so far enlightened respecting the real nature of their situation as to be aware that by aiding them in their schemes of renovation they would probably be promoting the ambitious views of others without in any respect benefiting themselves. The country gentlemen and men of property in England might securely return to a wholesome jealousy of the encroachments of power; and instead of daily sacrificing the liberties of the subject on the altar of public safety, might without any just apprehension from the people not only tread back their late steps, but firmly insist upon those gradual reforms which the lapse of time and the storms of the political world have rendered necessary to prevent the gradual destruction of the British constitution.

All improvements in governments must necessarily originate with persons of some education, and these will of course be found among the people of property. Whatever may be said of a few, it is impossible to suppose that the great mass of the people of property should be really interested in the abuses of government. They merely submit to them from the fear that an endeavour to remove them might be productive of greater evils. Could we but take away this fear, reform and improvement would proceed with as much facility as the removal of nuisances or the paving and lighting of the streets. In human life we are continually called upon to submit to a lesser evil in order to avoid a greater; and it is the part of a wise man to do this readily and cheerfully; but no wise man will submit to any evil if he can get rid of it without danger. Remove all apprehension from the tyranny or folly of the people, and the tyranny of government could not stand a moment. It would then appear in its proper deformity, without palliation, without pretext, without protector. Naturally feeble in itself, when it was once stripped naked and deprived of the support of public opinion and of the great plea of necessity, it would fall without a struggle. Its few interested defenders would hide their heads abashed, and would be ashamed any longer to support a cause for which no human ingenuity could invent a plausible argument.

The most successful supporters of tyranny are without doubt those general declaimers who attribute the distresses of the poor, and almost all the evils to which society is subject, to human institutions and the iniquity of governments. The falsity of these accusations and the dreadful consequences that would result from their being generally admitted and acted upon, make it absolutely necessary that they should at all events be resisted, not only on account of the immediate revolutionary horrors to be expected from a movement of the people acting under such impressions (a consideration which must at all times have very great weight), but also on account of the extreme probability that such a revolution would terminate in a much worse despotism than that which it had destroyed. On these grounds a genuine friend of freedom, a zealous advocate for the real rights of man, might be found among the defenders of a considerable degree of tyranny. A cause bad in itself might be supported by the good and the virtuous, merely because that which was opposed to it was much worse; and because it was absolutely necessary at the moment to make a choice between the two. Whatever therefore may be the intention of those indiscriminate accusations against governments, their real effect undoubtedly is to add a weight of talents and principles to the prevailing power which it never would have received otherwise.

It is a truth which I trust has been sufficiently proved in the course of this work, that under a government constructed upon the best and purest principles and executed by men of the highest talents and integrity, the most squalid poverty and wretchedness might universally prevail from an inattention to the prudential check to population. And as this cause of unhappiness has hitherto been so little understood that the efforts of society have always tended rather to aggravate than to lessen it, we have the strongest reasons for supposing that in all the governments with which we are acquainted a great part of the misery to be observed among the lower classes of the people arises from this cause.

The inference therefore which Mr. Paine and others have drawn against governments from the unhappiness of the people is palpably unfair; and before we give a sanction to such accusations it is a debt we owe to truth and justice to ascertain how much of this unhappiness arises from the principle of population, and how much is fairly to be attributed to government. When this distinction has been properly made, and all the vague, indefinite, and false accusations removed, government would remain, as it ought to be, clearly responsible for the rest; and the amount of this would still be such as to make the responsibility very considerable. Though government has but little power in the direct and immediate relief of poverty, yet its indirect influence on the prosperity of its subjects is striking and incontestable. And the reason is, that though it is comparatively impotent in its efforts to make the food of a country keep pace with an unrestricted increase of population, yet its influence is great in giving the best direction to those checks which in some form or other must necessarily take place. It has clearly appeared in the former part of this work that the most despotic and worst-governed countries, however low they might be in actual population, were uniformly the most populous in proportion to their means of subsistence, and the necessary effect of this state of things must of course be very low wages. In such countries the checks to population arise more from the sickness and mortality consequent on poverty than from the prudence and foresight which restrain the frequency and universality of early marriages. The checks are more of the positive and less of the preventive kind.

The first grand requisite to the growth of prudential habits is the perfect security of property, and the next perhaps is that respectability and importance which are given to the lower classes by equal laws and the possession of some influence in the framing of them. The more excellent therefore is the government, the more does it tend to generate that prudence and elevation of sentiment by which alone in the present state of our being poverty can be avoided.

It has been sometimes asserted that the only reason why it is advantageous that the people should have some share in the government is that a representation of the people tends best to secure the framing of good and equal laws, but that if the same object could be attained under a despotism the same advantage would accrue to the community. If, however, the representative system, by securing to the lower classes of society a more equal and liberal mode of treatment from their superiors, gives to each individual a greater personal respectability and a greater fear of personal degradation, it is evident that it will powerfully co-operate with the security of property in animating the exertions of industry and in generating habits of prudence, and thus more powerfully tend to increase the riches and prosperity of the lower classes of the community than if the same laws had existed under a despotism.

But though the tendency of a free constitution and a good government to diminish poverty be certain, yet their effect in this way must necessarily be indirect and slow, and very different from the direct and immediate relief which the lower classes of people are too frequently in the habit of looking forward to as the consequence of a revolution. This habit of expecting too much, and the irritation occasioned by disappointment, continually give a wrong direction to their efforts in favour of liberty, and constantly tend to defeat the accomplishment of those gradual reforms in government and that slow melioration of the condition of the lower classes of society which are really attainable. It is of the very highest importance therefore to know distinctly what government cannot do as well as what it can. If I were called upon to name the cause which in my conception had more than any other contributed to the very slow progress of freedom, so disheartening to every liberal mind, I should say that it was the confusion that had existed respecting the causes of the unhappiness and discontents which prevail in society, and the advantage which governments had been able to take and indeed had been compelled to take of this confusion to confirm and strengthen their power. I cannot help thinking therefore that a knowledge generally circulated that the principal cause of want and unhappiness is only indirectly connected with government and totally beyond its power directly to remove, and that it depends upon the conduct of the poor themselves, would, instead of giving any advantage to governments, give a great additional weight to the popular side of the question by removing the dangers with which from ignorance it is at present accompanied, and thus tend in a very powerful manner to promote the cause of rational freedom.

VII. Continuation of the Same Subject

The reasonings of the foregoing chapter have been strikingly confirmed by the events of the last two or three years [1815–17]. Perhaps there never was a period when more erroneous views were formed by the lower classes of society of the effects to be expected from reforms in the government when these erroneous views were more immediately founded on a total misapprehension of the principal cause of poverty, and when they more directly led to results unfavourable to liberty.

One of the main causes of complaint against the government has been that a considerable number of labourers, who are both able and willing to work, are wholly out of employment and unable consequently to command the necessaries of life. That this state of things is one of the most afflicting events that can occur in civilised life, that it is a natural and pardonable cause of discontent among the lower classes of society, and that every effort should be made by the higher classes to mitigate it, consistently with a proper care not to render it permanent, no man of humanity can doubt. But that such a state of things may occur in the best conducted and most economical government that ever existed is as certain as that governments have not the power of commanding with effect the resources of a country to be progressive when they are naturally stationary or declining.

It will be allowed that periods of prosperity may occur in any well-governed state, during which an extraordinary stimulus may be given to its wealth and population which cannot in its nature be permanent. If for instance new channels of trade are opened, new colonies are possessed, new inventions take place in machinery, and new and great improvements are made in agriculture, it is quite obvious that while the markets at home and abroad will readily take off at advantageous prices the increasing produce, there must be a rapid increase of capital and an unusual stimulus given to the population. On the other hand, if subsequently these channels of trade are either closed by accident or contracted by foreign competition; if colonies are lost, or the same produce is supplied from other quarters; if the markets, either from glut or competition, cease to extend with the extension of the new machinery; and if the improvements in agriculture from any cause whatever cease to be progressive, it is as obvious that just at the time when the stimulus to population has produced its greatest effect the means of employing and supporting this population may, in the natural course of things and without any fault whatever in the government, become deficient. This failure must unavoidably produce great distress among the labouring classes of society, but it is quite clear that no inference can be drawn from this distress that a radical change is required in the government, and the attempt to accomplish such a change might only aggravate the evil.

It has been supposed in this case that the government has in no respect by its conduct contributed to the pressure in question, a supposition which in practice perhaps will rarely be borne out by the fact. It is unquestionably in the power of a government to produce great distress by war and taxation, and it requires some skill to distinguish the distress which is the natural result of these causes from that which is occasioned in the way just described. In our own case unquestionably both descriptions of causes have combined, but the former in a greater degree than the latter. War and taxation, as far as they operate directly and simply, tend to destroy or retard the progress of capital, produce, and population; but during the late war these checks to prosperity have been much more than overbalanced by a combination of circumstances which has given an extraordinary stimulus to production: that for this overbalance of advantages the country cannot be considered as much indebted to the government is most certain. The government during the last twenty-five years has shown no very great love either of peace or liberty, and no particular economy in the use of the national resources. It has proceeded in a very straightforward manner to spend great sums in war and to raise them by very heavy taxes. It has no doubt done its part towards the dilapidation of the national resources. But still the broad fact must stare every impartial observer in the face that at the end of the war in 1814 the national resources were not dilapidated, and that not only were the wealth and population of the country considerably greater than they were at the commencement of the war, but that they had increased in the interval at a more rapid rate than was ever experienced before.

Perhaps this may justly be considered as one of the most extraordinary facts in history; and it certainly follows from it that the sufferings of the country since the peace have not been occasioned so much by the usual and most natural effects to be expected from war and taxation as by the sudden ceasing of an extraordinary stimulus to production, the distresses consequent upon which, though increased no doubt by the weight of taxation, do not essentially arise from it, and are not directly therefore and immediately to be relieved by its removal.

That the labouring classes of society should not be fully aware that the main causes of their distress are to a certain extent and for a certain time irremediable is natural enough, and that they should listen much more readily and willingly to those who confidently promise immediate relief rather than to those who can only tell them unpalatable truths is by no means surprising. But it must be allowed that full advantage has been taken by the popular orators and writers of a crisis which has given them so much power. Partly from ignorance and partly from design, everything that could tend to enlighten the labouring classes as to the real nature of their situation, and encourage them to bear an unavoidable pressure with patience, has been either sedulously kept out of their view or clamorously reprobated; and everything that could tend to deceive them, to aggravate and encourage their discontents, and to raise unreasonable and extravagant expectations as to the relief to be expected from reform, has been as sedulously brought forward. If under these circumstances the reforms proposed had been accomplished, it is impossible that the people should not have been most cruelly disappointed; and under a system of universal suffrage and annual parliaments, a general disappointment of the people would probably lead to every sort of experiment in government till the career of change was stopped by a military despotism. The warmest friends of genuine liberty might justly feel alarmed at such a prospect. To a cause conducted on such principles, and likely to be attended with such results, they could not of course consistently with their duty lend any assistance. And if with great difficulty, and against the sense of the great mass of petitioners, they were to effect a more moderate and more really useful reform, they could not but feel certain that the unavoidable disappointment of the people would be attributed to the half measures which had been pursued, and that they would be either forced to proceed to more radical changes or submit to a total loss of their influence and popularity by stopping short while the distresses of the people were unrelieved, their discontents unallayed, and the great *panacea* on which they had built their sanguine expectations untried.

These considerations have naturally paralysed the exertions of the best friends of liberty; and those salutary reforms which are acknowledged to be necessary in order to repair the breaches of time and improve the fabric of our constitution are thus rendered much more difficult and consequently much less probable.

But not only have the false expectations and extravagant demands suggested by the leaders of the people given an easy victory to government over every proposition for reform, whether violent or moderate, but they have furnished the most fatal instruments of offensive attack against the constitution itself. They are naturally calculated to excite some alarm and to check moderate reform; but alarm, when once excited, seldom knows where to stop, and the causes of it are particularly liable to be exaggerated. There is reason to believe that it has been under the influence of exaggerated statements, and of inferences drawn by exaggerated fears from these statements, that acts unfavourable to liberty have been passed without an adequate necessity. But the power of creating these exaggerated fears and of passing these acts has been unquestionably furnished by the extravagant expectations of the people. And it must be allowed that the present times furnish a very striking illustration of the doctrine that an ignorance of the principal cause of poverty is peculiarly unfavourable, and that a knowledge of it must be peculiarly favourable to the cause of civil liberty.

VIII. Plan of the Gradual Abolition of the Poor-Laws Proposed

If the principles in the preceding chapters should stand the test of examination, and we should ever feel the obligation of endeavouring to act upon them, the next inquiry would be in what way we ought practically to proceed. The first grand obstacle which presents itself in this country is the system of the poor-laws, which has been justly stated to be an evil, in comparison of which the national debt, with all its magnitude of terror, is of little moment. The rapidity with which the poor's rates have increased of late years presents us indeed with the prospect of such an extraordinary proportion of paupers in the society as would seem to be incredible in a nation flourishing in arts, agriculture, and commerce, and with a government which has generally been allowed to be the best that has hitherto stood the test of experience.

Greatly as we may be shocked at such a prospect, and ardently as we may wish to remove it, the evil is now so deeply seated, and the relief given by the poor-laws so widely extended, that no man of humanity could venture to propose their immediate abolition. To mitigate their effects, however, and stop their future increase, to which if left to continue upon their present plan we can see no probable termination, it has been proposed to fix the whole sum to be raised at its present rate, or any other that might be determined upon, and to make a law that on no account this sum should be exceeded. The objection to this plan is that a very large sum would be still to be raised and a great number of people to be supported, the consequence of which would be that the poor would not be easily able to distinguish the alteration that had been made. Each individual would think that he had as good a right to be supported when he was in want as any other person; and those who unfortunately chanced to be in distress when the fixed sum had been collected would think themselves particularly ill-used on being excluded from all assistance while so many others were enjoying this advantage. If the sum collected were divided among all that were in want, however their numbers might increase, though such a plan would not be so unfair with regard to those who became dependent after the sum had been fixed, it would undoubtedly be very hard upon those who had been in the habit of receiving a more liberal supply, and had done nothing to justify its being taken from them; and in both cases it would certainly be unjust in the society to undertake the support of the poor, and yet if their numbers increased to feed them so sparingly that they must necessarily die of hunger and disease.

I have reflected much on the subject of the poor-laws, and hope therefore that I shall be excused in venturing to suggest a mode of their gradual abolition, to which I confess that at present I can see no material objection. Of this indeed I feel nearly convinced, that should we ever become so fully sensible of the wide-spreading tyranny, dependence, indolence, and unhappiness which they create as seriously to make an effort to abolish them, we shall be compelled by a sense of justice to adopt the principle, if not the plan, which I shall mention. It seems impossible to get rid of so extensive a system of support, consistently with humanity, without applying ourselves directly to its vital principle, and endeavouring to counteract that deeply seated cause which occasions the rapid growth of all such establishments, and invariably renders them inadequate to their object.

As a previous step even to any considerable alteration in the present system, which would contract or stop the increase of the relief to be given, it appears to me that we are bound in justice and honour formally to disclaim the *right* of the poor to support.

To this end, I should propose a regulation to be made, declaring that no child born from any marriage taking place after the expiration of a year from the date of the law, and no illegitimate child born two years from the same date, should ever be entitled to parish assistance. And to give a more general knowledge of this law, and to enforce it more strongly on the minds of the lower classes of people, the clergyman of each parish should, after the publication of banns, read a short address, stating the strong obligation on every man to support his own children; the impropriety, and even immorality, of marrying without a prospect of being able to do this; the evils which had resulted to the poor themselves from the attempt which had been made to assist by public institutions in a duty which ought to be exclusively appropriated to parents, and the absolute necessity which had at length appeared of abandoning all such institutions on account of their producing effects totally opposite to those which were intended.

This would operate as a fair, distinct, and precise notice, which no man could well mistake, and without pressing hard on any particular individuals would at once throw off the rising generation from that miserable and helpless dependence upon the government and the rich, the moral as well as physical consequences of which are almost incalculable.

After the public notice which I have proposed had been given, and the system of poor-laws had ceased with regard to the rising generation, if any man choose to marry without a prospect of being able to support a family he should have the most perfect liberty so to do. Though to marry in this case is in my opinion clearly an immoral act, yet it is not one which society can justly take upon itself to prevent or punish; because the punishment provided for it by the laws of nature falls directly and most severely upon the individual who commits the act, and through him, only more remotely and feebly, on the society. When nature will govern and punish for us, it is a very miserable ambition to wish to snatch the rod from her hands, and draw upon ourselves the odium of executioner. To the punishment therefore of nature he should be left, the punishment of want. He has erred in the face of a most clear and precise warning, and can have no just reason to complain of any person but himself when he feels the consequences of his error. All parish assistance should be denied him, and he should be left to the uncertain support of private charity. He should be taught to know that the laws of nature, which are the laws of God, had doomed him and his family to suffer for disobeying their repeated admonitions; that he had no claim of *right* on society for the smallest portion of food beyond that which his labour would fairly purchase, and that if he and his family were saved from feeling the natural consequences of his imprudence, he would owe it to the pity of some kind benefactor, to whom therefore he ought to be bound by the strongest ties of gratitude.

If the plan which I have proposed were adopted, the poor's rates in a few years would begin very rapidly to decrease, and in no great length of time would be completely extinguished; and yet as far as it appears to me at present no individual would be either deceived or injured, and consequently no person could have a just right to complain.

The abolition of the poor-laws however is not of itself sufficient; and the obvious answer to those who lay too much stress on this system is, to desire them to look at the state of the poor in some other countries where such laws do not prevail, and to compare it with their condition in England. But this comparison it must be acknowledged is in many respects unfair; and would by no means decide the question of the utility or inutility of such a system. England possesses very great natural and political advantages, in which perhaps the countries that we should in this case compare with her, would be found to be palpably deficient. The nature of her soil and climate is such, that those almost universal failures in the crops of grain which are known in some countries never occur in England. Her insular situation and extended commerce are peculiarly favourable for importation. Her numerous manufactures employ nearly all the hands that are not engaged in agriculture, and afford the means of a regular distribution of the annual produce of the land and labour to the whole of her inhabitants. But above all, throughout a very large class of people, a decided taste for the conveniences and comforts of life, a strong desire of bettering their condition (that master spring of public prosperity), and in consequence a most laudable spirit of industry and foresight, are observed to prevail. These dispositions, so contrary to the hopeless indolence remarked in despotic countries, are generated by the constitution of the English government and the excellence of its laws, which secure to every individual the produce of his industry. When therefore on a comparison with other countries England appears to have the advantage in the state of her poor, the superiority is entirely to be attributed to these favourable circumstances and not to the poor-laws. A woman with one bad feature may greatly excel in beauty some other who may have this individual feature tolerably good, but it would be rather strange to assert in consequence that the superior beauty of the former was occasioned by this particular deformity. The poor-laws have constantly tended to counteract the natural and acquired advantages of this country. Fortunately these disadvantages have been so considerable that though weakened they could not be overcome, and to these advantages, together with the checks to marriage which the laws themselves create, it is owing that England has been able to bear up so long against this pernicious system. Probably there is not any other country in the world, except perhaps Holland before the revolution, which could have acted upon it so completely for the same period of time without utter ruin.

It has been proposed by some to establish poor-laws in Ireland, but from the depressed state of the common people there is little reason to doubt that, on the establishment of such laws, the whole of the landed property would very soon be absorbed or the system be given up in despair.

In Sweden, from the dearths which are not unfrequent owing to the general failure of crops in an unpropitious climate and the impossibility of great importations in a poor country, an attempt to establish a system of parochial relief such as that in England (if it were not speedily abandoned from the physical impossibility of executing it) would level the property of the kingdom from one end to the other, and convulse the social system in such a manner as absolutely to prevent it from recovering its former state on the return of plenty.

Even in France, with all her advantages of situation and climate, the tendency to population is so great and the want of foresight among the lower classes of the people so remarkable, that if poor-laws were established the landed property would soon sink under the burden, and the wretchedness of the people at the same time be increased. On these considerations the committee *de Mendicité,* at the beginning of the revolution, very properly and judiciously rejected the establishment of such a system which had been proposed.

The exception of Holland, if it were an exception, would arise from very particular circumstances—her extensive foreign trade and her numerous colonial emigrations, compared with the smallness of her territory, together with the extreme unhealthiness of a great part of the country, which occasions a much greater average mortality than is common in other states. These, I conceive, were the unobserved causes which principally contributed to render Holland so famous for the management of her poor, and able to employ and support all who applied for relief.

No part of Germany is sufficiently rich to support an extensive system of parochial relief, but I am inclined to think that from the absence of it the lower classes of the people, in some parts of Germany, are in a better situation than those of the same class in England. In Switzerland for the same reason their condition before the late troubles was perhaps universally superior; and in a journey through the duchies of Holstein and Sleswick belonging to Denmark, the houses of the lower classes of people appeared to me to be neater and better, and in general there were fewer indications of poverty and wretchedness among them, than among the same ranks in this country.

Even in Norway, notwithstanding the disadvantage of a severe and uncertain climate, from the little that I saw in a few weeks' residence in the country and the information that I could collect from others, I am inclined to think that the poor are on the average better off than in England. Their houses and clothing are often superior, and though they have no white bread they have much more meat, fish, and milk than our labourers, and I particularly remarked that the farmers' boys were much stouter and healthier-looking lads than those of the same description in England. This degree of happiness, superior to what could be expected from the soil and climate, arises almost exclusively from the degree in which the preventive check to population operates. The establishment of a system of poor-laws, which would destroy this check, would at once sink the lower classes of the people into a state of the most miserable poverty and wretchedness, would diminish their industry and consequently the produce of the land and labour of the country, would weaken the resources of ingenuity in times of scarcity, and ultimately involve the country in all the horrors of continual famines.

If, as in Ireland, Spain, and many countries of the more southern climates, the people are in so degraded a state as to propagate their species without regard to consequences, it matters little whether they have poor-laws or not. Misery in all its various forms must be the predominant check to their increase. Poor-laws indeed will always tend to aggravate the evil by diminishing the general resources of the country, and in such a state of things can exist only for a very short time; but with or without them no stretch of human ingenuity and exertion can rescue the people from the most extreme poverty and wretchedness.

IX. Of the Modes of Correcting the Prevailing Opinions on Population

It is not enough to abolish all the positive institutions which encourage population, but we must endeavour at the same time to correct the prevailing opinions which have the same or perhaps even a more powerful effect. This must necessarily be a work of time, and can only be done by circulating juster notions on these subjects in writings and conversation, and by endeavouring to impress as strongly as possible on the public mind that it is not the duty of man simply to propagate his species but to propagate virtue and happiness, and that if he has not a tolerably fair prospect of doing this he is by no means called upon to leave descendants.

Among the higher ranks of society we have not much reason to apprehend the too great frequency of marriage. Though the circulation of juster notions on this subject might even in this part of the community do much good and prevent many unhappy marriages, yet whether we make particular exertions for this purpose or not we may rest assured that the degree of proper pride and spirit of independence, almost invariably connected with education and a certain rank in life, will secure the operation of the prudential check to marriage to a considerable extent. All that the society can reasonably require of its members is that they should not have families without being able to support them. This may be fairly enjoined as a positive duty. Every restraint beyond this must be considered as a matter of choice and taste; but from what we already know of the habits which prevail among the higher ranks of life we have reason to think that little more is wanted to attain the object required than to award a greater degree of respect and of personal liberty to single women and to place them nearer upon a level with married women,—a change which, independently of any particular purpose in view, the plainest principles of equity seem to demand.

If among the higher classes of society the object of securing the operation of the prudential check to marriage to a sufficient degree appears to be attainable without much difficulty, the obvious mode of proceeding with the lower classes of society, where the point is of the principal importance, is to endeavour to infuse into them a portion of that knowledge and foresight which so much facilitates the attainment of this object in the educated part of the community.

The fairest chance of accomplishing this end would probably be by the establishment of a system of parochial education upon a plan similar to that proposed by Adam Smith [in the *Wealth of Nations*]. In addition to the usual subjects of instruction and those which he has mentioned, I should be disposed to lay considerable stress on the frequent explanation of the real state of the lower classes of society as affected by the principle of population, and their consequent dependence on themselves for the chief part of their happiness or misery. It would be by no means necessary or proper in these explanations to underrate in the smallest degree the desirableness of marriage. It should always be represented as what it really is, a state peculiarly suited to the nature of man, and calculated greatly to advance his happiness and remove the temptations to vice; but like property or any other desirable object its advantages should be shown to be unattainable except under certain conditions. And a strong conviction in a young man of the great desirableness of marriage, with a conviction at the same time that the power of supporting a family was the only condition which would enable him really to enjoy its blessings, would be the most effectual motive imaginable to industry and sobriety before marriage, and would powerfully urge him to save that superfluity of income which single labourers necessarily possess for the accomplishment of a rational and desirable object instead of dissipating it as is now usually done in idleness and vice.

If in the course of time a few of the simplest principles of political economy could be added to the instructions given in these schools the benefit to society would be almost incalculable. In some conversations with labouring men during the late scarcities, I confess that I was to the last degree disheartened at observing their inveterate prejudices on the subject of grain, and I felt very strongly the almost absolute incompatibility of a government really free with such a degree of ignorance. The delusions are of such a nature that if acted upon they must at all events be repressed by force, and it is extremely difficult to give such a power to the government as will be sufficient at all times for this purpose without the risk of its being employed improperly and endangering the liberty of the subject.

We have lavished immense sums on the poor, which we have every reason to think have constantly tended to aggravate their misery. But in their education and in the circulation of those important political truths that most nearly concern them, which are perhaps the only means in our power of really raising their condition, and of making them happier men and more peaceable subjects, we have been miserably deficient.

The principal argument which I have heard advanced against a system of national education in England is that the common people would be put in a capacity to read such works as those of Paine, and that the consequences would probably be fatal to government. But on this subject I agree most cordially with Adam Smith in thinking that an instructed and well-informed people would be much less likely to be led away by inflammatory writings, and much better able to detect the false declamation of interested and ambitious demagogues than an ignorant people. One or two readers in a parish are sufficient to circulate any quantity of sedition; and if these be gained to the democratic side, they will probably have the power of doing much more mischief by selecting the passages best suited to their hearers, and choosing the moments when their oratory is likely to have the most effect than if each individual in the parish had been in a capacity to read and judge of the whole work himself; and at the same time to read and judge of the opposing arguments which we may suppose would also reach him.

But in addition to this a double weight would undoubtedly be added to the observation of Adam Smith if these schools were made the means of instructing the people in the real nature of their situation; if they were taught what is really true, that without an increase of their own industry and prudence no change of government could essentially better their condition; that though they might get rid of some particular grievance, yet in the great point of supporting their families they would be but little or perhaps not at all benefited; that a revolution would not alter in their favour the proportion of the supply of labour to the demand, or the quantity of food to the number of the consumers; and that if the supply of labour were greater than the demand, and the demand for food greater than the supply, they might suffer the utmost severity of want under the freest, the most perfect, and best executed government that the human imagination could conceive.

A knowledge of these truths so obviously tends to promote peace and quietness, to weaken the effect of inflammatory writings, and to prevent all unreasonable and ill-directed opposition to the constituted authorities, that those who would still object to the instruction of the people may fairly be suspected of a wish to encourage their ignorance as a pretext for tyranny, and an opportunity of increasing the power and the influence of the executive government.

Besides explaining the real situation of the lower classes of society as depending principally upon themselves for their happiness or misery, the parochial schools would, by early instruction and the judicious distribution of rewards, have the fairest chance of training up the rising generation in habits of sobriety, industry, independence, and prudence, and in a proper discharge of their religious duties, which would raise them from their present degraded state, and approximate them in some degree to the middle classes of society, whose habits generally speaking are certainly superior.

In most countries, among the lower classes of people, there appears to be something like a standard of wretchedness, a point below which they will not continue to marry and propagate their species. This standard is different in different countries, and is formed by various concurring circumstances of soil, climate, government, degree of knowledge, civilisation, &c. The principal circumstances which contribute to raise it are liberty, security of property, the diffusion of knowledge, and a taste for the conveniences and the comforts of life. Those which contribute principally to lower it are despotism and ignorance.

In an attempt to better the condition of the labouring classes of society our object should be to raise this standard as high as possible by cultivating a spirit of independence, a decent pride, and a taste for cleanliness and comfort. The effect of a good government in increasing the prudential habits and personal respectability of the lower classes of society has already been insisted on; but certainly this effect will always be incomplete without a good system of education; and indeed it may be said that no government can approach to perfection that does not provide for the instruction of the people. The benefits derived from education are among those which may be enjoyed without restriction of numbers; and as it is in the power of governments to confer these benefits, it is undoubtedly their duty to do it.

X. Of the Direction of Our Charity

An important and interesting inquiry yet remains, relating to the mode of directing our private charity, so as not to interfere with the great object in view, of meliorating the condition of the labouring classes of people by preventing the population from pressing too hard against the limits of the means of subsistence.

The emotion which prompts us to relieve our fellow creatures in distress is like all our other natural passions general, and in some degree indiscriminate and blind. Our feelings of compassion may be worked up to a higher pitch by a well-wrought scene in a play or a fictitious tale in a novel than by almost any events in real life; and if among ten petitioners we were to listen only to the first impulses of our feelings without making further inquiries we should undoubtedly give our assistance to the best actor of the party. It is evident therefore that the impulse of benevolence, like the impulses of love, of anger, of ambition, the desire of eating and drinking, or any other of our natural propensities, must be regulated by experience and frequently brought to the test of utility, or it will defeat its intended purpose.

The apparent object of the passion between the sexes is the continuation of the species, and the formation of such an intimate union of views and interests between two persons as will best promote their happiness, and at the same time secure the proper degree of attention to the helplessness of infancy and the education of the rising generation; but if every man were to obey at all times the impulses of nature in the gratification of this passion without regard to consequences, the principal part of these important objects would not be attained, and even the continuation of the species might be defeated by a promiscuous intercourse.

The apparent end of the impulse of benevolence is to draw the whole human race together, but more particularly that part of it which is of our own nation and kindred, in the bonds of brotherly love, and by giving men an interest in the happiness and misery of their fellow creatures, to prompt them as they have power to mitigate the partial evils arising from general laws, and thus to increase the sum of human happiness; but if our benevolence be indiscriminate, and the degree of apparent distress be made the sole measure of our liberality, it is evident that it will be exercised almost exclusively upon common beggars, while modest, unobtrusive merit, struggling with unavoidable difficulties, yet still maintaining some slight appearances of decency and cleanliness, will be totally neglected. We shall raise the worthless above the worthy, we shall encourage indolence and check industry, and in the most marked manner subtract from the sum of human happiness.

Our experience has indeed informed us that the impulse of benevolence is not so strong as the passion between the sexes, and that generally speaking there is much less danger to be apprehended from the indulgence of the former than of the latter: but independently of this experience and of the moral codes founded upon it, we should be as much justified in a general indulgence of the former passion as in following indiscriminately every impulse of our benevolence. They are both natural passions excited by their appropriate objects, and to the gratification of which we are prompted by the pleasurable sensations which accompany them. As animals, or till we know their consequences, our only business is to follow these dictates of nature; but as reasonable beings we are under the strongest obligations to attend to their consequences; and if they be evil to ourselves or others, we may justly consider it as an indication that such a mode of indulging these passions is not suited to our state or conformable to the will of God. As moral agents therefore it is clearly our duty to restrain their indulgence in these particular directions; and by thus carefully examining the consequences of our natural passions, and frequently bringing them to the test of utility, gradually to acquire a habit of gratifying them only in that way which, being unattended with evil, will clearly add to the sum of human happiness and fulfil the apparent purpose of the Creator.

Though utility therefore can never be the immediate excitement to the gratification of any passion, it is the test by which alone we can know, independently of the revealed will of God, whether it ought or ought not to be indulged, and is therefore the surest criterion of moral rules which can be collected from the light of nature. All the moral codes which have inculcated the subjection of the passions to reason have been as I conceive really built upon this foundation, whether the promulgators of them were aware of it or not.

I remind the reader of these truths in order to apply them to the habitual direction of our charity; and if we keep the criterion of utility constantly in view, we may find ample room for the exercise of our benevolence without interfering with the great purpose which we have to accomplish.

One of the most valuable parts of charity is its effect upon the giver. It is more blessed to give than to receive. Supposing it to be allowed that the exercise of our benevolence in acts of charity is not upon the whole really beneficial to the poor, yet we could never sanction any endeavour to extinguish an impulse, the proper gratification of which has so evident a tendency to purify and exalt the human mind. But it is particularly satisfactory and pleasing to find that the mode of exercising our charity, which when brought to the test of utility will appear to be most beneficial to the poor, is precisely that which will have the best and most improving effect on the mind of the donor.

The quality of charity, like that of mercy,

> *Is not strained;*
> *It droppeth as the gentle rain from Heav'n*
> *Upon the earth beneath.*

The immense sums distributed to the poor in this country by the parochial laws are improperly called charity. They want its most distinguishing attribute; and as might be expected from an attempt to force that which loses its essence the moment it ceases to be voluntary, their effects upon those from whom they are collected are as prejudicial as on those to whom they are distributed. On the side of the receivers of this miscalled charity, instead of real relief, we find accumulated distress and more extended poverty; on the side of the givers, instead of pleasurable sensations, unceasing discontent and irritation.

In the great charitable institutions supported by voluntary contributions, some of which are certainly of a prejudicial tendency, the subscriptions I am inclined to fear are sometimes given grudgingly, and rather because they are expected by the world from certain stations and certain fortunes than because they are prompted by motives of genuine benevolence; and as the greater part of the subscribers do not interest themselves in the management of the funds or in the fate of the particular objects relieved, it is not to be expected that this kind of charity should have any strikingly beneficial influence on the minds of the majority who exercise it.

Even in the relief of common beggars we shall find that we are often as much influenced by the desire of getting rid of the importunities of a disgusting object as by the pleasure of relieving it. We wish that it had not fallen in our way rather than rejoice in the opportunity given us of assisting a fellow creature. We feel a painful emotion at the sight of so much apparent misery, but the pittance we give does not relieve it. We know that it is totally inadequate to produce any essential effect. We know besides that we shall be addressed in the same manner at the corner of the next street, and we know that we are liable to the grossest impositions. We hurry therefore sometimes by such objects, and shut our ears to their importunate demands. We give no more than we can help giving without doing actual violence to our feelings. Our charity is in some degree forced, and like forced charity it leaves no satisfactory impression on the mind, and cannot therefore have any very beneficial and improving effect on the heart and affections.

But it is far otherwise with that voluntary and active charity which makes itself acquainted with the objects which it relieves; which seems to feel and to be proud of the bond that unites the rich with the poor; which enters into their houses, informs itself not only of their wants but of their habits and dispositions, checks the hopes of clamorous and obtrusive poverty with no other recommendation but rags, and encourages with adequate relief the silent and retiring sufferer labouring under unmerited difficulties. This mode of exercising our charity presents a very different picture from that of any other; and its contrast with the common mode of parish relief cannot be better described than in the words of Mr. [Joseph] Townsend in the conclusion of his admirable *Dissertation on the Poor-laws:*—"Nothing in nature can be more disgusting than a parish pay table, attendant upon which, in the same objects of misery, are too often found combined snuff, gin, rags, vermin, insolence, and abusive language; nor in nature can anything be more beautiful than the mild complacency of benevolence hastening to the humble cottage to relieve the wants of industry and virtue, to feed the hungry, to clothe the naked, and to soothe the sorrows of the widow with her tender orphans; nothing can be more pleasing unless it be their sparkling eyes, their bursting tears, and their uplifted hands, the artless expressions of unfeigned gratitude for unexpected favours. Such scenes will frequently occur whenever men shall have power to dispose of their own property."

I conceive it to be almost impossible that any person could be much engaged in such scenes without daily making advances in virtue. No exercise of our affections can have a more evident tendency to purify and exalt the human mind. It is almost exclusively this species of charity that blesseth him that gives; and in a general view it is almost exclusively this species of charity which blesseth him that takes; at least it may be asserted that there are but few other modes of exercising our charity, in which large sums can be distributed, without a greater chance of producing evil than good.

The discretionary power of giving or withholding relief, which is to a certain extent vested in parish officers and justices, is of a very different nature and will have a very different effect from the discrimination which may be exercised by voluntary charity. Every man in this country under certain circumstances is entitled by law to parish assistance; and unless his disqualification is clearly proved, has a right to complain if it be withheld. The inquiries necessary to settle this point, and the extent of the relief to be granted, too often produce evasion and lying on the part of the petitioner, and afford an opening to partiality and oppression in the overseer. If the proposed relief be given, it is of course received with unthankfulness; and if it be denied the party generally thinks himself severely aggrieved and feels resentment and indignation at his treatment.

In the distribution of voluntary charity nothing of this kind can take place. The person who receives it is made the proper subject of the pleasurable sensation of gratitude; and those who do not receive it cannot possibly conceive themselves in the slightest degree injured. Every man has a right to do what he will with his own, and cannot in justice be called upon to render a reason why he gives in the one case and abstains from it in the other. This kind of despotic power, essential to voluntary charity, gives the greatest facility to the selection of worthy objects of relief without being accompanied by any ill consequences; and has further a most beneficial effect from the degree of uncertainty which must necessarily be attached to it. It is in the highest degree important to the general happiness of the poor that no man should look to charity as a fund on which he may confidently depend. He should be taught that his own exertions, his own industry and foresight, are his only just grounds of dependence; that if these fail assistance in his distresses can only be the subject of rational hope; and that even the foundation of this hope will depend in a considerable degree on his own good conduct, and the consciousness that he has not involved himself in these difficulties by his indolence or imprudence.

That in the distribution of our charity we are under a strong moral obligation to inculcate this lesson on the poor by a proper discrimination is a truth of which I cannot feel a doubt. If all could be completely relieved, and poverty banished from the country, even at the expense of three fourths of the fortunes of the rich, I would be the last person to say a single syllable against relieving all, and making the degree of distress alone the measure of our bounty. But as experience has proved, I believe without a single exception, that poverty and misery have always increased in proportion to the quantity of indiscriminate charity, are we not bound to infer, reasoning as we usually do from the laws of nature, that it is an intimation that such a mode of distribution is not the proper office of benevolence?

The laws of nature say with St. Paul, "If a man will not work, neither shall he eat." They also say that he is not rashly to trust to Providence. They appear indeed to be constant and uniform for the express purpose of telling him what he is to trust to, and that if he marry without a reasonable prospect of supporting a family he must expect to suffer want. These intimations appear from the constitution of human nature to be absolutely necessary and to have a strikingly beneficial tendency. If in the direction either of our public or our private charity we say that though a man will not work yet he shall eat; and though he marry without being able to support a family, yet his family shall be supported; it is evident that we do not merely endeavour to mitigate the partial evils arising from general laws, but *regularly* and *systematically* to counteract the obviously beneficial effects of these general laws themselves. And we cannot easily conceive that the Deity should implant any passion in the human breast for such a purpose.

In the great course of human events, the best-founded expectations will sometimes be disappointed; and industry, prudence, and virtue not only fail of their just reward but be involved in unmerited calamities. Those who are thus suffering in spite of the best-directed endeavours to avoid it, and from causes which they could not be expected to foresee, are the genuine objects of charity. In relieving these we exercise the appropriate office of benevolence, that of mitigating the partial evils arising from general laws; and in this direction of our charity therefore we need not apprehend any ill consequences. Such objects ought to be relieved, according to our means, liberally and adequately, even though the worthless were in much more severe distress.

When indeed this first claim on our benevolence was satisfied, we might then turn our attention to the idle and improvident; but the interests of human happiness most clearly require that the relief which we afford them should not be abundant. We may perhaps take upon ourselves with great caution to mitigate the punishments which they are suffering from the laws of nature, but on no account to remove them entirely. They are deservedly at the bottom in the scale of society; and if we raise them from this situation, we not only palpably defeat the end of benevolence, but commit a most glaring injustice to those who are above them. They should on no account be enabled to command so much of the necessaries of life as can be obtained by the wages of common labour.

It is evident that these reasonings do not apply to those cases of urgent distress arising from disastrous accidents, unconnected with habits of indolence and improvidence. If a man break a leg or an arm, we are not to stop to inquire into his moral character before we lend him our assistance; but in this case we are perfectly consistent, and the touchstone of utility completely justifies our conduct. By affording the most indiscriminate assistance in this way we are in little danger of encouraging people to break their arms and legs. According to the touchstone of utility, the high approbation which Christ gave to the conduct of the good Samaritan, who followed the immediate impulse of his benevolence in relieving a stranger in the urgent distress of an accident, does not in the smallest degree contradict the expression of St. Paul, "If a man will not work, neither shall he eat."

We are not, however, in any case to lose a present opportunity of doing good from the mere supposition that we may meet possibly with a worthier object. In all doubtful cases it may safely be laid down as our duty to follow the natural impulse of our benevolence; but when in fulfilling our obligations as reasonable beings to attend to the consequences of our actions, we have from our own experience and that of others drawn the conclusion that the exercise of our benevolence in one mode is prejudicial and in another is beneficial in its effects, we are certainly bound as moral agents to check our natural propensities in the one direction, and to encourage them and acquire the habits of exercising them in the other.

XI. Of Our Rational Expectations Respecting the Future Improvement of Society

In taking a general and concluding view of our rational expectations respecting the mitigation of the evils arising from the principle of population, it may be observed that though the increase of population in a geometrical ratio be incontrovertible, and the period of doubling when unchecked has been uniformly stated in this work rather below than above the truth; yet there are some natural consequences of the progress of society and civilisation, which necessarily repress its full effects. These are more particularly great towns and manufactures, in which we can scarcely hope, and certainly not expect to see any very material change. It is undoubtedly our duty and in every point of view highly desirable, to make towns and manufacturing employments as little injurious as possible to the duration of human life; but after all our efforts it is probable that they will always remain less healthy than country situations and country employments, and consequently operating as positive checks will diminish in some degree the necessity of the preventive check.

In every old state it is observed that a considerable number of grown-up people remain for a time unmarried. The duty of practising the common and acknowledged rules of morality during this period has never been controverted in theory, however it may have been opposed in practice. This branch of the duty of moral restraint has scarcely been touched by the reasonings of this work. It rests on the same foundation as before, neither stronger nor weaker. And knowing how incompletely this duty has hitherto been fulfilled, it would certainly be visionary to expect that in future it would be completely fulfilled.

The part which has been affected by the reasonings of this work is not therefore that which relates to our conduct during the period of celibacy, but to the duty of extending this period till we have a prospect of being able to maintain our children. And it is by no means visionary to indulge a hope of some favourable change in this respect; because it is found by experience that the prevalence of this kind of prudential restraint is extremely different in different countries, and in the same countries at different periods.

It cannot be doubted that throughout Europe in general, and most particularly in the northern states, a decided change has taken place in the operation of prudential restraint, since the prevalence of those warlike and enterprising habits which destroyed so many people. In later times the gradual diminution and almost total extinction of the plagues, which so frequently visited Europe in the seventeenth and beginning of the eighteenth centuries, produced a change of the same kind. And in this country it is not to be doubted that the proportion of marriages has become smaller since the improvement of our towns, the less frequent returns of epidemics, and the adoption of habits of greater cleanliness. During the late scarcities it appears that the number of marriages diminished; and the same motives which prevented many people from marrying during such a period, would operate precisely in the same way, if in future the additional number of children reared to manhood from the introduction of the cowpox, were to be such as to crowd all employments, lower the price of labour, and make it more difficult to support a family.

Universally, the practice of mankind on the subject of marriage has been much superior to their theories; and however frequent may have been the declamations on the duty of entering into this state, and the advantage of early unions to prevent vice, each individual has practically found it necessary to consider of the means of supporting a family before he ventured to take so important a step. That great *vis medicatrix reipublicæ,* the desire of bettering our condition, and the fear of making it worse, has been constantly in action, and has been constantly directing people into the right road in spite of all the declamations which tended to lead them aside. Owing to this powerful spring of health in every state, which is nothing more than an inference from the general course of the laws of nature irresistibly forced on each man's attention, the prudential check to marriage has increased in Europe; and it cannot be unreasonable to conclude that it will still make further advances. If this take place without any marked and decided increase of a vicious intercourse with the sex, the happiness of society will evidently be promoted by it; and with regard to the danger of such increase, it is consolatory to remark that those countries in Europe where marriages are the latest or least frequent, are by no means particularly distinguished by vices of this kind. It has appeared that Norway, Switzerland, England, and Scotland, are above all the rest in the prevalence of the preventive check; and though I do not mean to insist particularly on the virtuous habits of these countries, yet I think that no person would select them as the countries most marked for profligacy of manners. Indeed from the little that I know of the continent, I should have been inclined to select them as most distinguished for contrary habits, and as rather above than below their neighbours in the chastity of their women, and consequently in the virtuous habits of their men. Experience therefore seems to teach us that it is possible for moral and physical causes to counteract the effects that might at first be expected from an increase of the check to marriage; but allowing all the weight to these effects which is in any degree probable, it may be safely asserted that the diminution of the vices arising from indigence would fully counterbalance them; and that all the advantages of diminished mortality and superior comforts, which would certainly result from an increase of the preventive check, may be placed entirely on the side of the gains to the cause of happiness and virtue.

It is less the object of the present work to propose new plans of improving society than to inculcate the necessity of resting contented with that mode of improvement which already has in part been enacted upon as dictated by the course of nature, and of not obstructing the advances which would otherwise be made in this way.

It would be undoubtedly highly advantageous that all our positive institutions, and the whole tenor of our conduct to the poor, should be such as actively to co-operate with that lesson of prudence inculcated by the common course of human events; and if we take upon ourselves sometimes to mitigate the natural punishments of imprudence, that we could balance it by increasing the rewards of an opposite conduct. But much would be done if merely the institutions which directly tend to encourage marriage were gradually changed and we ceased to circulate opinions and inculcate doctrines which positively counteract the lessons of nature.

The limited good which it is sometimes in our power to effect is often lost by attempting too much, and by making the adoption of some particular plan essentially necessary even to a partial degree of success. In the practical application of the reasonings of this work I hope that I have avoided this error. I wish to press on the recollection of the reader that though I may have given some new views of old facts, and may have indulged in the contemplation of a considerable degree of *possible* improvement that I might not shut out that prime cheerer hope, yet in my expectations of probable improvement and in suggesting the means of accomplishing it I have been very cautious. The gradual abolition of the poor-laws has already often been proposed in consequence of the practical evils which have been found to flow from them, and the danger of their becoming a weight absolutely intolerable on the landed property of the kingdom. The establishment of a more extensive system of national education has neither the advantage of novelty with some nor its disadvantages with others to recommend it. The practical good effects of education have long been experienced in Scotland, and almost every person who has been placed in a situation to judge has given his testimony that education appears to have a considerable effect in the prevention of crimes, and the promotion of industry, morality, and regular conduct. Yet these are the only plans which have been offered, and though the adoption of them in the modes suggested would very powerfully contribute to forward the object of this work and better the condition of the poor, yet if nothing be done in this way I shall not absolutely despair of some partial good resulting from the general effects of the reasoning.

If the principles which I have endeavoured to establish be false I most sincerely hope to see them completely refuted; but if they be true, the subject is so important and interests the question of human happiness so nearly, that it is impossible they should not in time be more fully known and more generally circulated, whether any particular efforts be made for the purpose or not.

Among the higher and middle classes of society the effect of this knowledge will I hope be to direct without relaxing their efforts in bettering the condition of the poor; to show them what they can and what they cannot do; and that although much may be done by advice and instruction, by encouraging habits of prudence and cleanliness, by discriminate charity, and by any mode of bettering the present condition of the poor which is followed by an increase of the preventive check; yet that without this last effect all the former efforts would be futile; and that in any old and well-peopled state to assist the poor in such a manner as to enable them to marry as early as they please and rear up large families, is a physical impossibility. This knowledge, by tending to prevent the rich from destroying the good effects of their own exertions and wasting their efforts in a direction where success is unattainable, would confine their attention to the proper objects, and thus enable them to do more good.

Among the poor themselves its effects would be still more important. That the principal and most permanent cause of poverty has little or no *direct* relation to forms of government or the unequal division of property; and that as the rich do not in reality possess the *power* of finding employment and maintenance for the poor, the poor cannot in the nature of things possess the *right* to demand them, are important truths flowing from the principle of population which when properly explained would by no means be above the most ordinary comprehensions. And it is evident that every man in the lower classes of society who became acquainted with these truths would be disposed to bear the distresses in which he might be involved with more patience; would feel less discontent and irritation at the government and the higher classes of society on account of his poverty; would be on all occasions less disposed to insubordination and turbulence; and if he received assistance either from any public institution or from the hand of private charity, he would receive it with more thankfulness, and more justly appreciate its value.

If these truths were by degrees more generally known (which in the course of time does not seem to be improbable from the natural effects of the mutual interchange of opinions), the lower classes of people as a body would become more peaceable and orderly, would be less inclined to tumultuous proceedings in seasons of scarcity, and would at all times be less influenced by inflammatory and seditious publications from knowing how little the price of labour and the means of supporting a family depend upon a revolution. The mere knowledge of these truths, even if they did not operate sufficiently to produce any marked change in the prudential habits of the poor with regard to marriage, would still have a most beneficial effect on their conduct in a political light; and undoubtedly one of the most valuable of these effects would be the power that would result to the higher and middle classes of society of gradually improving their governments without the apprehension of those revolutionary excesses, the fear of which at present threatens to deprive Europe even of that degree of liberty which she had before experienced to be practicable, and the salutary effects of which she had long enjoyed.

From a review of the state of society in former periods compared with the present, I should certainly say that the evils resulting from the principle of population have rather diminished than increased, even under the disadvantage of an almost total ignorance of the real cause. And if we can indulge the hope that this ignorance will be gradually dissipated, it does not seem unreasonable to expect that they will be still further diminished. The increase of absolute population, which will of course take place, will evidently tend but little to weaken this expectation, as everything depends upon the relative proportion between population and food, and not on the absolute number of people. In the former part of this work it appeared that the countries which possessed the fewest people often suffered the most from the effects of the principle of population; and it can scarcely be doubted that, taking Europe throughout, fewer famines and fewer diseases arising from want have prevailed in the last century than in those which preceded it.

On the whole, therefore, though our future prospects respecting the mitigation of the evils arising from the principle of population may not be so bright as we could wish, yet they are far from being entirely disheartening, and by no means preclude that gradual and progressive improvement in human society, which before the late wild speculations on this subject was the object of rational expectation. To the laws of property and marriage, and to the apparently narrow principle of self-interest which prompts each individual to exert himself in bettering his condition, we are indebted for all the noblest exertions of human genius, for everything that distinguishes the civilised from the savage state. A strict inquiry into the principle of population obliges us to conclude that we shall never be able to throw down the ladder by which we have risen to this eminence; but it by no means proves that we may not rise higher by the same means. The structure of society in its great features will probably always remain unchanged. We have every reason to believe that it will always consist of a class of proprietors and a class of labourers; but the condition of each and the proportion which they bear to each other may be so altered as greatly to improve the harmony and beauty of the whole. It would indeed be a melancholy reflection that, while the views of physical science are daily enlarging so as scarcely to be bounded by the most distant horizon, the science of moral and political philosophy should be confined within such narrow limits, or at best be so feeble in its influence as to be unable to counteract the obstacles to human happiness arising from a single cause. But however formidable these obstacles may have appeared in some parts of this work, it is hoped that the general result of the inquiry is such as not to make us give up the improvement of human society in despair. The partial good which seems to be attainable is worthy of all our exertions, is sufficient to direct our efforts and animate our prospects. And although we cannot expect that the virtue and happiness of mankind will keep pace with the brilliant career of physical discovery; yet if we are not wanting to ourselves, we may confidently indulge the hope that to no unimportant extent they will be influenced by its progress and will partake in its success.

Catalog

If you are interested in a list of fine Paperback
books, covering a wide range of subjects
and interests, send your name and address,
requesting your free catalog, to:

McGraw-Hill Paperbacks
1221 Avenue of Americas
New York, N.Y. 10020